GAZA IN CRISIS

GAZA IN CRISIS

REFLECTIONS ON ISRAEL'S WAR
AGAINST THE PALESTINIANS

ILAN PAPPÉ AND NOAM CHOMSKY
EDITED BY FRANK BARAT

Haymarket Books
Chicago, Illinois

© 2010 Noam Chomsky and Ilan Pappé

First published by Haymarket Books in 2010
P.O. Box 180165
Chicago, IL 60618
773-583-7884
www.haymarketbooks.org
info@haymarketbooks.org

ISBN: 978-1608460-97-7

Trade distribution:
In the U.S., Consortium Book Sales, www.cbsd.com
In Canada, Publishers Group Canada, www.pgcbooks.ca
In the UK, Turnaround Publisher Services, www.turnaround-uk.com
In Australia, Palgrave MacMillan, www.palgravemacmillan.com.au
All other countries, Publishers Group Worldwide, www.pgw.com

Cover design by Josh On. Cover photo of a Palestinian woman standing on the
rubble of her home in the aftermath of Israeli bombing in January 2009 by Patrick
Baz/AFP/Getty Images.

This book was published with the generous support of Lannan Foundation and
the Wallace Global Fund.

Printed in Canada by union labor on recycled paper containing 100 percent post-
consumer waste, in accordance with the guidelines of the Green Press Initiative,
www.greenpressinitiative.org.

Library of Congress Cataloging in Publication data is available.

10 9 8 7 6 5 4 3 2 1

CONTENTS

INTRODUCTION

When Noam Chomsky first answered my email in December 2005, I would never have imagined that five years later I would be working on a book with him. Since then, Chomsky has continued to reply to my emails and questions and we have slowly developed a steady "written" relationship.

A few years after that first email, thinking about how to raise awareness and reach a wider audience on the Palestine question, I asked him if he would agree to an interview. He did, and a few months later sent me his answers, which as usual were more detailed and researched than I could have expected.

The interview was well received and published on various Web sites and in publications, prompting me to consider the format an excellent way to inform and educate a public that too often has to rely on information from a corporate and profit-driven media system.

The idea of another interview slowly made its way in my head, but this time I wanted something different, something more interactive. I decided to ask the renowned Israeli historian Ilan Pappé if he would participate in a joint interview/dialogue with Professor Chomsky. Pappé agreed and during the next few months I worked with both of them on various questions and key topics of what is usually referred to as the "Israel-Palestine conflict."

When that interview came out, probably because it was the first Chomsky-Pappé interview ever conducted, it appeared in even more publications and Web sites than the first one and came to the attention of a Belgian publisher, Gilles Martin, who consequently published the interview as a booklet entitled *Le Champ du possible* (Aden Editions, November 2008).

Then came an offer to create an English version of that booklet. But it needed more work. I started to think about what type of book I wanted, what would be its goal and its substance. The last thing I wanted was to publish a book merely for the sake of it. Hundreds of books on the "Israel-Palestine conflict" already exist, some exceptional, so how would this one be different?

To answer this, I asked myself: "Why has this 'conflict' lasted for so long, who can stop it, and how?" Ignorance, the people, and by popular resistance and a refusal to remain silent were the first answers that came to mind. I sincerely believe that what is happening in Palestine would never have lasted this long if the public were properly informed about what had been really taking place in this part of the Middle East.

Noam, Ilan, and I worked on the dialogue, now titled "The Ghettoization of Palestine," again, gave it more insight, edited some questions, and added new ones. Ilan additionally contributed several articles addressing various crucial aspects of the Israel-Palestine question and Noam reworked his astonishing piece "'Exterminate All the Brutes': Gaza 2009."

Combining interviews and essays was important. On one hand, the interactive joint interview/dialogue form is a means to express and explore researched analysis and opinions in an accessible way. It also offers a more flexible and lively vehicle to share expert knowledge. The joint interview, with two of the most respected people in this field of study, one an American professor and one an

Israeli historian, could fill in gaps of understanding and reach a wider audience. Both interviews address multiple topics related to the Israel-Palestine question as well as the recent Israeli Army attack on the "Freedom Flotilla" and, hopefully, allow readers to draw their own conclusions from two compatible yet different views.

On the other hand, the solely authored essays give the book a more in-depth analysis, scrutinizing specific periods and events in history in a new light, challenging (even more well-versed) readers in the process. Selected articles by Ilan Pappé give the necessary historical background that is key to understanding Palestine today. In chapters two and three, Ilan Pappé traces the historical development of U.S. involvement in the question of Palestine and the importance of *Nakbah* ("catastrophe" in Arabic) denial for Israel. Understanding the Nakbah is crucial to understanding Palestinian-Israeli history.

Chapter four is the updated and superb essay "'Exterminate All the Brutes': Gaza 2009" by Chomsky. This groundbreaking piece focuses primarily on the December 2008–January 2009 Israeli assault on Gaza, but also gives a thorough analysis of Israel's relations with the United States and Europe, and the role of social and military resistance in Arab countries.

We return to Pappé in chapters five and seven where he charts the progress of the movement for one state, and lastly, the Israeli Army's massacres in Gaza. These articles offer an alternative narrative to that which is presented by the Israeli government and I am sure will help people to reframe the "conflict." The book closes with Chomsky's latest reflections on the peace process.

My hope is that this book can be used as a guide in excavating the past for the benefit of a more clear-sighted present and a justice-centered future in which human rights are universal and justice restored.

Frank Barat

London, July 2010

ONE

THE FATE OF PALESTINE:
AN INTERVIEW WITH NOAM CHOMSKY
(2007)

What is your view of the situation in Gaza today? Could it mark the beginning of the end for the Palestinian Authority?

Some background is necessary.

Let's begin with January 2006, when Palestinians voted in a carefully monitored election, pronounced to be free and fair by international observers, despite U.S. efforts to swing the election toward their favorite, Mahmoud Abbas and his Fatah party. But Palestinians committed a grave crime, by Western standards. They voted "the wrong way." The United States instantly joined Israel in punishing Palestinians for their misconduct, with Europe toddling along behind as usual. There is nothing novel about the reaction to these Palestinian "misdeeds." Though it is obligatory to hail our leaders for their sincere dedication to bringing democracy to a suffering world, perhaps in an excess of idealism, the more serious scholar/advocates of the mission of "democracy promotion" recognize that there is a "strong line of continuity" running through all administrations: the United States supports democracy if and only if it conforms to U.S. strategic and economic interests.[1] In short, the project is pure cynicism, if viewed honestly. And quite commonly, the U.S. project should be described as one of blocking democracy, not promoting it. Dramatically so in the case of Palestine.

The punishment of Palestinians for the crime of voting the wrong way was severe. With constant U.S. backing, Israel increased its violence in Gaza, withheld funds that it was legally obligated to transmit to the Palestinian Authority, tightened its siege, and in a gratuitous act of cruelty, even cut off the flow of water to the arid Gaza Strip. The Israeli attacks became far more severe after the capture of Corporal Gilad Shalit on June 25, 2006, which the West portrayed as a terrible crime. Again, pure cynicism. Just one day before, Israel kidnapped two civilians in Gaza—a far worse crime than capturing a soldier—and transported them to Israel (in violation of international law, but that is routine), where they presumably joined the roughly one thousand prisoners held by Israel without charges, hence kidnapped.[2] None of this merits more than a yawn in the West.

There is no need here to run through the ugly details, but the U.S.-Israel made sure that Hamas would not have a chance to govern. And of course, the two leaders of the rejectionist camp flatly rejected Hamas's call for a long-term cease-fire to allow for negotiations in terms of the international consensus on a two-state settlement, which the United States and Israel reject, as they have done in virtual isolation for over thirty years, with rare and temporary departures.

Meanwhile, Israel stepped up its programs of annexation, dismemberment, and imprisonment of shrinking Palestinian cantons in the West Bank, always with decisive U.S. backing despite occasional minor complaints, accompanied by the wink of an eye and munificent funding. The programs were formalized in Prime Minister Ehud Olmert's "convergence" program, which spells the end of any viable Palestinian state. His program was greeted in the West with much acclaim as "moderate" because it did not satisfy the demands of "Greater Israel" extremists. It was soon abandoned as "too moderate," again with understanding if mild notes of disapproval by Western hypocrites.

There is a standard operating procedure for overthrowing an unwanted government: arm the military to prepare for a military coup. The U.S.-Israel adopted this conventional plan, arming and training Fatah to win by force what it lost at the ballot box. The United States also encouraged Mahmoud Abbas to amass power in his own hands, steps that are quite appropriate in the eyes of Bush administration advocates of presidential dictatorship. As for the rest of the Quartet, Russia has no principled objection to such steps, the UN is powerless to defy the Master, and Europe is too timid to do so. Egypt and Jordan supported the effort, consistent with their own programs of internal repression and barring of democracy, with U.S. backing.

The strategy backfired. Despite the flow of military aid, Fatah forces in Gaza were defeated in a vicious and brutal conflict, which many close observers describe as a preemptive strike targeting primarily the security forces of the brutal Fatah strongman Muhammad Dahlan.[3] However, those with overwhelming power can often snatch victory from the jaws of defeat, and the U.S.-Israel quickly moved to turn the outcome to their benefit. They now have a pretext for tightening the stranglehold on the people of Gaza, cheerfully pursuing policies that the prominent international law scholar Richard Falk describes as a prelude to genocide that "should remind the world of the famous post-Nazi pledge of 'never again.'"[4]

The U.S.-Israel can pursue the project with international backing unless Hamas meets the three conditions imposed by the "international community"—a technical term referring to the U.S.

government and whoever goes along with it. For Palestinians to be permitted to peek out of the walls of their Gaza dungeon, Hamas must: (1) recognize Israel, or in a more extreme form, Israel's "right to exist," that is, the legitimacy of Palestinians' expulsion from their homes; (2) renounce violence; (3) accept past agreements, in particular, the Road Map of the Quartet.

The hypocrisy again is stunning. No such conditions are imposed on those who wear the jackboots. (1) Israel does not recognize Palestine, in fact, is devoting extensive efforts to ensure that there will be no viable Palestine ever, always with decisive U.S. support; (2) Israel does not renounce violence, and it is ridiculous even to raise the question with regard to the United States; (3) Israel firmly rejects past agreements, in particular, the Road Map, with U.S. support. The first two points are obvious. The third is correct, but scarcely known. While Israel formally accepted the Road Map, it attached fourteen reservations that completely eviscerate it. To take just the first, Israel demanded that for the process to commence and continue, the Palestinians must ensure full quiet, education for peace, cessation of incitement, dismantling of Hamas and other organizations, and other conditions; and even if they were to satisfy this virtually impossible demand, the Israeli cabinet proclaimed that "the road map will not state that Israel must cease violence and incitement against the Palestinians."[5] The other reservations continue in the same vein.

Israel's instant rejection of the Road Map, with U.S. support, is unacceptable to the Western self-image, so it has been suppressed. The facts did finally break into the mainstream with the publication of Jimmy Carter's *Palestine: Peace Not Apartheid*. The book elicited a torrent of abuse and desperate efforts to discredit it, but these sections—the only part of the book that would have been new to readers with some familiarity with the topic—were scrupulously avoided.

It would, rightly, be considered utterly ludicrous to demand that a political party in the United States or Israel meet such conditions, though it would be fair to ask that the two states with overwhelming power meet them. But the imperial mentality is so deeply embedded in Western culture that this travesty passes without criticism, even notice.

While now in a position to crush Gaza with even greater cruelty, Israel can also proceed, with U.S. backing, to implement its plans in the West Bank, expecting to have the tacit cooperation of Fatah leaders who will be amply rewarded for their capitulation. Among other steps, Israel began to release the funds—estimated at $600 million—that it had stolen in reaction to the January 2006 election, and is making a few other gestures. The programs of undermining democracy are proceeding with shameless self-righteousness and ill-concealed pleasure, with gestures to keep the natives contented—at least those who play along, while Israel continues its merciless repression and violence, and, of course, its immense projects to ensure that it will take over whatever is of value to it in the West Bank. All thanks to the benevolence of the gracious rich uncle.

To turn finally to your question, the end of the Palestinian Authority might not be a bad idea for Palestinians, in the light of U.S.-Israeli programs of rendering it nothing more than a quisling regime to oversee their extreme rejectionist designs. What should concern us much more is that U.S.-Israeli triumphalism, and European cowardice, might be the prelude to the death of a nation, a rare and somber event.

Do you think that there are any conditions under which the United States might change its policy of unconditional support to Israel?

A large majority of Americans oppose U.S. government policy and support the international consensus on a two-state settlement—in recent polls, it's called the "Saudi Plan," referring to the position of the Arab League, supported by virtually the entire world apart from the United States and Israel. Furthermore, a large majority think that the United States should deny aid to either of the contending parties—Israel and the Palestinians—if they do not negotiate in good faith toward this settlement. This is one of a great many illustrations of a huge gap between public opinion and public policy on critical issues.

It should be added that few people are likely to be aware that their preferences would lead to cutting off all aid to Israel. To understand this consequence one would have to escape the grip of the powerful and largely uniform doctrinal system, which labors to project an image of U.S. benevolence, Israeli righteousness, and Palestinian terror and obstructionism, whatever the facts.

To answer your question, U.S. policy might well change if the United States became a functioning democratic society, in which an informed public has a meaningful voice in policy formation. That's the task for activists and organizers, not just in this case. One can think of other possible conditions that might lead to a change in U.S. policy, but none that holds anywhere near as much promise as this one.

Al Jazeera reported that Tony Blair could soon be appointed the Middle East Quartet's envoy. What message do you think this will send to the Palestinians and others around the region?

Perhaps the most apt comment was by the fine Lebanese political analyst Rami Khouri. He said that "Appointing Tony Blair as special envoy for Arab-Israeli peace is something like appointing the Emperor Nero to be the chief fireman of Rome."[6] Blair was indeed appointed as an envoy, but not as the Quartet's envoy, except in name. The Bush administration made it very clear at once that he is Washington's envoy, with a very limited mandate. It announced in no uncertain terms that Secretary of State Rice (and the president) would retain unilateral control over the important issues, while Blair would be permitted to deal only with problems of institution building, an impossible task as long as Washington maintains its extreme rejectionist policies. Europe had no noticeable reaction to yet another slap in the face. Washington evidently assumes that Blair will continue to be "the spear carrier for the *pax americana*," as his role was described in the journal of Britain's Royal Institute of International Affairs.[7]

Do you think that the corporate media in the United States should worry about its lies and fantasies being exposed in online independent media (ZNet, CounterPunch, etc.), or is there a finite limit on how far these alternative media can ever penetrate the consciousness of a population like that in the United States?

For the present, the media—and the intellectual community—need not be too concerned about the exposure of "lies and fantasies." The limit is determined by the strength and commitment of popular movements. They certainly face barriers, but there is no reason to think they are insurmountable ones.

Due to constant pressure and lobbying by Professor Alan Dershowitz, Professor Norman Finkelstein was recently denied tenure at DePaul. Why does someone like Dershowitz have so much influence that he can make an institution break its own rules?

Dershowitz has been repeatedly exposed as a dedicated liar, charlatan, and opponent of elementary civil rights, and he is, uncontroversially, an extreme apologist for the crimes and violence of the State of Israel. But he is taken seriously by the media and the academic world. That tells us quite a lot about the reigning intellectual culture. As to why institutions succumb, few are willing to endure the deluge of slanders, lies, and defamation poured out by Dershowitz, the Anti-Defamation League, and other apologists for the crimes of their favored state, who are granted free rein with little concern about response. Merely to illustrate, Dershowitz's books are treated with reverence by the *Boston Globe*, probably the most liberal paper in the country, but they refuse even to review Norman Finkelstein's carefully documented demonstration that they are an absurd collection of fabrication and deceit. Authentic scholarship knows better, as the record clearly shows. But it receives little attention.

For the late Edward W. Said, the solution was one state where all the citizens (Arabs, Jews, Christians, etc.) would have the same democratic rights. Do you think that because of the situation in Gaza and the ever-spreading settlements, the pendulum will now swing toward a one-state solution as being the only possible end point to the conflict?

Two points of clarification are necessary. First, there is a crucial difference between a one-state solution and a binational state. In general, nation-states have been imposed with substantial violence and repression for one reason—because they seek to force varied and complex populations into a single mold. One of the more healthy developments in Europe today is the revival of some degree of regional autonomy and cultural identity, reflecting somewhat more closely the nature of the populations. In the case of Israel-Palestine, a one-state solution will arise only on the U.S. model: with extermination or expulsion of the indigenous population. A sensible approach would be advocacy of a binational solution, recognizing that the territory now includes two fairly distinct societies.

The second point is that Edward Said—an old and close friend—was one of the earliest and most outspoken supporters of a two-state solution. By the 1990s, he felt that the opportunity had been lost, and he proposed, without much specification, a unitary state, by which I am sure he would have meant a binational state. I purposely use the word "propose," not "advocate." The distinction is crucial. We can propose that everyone should live in peace and harmony. The proposal rises to the level of advocacy when we sketch a path from here to there. In the case of a unitary (binational) solution, the only advocacy I know of passes through a number of stages: first a two-state settlement in terms of the international consensus that the United States and Israel have prevented, followed by moves toward binational federation, and finally closer integration, perhaps to a binational democratic state, as circumstances allow.

It is of some interest that when binationalist federation, opening the way to closer integration, was feasible—from 1967 to the mid-1970s—suggestions to this effect (my own writings, for example) elicited near hysteria. Today, when they are completely unfeasible, they are treated with respect in the mainstream (*New York Times*, *New York Review of Books*, etc.). The reason, I suspect, is that a call today for a one-state settlement is a gift to the jingoist right, who can then wail that "they are trying to destroy us" so we must destroy them in self-defense. But true advocacy of a binational state seems to me just as appropriate as it has always been. That has been my unchanged opinion since the 1940s. Advocacy, that is, not mere proposal.

Looking ahead, what do you consider to be the best-case, worst-case, and most likely scenarios for the boundaries and control of occupied Palestine in the next ten years?

The worst case would be the destruction of Palestine. The best case in the short term would be a two-state settlement in terms of the international consensus. That is by no means impossible. It is supported by virtually the entire world, including the majority of the U.S. population. It has come rather close, once, during the last month of Clinton's presidency, the sole U.S. departure from extreme rejectionism in the past thirty years. The United States lent its support to the negotiations in Taba, Egypt (in January 2001), which came very close to a settlement in the general terms of the international consensus, before they were called off prematurely by Israeli prime minister Ehud Barak. In their final press conference, the negotiators expressed some hope that if they had been permitted to continue their joint work, a settlement could have been reached. The years since have seen many horrors, but the possibility remains. As for the most likely scenario, it looks unpleasantly close to the worst case, but human affairs are not predictable: too much depends on will and choice.

Would you agree with Edward Said when he said, "The most demoralising aspect of the Zionist-Palestinian conflict is the almost total opposition between the mainstream Israeli and Palestinian points of view…Might it not make sense for a group of universally respected historians and intellectuals, composed equally of Palestinians and Israelis to hold a series of meetings to try to agree [to] a modicum of truth about where this conflict actually lies…for them to agree on a body of facts…who took what from whom, who did what to whom…something like a Historical Truth and Political Justice Committee"[8]?

Who are the "respected historians and intellectuals"? Edward had much more faith in the importance and the integrity of respected intellectuals than I do. That aside, I do not think there is very much dispute about the bare facts, except for fringe liars. Disputes have to do with selection and interpretation.

The University and College Union in Britain voted in favor of considering an academic boycott of Israeli universities. Do you think that this and other

types of boycotts (of Israeli products, for example) are appropriate measures and could have a positive effect on Israeli policies?

I have always been skeptical about academic boycotts. There may be overriding reasons, but in general I think that those channels should be kept open. As for boycotts in general, they are a tactic, not a principle. Like other tactics, we have to evaluate them in terms of their likely consequences. That is a matter of prime importance, at least for those who care about the fate of the victims. And circumstances have to be considered with care.

Let's consider South Africa and Israel, which are often compared in this context. In the case of South Africa, boycotts had some impact, but it is worth remembering that they were implemented after a long period of education and organizing, which had led to widespread condemnation of apartheid, even within mainstream opinion and powerful institutions. That included the U.S. corporate sector, which has an overwhelming influence on policy formation, transparently. At that stage, boycott became an effective instrument. The case of Israel is radically different. The preparatory educational and organizing work has scarcely been done. The result is that calls for boycott can easily turn out to be weapons for the hard right, and in fact that has regularly (and predictably) happened. Those who care about the fate of Palestinians will not undertake actions that harm them.

Nevertheless, carefully targeted boycotts, which are comprehensible to the public in the current state of understanding, can be effective instruments. One example is calls for university divestment from corporations that are involved in U.S.-Israeli repression and violence and denial of elementary human rights. In Europe, a sensible move would be to call for an end to preferential treatment for Israeli exports until Israel stops its systematic destruction of Palestinian

agriculture and its barring of economic development. In the United
States, it would make good sense to call for reducing U.S. aid to Israel by the estimated $600 million that Israel has stolen by refusing
to transmit funds to the elected government—and the cynicism of
funneling aid to the faction it supports should be exposed as just another exercise in undermining democracy. Looking farther ahead, a
sensible project would be to support the stand of the majority of
Americans that all aid to Israel should be canceled until it agrees to
negotiate seriously for a peaceful diplomatic settlement, instead of
continuing to act vigorously to undermine the possibility of realiz-
ing the international consensus on a two-state settlement. That,
however, will require serious educational and organizational efforts. Readers of the mainstream press were well aware of the shocking nature of apartheid. But they are presented daily with the
picture of Israel desperately seeking peace but under constant attack
by Palestinian terrorists who want to destroy it.

That is not just the media, incidentally. Just to illustrate, Harvard University's Kennedy School of Government published a research paper on the 2006 Lebanon war that has to be read to be
believed, but is not atypical. It's by Marvin Kalb, a highly respected
figure in journalism, head of the Kennedy School's media program. According to his account, the media were almost totally
controlled by Hezbollah, and failed to recognize that Israel was
"engaged in an existential struggle for survival," fighting a two-
front war of self-defense against attacks in Lebanon and Gaza.[9]
The attack on the pathetic victim from the south was the capture
of Corporal Shalit. The kidnapping of Gazan civilians the day before, and innumerable other crimes like it, are more self-defense.
The attack from the north was the Hezbollah capture of two soldiers on July 12. More cynicism. For decades Israel has been kidnapping and killing civilians in Lebanon, or on the high seas

between Lebanon and Cyprus, holding many for long periods as hostages while unknown numbers of others were sent to secret prison-torture chambers like Facility 1391 (not reported in the United States).[10] No one has ever condemned Israel for aggression or called for massive terror attacks in retaliation. As always, the cynicism reeks to the skies, illustrating imperial mentality so deeply rooted as to be imperceptible.

Continuing with the Kennedy School version of the war, it demonstrates the extreme bias of the Arab press with the horrified revelation that it portrayed Lebanese to Israeli casualties in the ratio of 22 to 1, whereas objective Western journalism would of course be neutral; the actual ratio was about 25 to 1. Kalb quotes *New York Times* correspondent Steven Erlanger, who was greatly disturbed that photos of destruction in South Beirut lacked context: they did not show that the rest of Beirut was not destroyed. By the same logic, photos of the World Trade Center on 9/11 revealed the extreme bias of Western journalism by failing to show that the rest of New York was untouched. The falsification and deceit, of which these examples are a small sample, would be startling if they were not so familiar. Until that is overcome, punitive actions that are well merited are likely to backfire.

All this raises another point. For the most part, Israel can act only within the framework established by the great power on which it has chosen to rely ever since it made the fateful decision in 1971 to prefer expansion to peace, rejecting Egyptian president Anwar Sadat's proposal for a full Israel-Egyptian peace treaty in favor of settlement in the Egyptian Sinai. We can debate the extent to which Israel relies on U.S. support, but there can be little doubt that its crushing of Palestinians and other violent crimes are possible only because the United States provides it with unprecedented economic, military, diplomatic, and ideological support. So if there are to be boycotts, why not of the United States, whose support of Israel is the least of its crimes? Or of the UK, or other criminal states? We know the answer, and it is not an attractive one, undermining the integrity of the call for boycott.

Finally, in April 2003, Gilbert Achcar wrote a "Letter to a Slightly Depressed Antiwar Activist," which ended with "This movement's spectacular growth has only been possible because it rested on the foundations of three years of progress by the global movement against neoliberal globalization born in Seattle. These two dimensions will continue to fuel each other, to strengthen people's awareness that neoliberalism and war are two faces of the same system of domination—which must be overthrown."[11] What would be your message today to antiwar and human rights activists around the world about their role in this worldwide struggle?

Gilbert Achcar is quite right, though we should recognize, as he surely does, that the North is a latecomer to the very promising global justice movements. They originated in the South, which is why the meetings of the World Social Forum have been held in Brazil, India, Venezuela, Kenya. Also of great significance are the solidarity movements that developed, primarily in the United States, in the 1980s, something quite new in the hundreds of years of Western imperialism, and have since proliferated in many ways. The lesson to activists is stark and simple: the future lies in their hands, including the question of the fate of Palestine.

TWO

CLUSTERS OF HISTORY: U.S. INVOLVEMENT IN THE PALESTINE QUESTION

A thought-provoking article was published by John Mearsheimer and Stephen Walt. Based on extended research, it discussed the power of the American Israel Public Affairs Committee (AIPAC), the Israeli lobby in Washington, in shaping American policy in the Middle East in general and toward Israel in particular.[1] Their basic argument was that the lobby directs American policy in a way that undermines the United States' national interest. Not since the 1960s would one have come across such a harsh criticism of either Zionism or U.S. policy from within the heart of American academia or the media.

The role of the lobby in shaping U.S. policy in the Middle East is undoubtedly crucial. But American policy in the Middle East, like any regional policy of a great power in the past, is the outcome of more than one factor. For those, like myself, for whom the analysis of such a policy is not just academic but a matter of life and death, an expanded analysis is called for, not only for the sake of understanding that policy more clearly, but also as a way of coping with its dangerous outcomes. As a historian by profession, I hope that seeing the development of this policy in a wider historical spectrum may help those of us who live in the area and in Palestine to better comprehend what one may or may not do vis-à-vis such a powerful factor in our daily lives—one that is likely to remain so for the foreseeable future.

A scholarly narrative of chaotic historical processes, such as the development of a particular foreign policy, requires an organizational method that might raise suspicions about a considerable gap between the structured representation of the policy and its actual implementation on the ground. This gap stems from the modern historiographical impulse to—in the words of Hayden White—organize reality with the same clarity as a novelist seeking to construct a lucid world in which a plot has a clear beginning and an end. Historiography is a constructive effort that is meant to expose the past as it really was—if we believe in such a possibility—or, for the sake of making a contemporary point, if we doubt that possibility. But anyone who dares to dive into the ocean of words to be found in the political and diplomatic documents in the various national archives understands how precarious is the story extracted from these heaps of documents, left behind by the chattering classes, that shaped our lives over the last two centuries. Technically, mapping a clear narrative out of the paperwork requires reliance on only a very small number of documents—chosen according to the subjective preference of the historian and not according to any objective criterion.

A middle ground between relativist and positivist views of foreign policy historiography consists of providing readers interested in a particular chapter of such policy with clusters of facts and evidence from the past, each providing a certain insight into the phenomenon being researched. In this article, which follows the history of the American involvement in the Middle East in general and in Palestine in particular, the clusters, when fused together, can supply an expanded explanation for this policy. Any attempt to focus on one cluster alone is problematic, as Mearsheimer and Walt learned from criticism directed at them by friends and foes alike. In what follows, there is an attempt to expand the historical panorama and present five clusters of facts and contexts. These are actually five legacies that feed into American policy in the Middle East today. At first, these processes developed discretely but, at a certain historical juncture, they met and fused into one powerful impulse that formulated American policy in this area.

THE BLACKSTONE-SCOFIELD LEGACY

If you ignore a no-entry sign on your right when you ascend toward the Jaffa Gate in the Old City of Jerusalem and take the forbidden turn alongside the old Ottoman wall, driving through the Citadel, you will reach one of Jerusalem's hidden gems. On the mountain's slope looking west lies the old Gobat School. Samuel Gobat was an Anglican bishop who built a boys' school there in the mid-nineteenth century that became the main preparatory school for the Palestinian elite. Today it is an American college and, among the beautiful buildings left behind by the Anglicans, the modern-day Americans have planted posters supporting the "Great Israel" idea and a Zionist Jerusalem, which would not have shamed the most ultra-right Zionist settler movement in Israel.

Gobat came to Palestine, as the Americans do today, because he believed that the return of the Jews would precipitate the Second Coming of the Messiah and the unfolding apocalypse of the "end times." But, unlike his contemporary successors, he fell in love with the local population and helped tie them into the global educational system. In a way, he forsook his missionary task for the sake of granting them a more universal education. His efforts helped the embryonic Palestinian national movement to emerge.

Gobat was, in many ways, a student of the Irishman John Nelson Darby and the Scot Edward Irving, the fathers of pre-millenarianist dogma at the beginning of the nineteenth century. Theirs was a doomsday vision that included the return of the Jews to their biblical homeland, followed by their conversion to Christianity on the way to a full realization of the apocalyptic prophecies. The source, as of so many of these Judeo-Christian dogmas, was Jewish and its origins can be found in the apocalyptic Jewish thought that evolved around the coming of the Messiah. These Irish and Scottish visions emerged, in an even more zealous form, in the United States. They seem to have rooted themselves in Newton, Massachusetts, once a city of its own, today part of Greater Boston. Newton is a circular suburb and at its center, in a typical New England wood, lies the theological seminary of Andover. In its early days, it hosted a Presbyterian brotherhood that wished to bring "the word of God to the heathen."[2] Two hundred and fifty enthusiastic boys were enlisted for the purpose; a decade later, they were in Palestine and the surrounding area, trying to convert a society that had already encountered the Jesuits and the Greek Orthodox missionaries who had arrived years before. The Andoverians built institutes that, in time, would become the American universities of Cairo and Beirut, the alma maters of the Arab national movement's first generation of leaders. The gospel they brought was, thus, not only that of Jesus but also that of the youngest state in the world, just liberated from the British colonialist yoke. The historian George Antonious, author of the famous *Arab Awakening* and a senior clerk in the British mandate government in Palestine, asserted that these missionaries were the principal agents of modernization and nationalization in the formative period of the modern Middle East.[3] With the advent of a more complex theoretical view of how nations are born, the role of the Presbyterian missionaries was diminished, but they are still regarded as a meaningful factor in this story.[4]

This ambivalence in the American theological view between a millenarianist vision and identification with the awakening Arab peoples continued until the First World War. We find, at the end of the nineteenth century, a debate between the two positions. On one side stood the preacher William Blackstone who, in the famous Protestant Convention of 1891, demanded of President Benjamin Harrison that the United States should "consider the condition of the Israelites and their claims to Palestine as their ancient home."[5] On the other side stood the American consul in Jerusalem, Selah Merrill, who attempted to counterbalance the growing influence of the "return of the Jews" notion. Merrill wrote to the president that, in his view (which was shared by his friends, the Muslim notables of Jerusalem), Zionism was neither a holy nor a religious phenomenon but, rather, a colonialist project that, he predicted, would not last because it pertained to the Jewish Eastern European world. While the definition is apt, the prediction seems, in hindsight, to be wrong.[6]

The millenarianists seemed to gain the upper hand as the years went by. Within the American evangelical scene, the voices of the "Merrills" weakened and were almost silenced by the vociferous sermons of the "Blackstones," whose numbers increased enormously in the twentieth century. Their positive view of Zionism was reinforced by the growing tension between the missionaries and the Islamic religious establishments in the eastern Mediterranean. The missionaries, who once preached for liberation from European colonialism, hoped that American Christianity and not the Islamic tradition would become the leading light of the new nations, as indeed would become the case. In many ways, the second and third generations of missionaries became the first "Orientalists"—in the full negative meaning of the term. But even before Edward Said attracted our attention to this group, another Edward was warning, forty years before Said's *Orientalism* appeared, of the dubious impact of the Orientalist missionary. This was Edward Earle who, like Said, also taught at Columbia University and who wrote in *Foreign Affairs* in 1929 that

> for almost a century American Public Opinion concerning the Near East was formed by missionaries. If American opinion has been uninformed, misinformed and prejudiced, the missionaries are largely to blame. Interpreting history in terms of the advance of Christianity, they have given an inadequate, distorted, and occasionally a grotesque picture of Moslems and Islam. [7]

The missionaries presented an even more distorted picture when they focused on Palestine. Their biased and negative descriptions faithfully echoed their immense disappointment at their first physical encounters with the Holy Land. Like Mark Twain, they found it difficult to digest the gap between what they discovered and the vision that the Holy Scriptures had led them to imagine. Like the Zionists who would follow them, as well as the British and Germans who came with them, they did not perceive the locals as a "people" or a group with rights or claims to the country, but rather as, at best, an exotic specter and, at worst, an ecological nuisance. The Zionist movement, having developed a similar view, immediately won their support, although it would take years before this link became a solid alliance between Christian fundamentalism and the State of Israel—an alliance that would greatly affect American policy in the Middle East as a whole.

That alliance was forged when Israel was established in 1948. In the eyes of the messianic Christians in America, the creation of the

State of Israel was the final and decisive proof that the divine apoc-alyptic schemes were about to materialize in front of their eyes: the return of the Jews, their conversion to Christianity, and the second coming of the Messiah.

Cyrus Scofield, a preacher from Dallas, Texas, was another link in the chain that connected missionary theology on both sides of the Atlantic. This violent priest produced an annotated, funda-mentalist version of the Bible that was published by Oxford University Press in 1909. It was, in a way, the most explicit sketch of the three prongs that form the basis for U.S. policy today: the return of the Jews, the decline of Islam, and the rising fortunes of the United States as a world power.[8] Parts of Scofield's sermons sound like contemporary speeches by George W. Bush. The Zionist move-ment could not have asked for more; the enthusiasm that now gripped Protestants in Britain and the United States was what it most needed to push forward an idea that had, before the Second World War, failed to enthuse most Jews.

Texas was indeed an important hub for this activity. It became a spouting fountain of fundamentalist hallucinations that, today, have turned into the policies of another Texan, George W. Bush. As the twentieth century marched on, the southern preachers pushed aside their eastern colleagues and wrote and prophesied, like the fa-mous Hal Lindsey, that, after Armageddon, millions of Jews would kneel before the returning Christ. This sermon reappears in the ceremonies conducted by Christian Zionists, who flock every year to the ancient ruins of Tel-Megiddo, where the final battle between good and evil is supposed to be played out; the delegations are re-ceived in Israel as the state's new saviors. Lindsey's book, *The Late, Great Planet Earth*, is today a hit—an apocalyptic bestseller and the bible of the average Christian Zionist.[9] In it, unconditional support for an aggressive and destructive Israel is a divine law: "What Israel wants is what God wants" is the statement that guided, at its onset, the fundamentalist pilgrimage to Jerusalem in the mid-1980s.

And thus, in September 2001, a century after Scofield's Bible appeared, his phantasm became a real policy when the U.S. administration faced a small group of terrorists who came from Saudi Arabia and Egypt and were trained in Afghanistan. The American leadership did not send forces to seek or arrest the terrorists but, instead, waged a total war against Islam, using destructive military force. Substantial aid to, and fortification of, Israel was conceived as the most significant part of the "war on terror." The ideological infrastructure of this Bush policy is very much the legacy of Scofield and his fundamentalist friends.

It is possible that the hidden but staunch anti-Semitic element within millenarian dogma deterred the pro-Israeli lobby at first from associating too strongly with the expanding network of Christian fundamentalist organizations. But in the 1970s all this changed. The Israeli government could not resist the temptation. Menachem Begin led the way, with the help of an enthusiastic young Likudnik, Binyamin Netanyahu. In 1978, the Likud government declared its intention of strengthening the connection with the Christian fundamentalists. It allowed them to open a TV station in southern Lebanon when it was occupied by Israel in Operation Litani. More important was the consent of the government for the opening, in 1980, of the international Christian embassy in Jerusalem. The stronghold of fundamentalism in Israel today, it was built in what must have been the "best seat in town": an excellent location overlooking the valley in which the prophesied resurrection would take place. In 1985, Netanyahu, then Israel's ambassador to the UN, declared to the annual convention of Christian Zionists that the latter's support for Israel was a superior moral deed. That night he became the blue-eyed boy for all those who wished to burn the

Jews in hell unless they converted to Christianity on Judgment Day. The churches were not content with words alone and established a special outfit that focused on helping Israel inside the United States, which Netanyahu made effective use of when he became prime minister.[10]

While the pro-Israeli lobby (see below) concentrated its efforts on wooing the Democratic Party toward Israel, these Christians turned the Republican Party into a sympathizer, at the very least. And one should not underrate this achievement; for the businessmen linked to the Republican Party were more inclined to accept the Arabists' point of view (on which more later) and support a pro-American axis in the Middle East, built on friendly Arab regimes. But this position was neutralized toward the end of the twentieth century due to the immense power accumulated by the fundamentalists who, by then, were officially dubbed "Christian Zionists." It is noteworthy that the pro-Israeli lobby was established, according to the declared aims of its founder, to eliminate pro-Arab influence in the State Department. This particular mission was accomplished, it seems, not so much by the lobby's effort as by the successful endeavors of the Christian Zionists.

History, quite often, is an explosive fusion of discrete processes that produce events later considered to be formative and significant. The Reaganite foreign policy of the 1980s and the historical narrative that accompanied it—which claimed that this American president and his UK colleague Margaret Thatcher were leading a hawkish West into decisive victory over the great Satan in Moscow—reinforced Christian Zionism even more. It was also fed by a TV revolution that bowdlerized the American value system and collapsed fundamentalist Christianity into the dimensions of the small screen. Flamboyant men appeared as preachers and succeeded, in the typical discourse of this shallow medium, in conveying even more simplified messages from the Christian Zionist pulpit. Thus, the transformations in a bipolar world, the communications revolution, and the rise of the Right to power in Israel turned the Jewish state's influence in the United States into a formidable, if not undefeatable, fact of life.

Jerry Falwell's shows on TV epitomize this latest transformation in the fundamentalist experience. In 1981, he said on one of his shows: "He who stands against Israel stands against God." In the same year, he received the Jabotinsky Prize from Menachem Begin. The various groups that fell within the category of Christian Zionism won an unprecedented place in the Israeli political system. So, despite vigorous opposition from the ultra-Orthodox Jews in Jerusalem to any missionary work in the city, Falwell and his friends shifted the focus of Christian Zionist activity to Jerusalem. Ever since, every few years the city has hosted the main convention of American Christian Zionists—a body that has adopted a host of resolutions calling upon Israel to pursue an expansionist policy in the occupied territories and encouraging the United States to wage continuous war against Islam and the Arab world. These positions were taken long before the United States was attacked by al-Qaeda.[11]

The outcome is that, today, tens of millions (probably around forty million) of Americans support Israel unreservedly, even expecting it to pursue a maximalist policy against the Arab world and the Palestinians. This body of people brings with it the money that helped install George W. Bush in the White House; its members are represented in all the important committees on Capitol Hill and in the American media. Ever since the outbreak of the second Intifada, most of the churches of this persuasion consider volunteering in Israel as mandatory.

As if this were not enough, since September 2001, this theology has also adopted a clear anti-Islamic line. In his important work on the subject, Stephen Sizer has revealed how Christian Zionists have constructed a historical narrative that describes the Muslim attitude to Christianity throughout the ages as a kind of a genocidal campaign, first against the Jews and then against the Christians.[12] Hence, what were once hailed as moments of human triumph in the Middle East—the Islamic renaissance of the Middle Ages, the golden era of the Ottomans, the emergence of Arab independence and the end of European colonialism—were recast as the satanic, anti-Christian acts of heathens. In the new historical view, the United States became St. George, Israel his shield and spear, and Islam their dragon.

THE KING-CRANE LEGACY

In the heart of Ohio lies the town of Oberlin. At the beginning of the nineteenth century it was still a typical Midwest American village, surrounded by infinite cornfields, away from the ivy towers of the East and West coasts. A pastoral part of the world, it would have escaped a place in the collective American memory had it not been for a unique theological college that was established there in 1833. Oberlin College was opened by a clergy very different from those already discussed. Its members were motivated by a commitment to peace and equality, both in the United States and in the world at large. In its early years, the college fought against racial segregation and discrimination against women in American academia. There, in the Gothic-like building of the college, Henry King taught for many years but, as was common for researchers then, he did not specialize in one particular area. At first King was attracted to theological education, then mathematics, and finally philosophy. In 1902 he became the college's president, then, during the First World War, he left this comfortable position to become the head of the YMCA in Paris. In the photo gallery of the college, one can see a tall man with a Groucho-like moustache decorating his long face, sitting next to a table made fit, lean, and long, to the man's proportions. This was taken at the Paris YMCA. It was while there that King was asked by his good friend, President Woodrow Wilson, to become involved in world politics. The American president wished to exploit the results of the war by disintegrating the big colonial empires in the name of the right to independence and self-determination. In the Wilsonian vision, the Arab peoples, too, were entitled to the national liberation denied them during four hundred years of Ottoman rule. Wilson suspected that Britain and France wanted to replace Turkish imperialism with European colonialism. He therefore asked the Peace Conference in Versailles to send a commission of inquiry to the Arab world to ascertain the peoples' aspirations there. The survey included Palestine, and King was his favored candidate to head the mission.[13]

King's partner for the mission came from a very different place. In the northeastern part of Istanbul, the University of Bogazici overlooks the straits of the Bosphorus. Its buildings, clinging to the hill slopes that descend to the straits' bank, resemble those of Oberlin College, which is no surprise as they were built by American clergymen too. This campus was opened in 1839 and was first named Roberts College.[14] It survived the Great War, which positioned the United States and Turkey as enemies, remaining an American cultural center at the heart of Istanbul. Charles Crane, a businessman from Chicago and a diplomat of sorts, was the campus's main trustee. He was about to invest more time in it as part of his plan to expand an all-American campus system in the Arab world, when he, too, was called on by President Wilson to assist King in his Middle East peace mission.[15] Crane gladly agreed to take part in what was an effort to enhance the independence of the Arab peoples according to the principle of self-determination, as articulated by the president in his famous 1914 speech at Mount Vermont.

When King and Crane arrived at the offices of the Peace Conference, they found that their mission was to be much more modest.

Most of the Arab world had already been divided into new nation-states by the colonialist powers, even before Versailles had been convened. Only one area remained without clear definition: the Levant. The British and French had already carved it out between themselves in the Sykes-Picot agreement of 1916. However, President Wilson hoped to calm colonialist hunger by peppering the dish with a bit of liberalism. It was still necessary to know what were the real ambitions of the people living in the areas that Britain and France coveted. And thus, despite demonstrable hostility from Britain and France, the Peace Conference agreed to delay the establishment of mandate regimes in Syria, Lebanon, and Palestine. King and Crane enlisted seven experts in different fields and set out for the area on June 10, 1919, staying there for forty-two days. They visited more than 1,500 locations—an amazing achievement for such a small delegation. They met urban elites, Jewish settlers, and Christian missionaries. They were in Jaffa, Rishon Le-Zion, Jerusalem, Ramallah, Nablus, Jenin, Nazareth, Haifa, and Acre until they returned to Turkey on board the U.S. Navy destroyer *Hazelwood*. They were surprised by the sincerity of the urban and rural inhabitants of Palestine. They discovered that most of them were happy to be part of an all-Syrian Arab state, although quite a few of the urban inhabitants hoped that an independent Palestine would eventually be established. They mainly knew what they did not want: a Zionist presence, the Balfour Declaration, and a British or French mandate. King and Crane's final report was undecided, except on one point: the negative impact the Balfour Declaration would have on the people of Palestine.[16]

Their report troubled the governments in Paris and London. Ever since 1912, both had toiled over a network of secret agreements that divided up the Greater Syria area (Palestine, Lebanon, Syria, and Jordan) between themselves. The Balfour Declaration was thrown into the deal, granting the establishment of a Jewish homeland in Palestine as well as the creation of a Hashemite kingdom in Jordan. The members of the King-Crane commission discovered that the people who were themselves living in Greater Syria had a different dream and innocently believed that it would fit with the wider vision of President Wilson.

No wonder, then, that the reports were shelved. When President Wilson fell seriously ill and collapsed that summer, the energetic American involvement in the Middle East petered out and with it disappeared the only American scheme in modern times that attempted to build a new Middle East according to the aspirations of the local population rather than those of Washington and its allies. Sparks of this positive energy would reappear now and again among the more pro-Arab American diplomats and officials of the State Department. This was particularly true in the mandate period of Palestine. When such experts were asked by President Franklin Roosevelt to provide an assessment of the Zionist movement, they wrote: "It has never been considered [by the U.S. government] that the realization of a Jewish National Home was connected with safeguarding American rights and interests."[17] But they mainly recommended pursuing a neutral policy and clandestinely assisting the British. This line held until 1942, when the Zionist leadership in Palestine succeeded for the first time in eliciting overwhelming support from the American Jewish community. This was immediately translated into pressure on the White House to change its position on Palestine and refuse to contemplate ideas such as those proposed by King and Crane.

It did not happen in a day. King and Crane's heirs were a professional group of university graduates who manned the State Department sections dealing with the Near East, as they called the area. They were the famous "Arabists." Their last significant impact on U.S. policy, which came toward the end of the British mandate in Palestine (1948), can tell us something about potential changes to American policy in the near and more distant future.

The scene for the last success of the Arabists was the town of Lake Success on Long Island. Contrary to what its name suggests, it is an ancient arena of defeat—that of the Native American Montauketts, who were destroyed in the U.S. genocide. Like so many other locations in the United States, this, too, is named after the chief of the defeated tribe, Sacut. Since the end of colonization, the area has been a military-industrial complex, which armed U.S. forces in both world wars. In 1946, the fledgling United Nations addressed, quite unexpectedly, the mayor of the little town of Lake Success and asked to rent some of the industrial areas, including huge hangars, as a temporary home. In one of them, in November 1947, the UN General Assembly announced the establishment of a Jewish state. But these pleasant Zionist memories disappeared into thin air when, a few months later in the very same hangar, a different spectacle took place. On February 24, 1948, the American delegate to the UN, Warren Austin, declared that his government wished to annul the partition resolution (which included the declaration of the Jewish state) as it wrought havoc and destruction instead of enhancing peace. Austin suggested imposing an international trusteeship over Palestine, pending a better solution. This was a step that ended a long process of rethinking in the State Department in the face of the new reality unfolding in Palestine. The Arabists saw how, under the umbrella of the UN partition resolution, the Zionist movement had begun ethnically cleansing Palestine of its native population. And so, on that day in February—within a week of the first significant Israeli ethnic cleansing operation, focusing on five coastal villages and a massacre in the north—Austin gave his speech.[18]

President Harry Truman knew very well what was in store for him. He had already developed an antipathy toward the Zionist leaders in his country, such as Aba Hillel Silver, whom his Jewish advisers invited into his chambers every now and then to complain about the State Department. This troubling activity was part of the new pro-Zionist campaign that Jews in the United States had initiated after David Ben-Gurion visited them in 1942. In that year, the Zionist leader convened a meeting in the Biltmore Hotel in New York that was meant to institutionalize the pro-Zionist lobby in the United States. And, indeed, the Zionist retaliation was not long in coming. Aba Hillel Silver arrived, followed by Chaim Weizmann and, although the president told his advisers that he would not be shouted at anymore, the ploy worked well—it had, after all, been an election year. The United States retracted its policy and Israeli ethnic cleansing raged on.[19]

However, the State Department continued to refer to the 1948 ethnic cleansing of Palestine as the root cause of the conflict. Under its guidance, the Palestinian right of return was the backbone of a new UN peace initiative attempted throughout 1949. Then, as they had in February 1948, the White House and other bodies involved in formulating U.S. policy on the question of Palestine at first accepted the department's lead. One month was noteworthy: May 1949. In that month, the United States demanded that Israel allow the repatriation of hundreds of thousands of Palestinian refugees, regardless of the cause of their flight and not even pending the conclusion of a final settlement. On May 29, 1949, the U.S. ambassador to Israel, James McDonald, conveyed a very sharp letter from President Truman to David Ben-Gurion, which made an explicit threat of severe sanctions if Israel did not adjust its polices. This was accompanied by the suspension of a promised loan.

In June 1949, Israel succeeded in conveying the impression that it was about to heed the pressure but asked for time to deal with some technical aspects of the request. In the meantime, conflicts broke out in different parts of the globe as the cold war began to heat up; hence, until the end of Truman's administration, that pressure was never attempted again. One could argue, though, that, to this day, there has been no official U.S. retraction from the Palestinian right of return.

The Arabist legacy seemed also to influence Truman's successor, Dwight Eisenhower, but this proved too much for both Israel and the Jewish community; they retaliated with the establishment of AIPAC (the American Israel Public Affairs Committee). This was the Arabists' swan song. Here and there, criticism popped out demanding recognition of the Palestinian people and their claims, especially during George Bush Sr.'s term in the White House. Today, the Arabists hold only very junior positions and play no role in the decision-making process of U.S. Middle East policy. In 2003, the veterans among the Arabists dispatched an impressive petition that accused George Bush Jr. of severely damaging the American national interest by occupying Iraq and uncritically backing Israeli policies. But even Michael Moore has more influence on American policy than they do—despite the long service they underwent in the area, their knowledge of its languages, and their solidarity with the people's basic aspirations there. Since that summer in 1919 when King and Crane tried to translate these qualifications into policy, America's Arab and Palestine policies have become confined to the narrow route efficiently delineated for them by AIPAC as the years have gone by.

THE LAGUARDIA AND KENEN LEGACY

Fiorello H. LaGuardia was born in the Bronx, New York, in 1882. His father emigrated from Italy and his mother was a Hungarian Jew. This double ethnicity became a useful political tool during LaGuardia's career in the American Labor Party, culminating in his becoming a member of the House of Representatives and mayor of New York. At every stage of his political career, until he died in 1947, he drew on his ethnic identity card—Italian or Jewish—to enhance his chances of being elected to coveted positions. He mastered Italian and Yiddish, and some claim his Hebrew was not at all bad. His legacy was such that those who followed him understood how useful were the politics of identity in the overall political scene. LaGuardia unhesitatingly accused opponents of trying to undermine the position of ethnic groups he happened to represent at the time: first the Italians in New York (in East Harlem), then the Jews in Brooklyn, and, even later, the Irish wherever they were.[20] In the 1950s, the next generation of politicians focused on the three "I"s—Israel, Italy, and Ireland—as the safe bets in local electoral races. From this angle, American foreign policy seems often a reflection of the domestic ethnic balance of power. And within this framework, the pro-Israeli lobby was born.

The use that political aspirants in an immigrant society make of their group identity as a career launchpad connects to another phenomenon in American politics: lobbying. The original lobby was the foyer leading to the Congress Hall. In 1830, for the first time, it became packed with people trying physically to influence their representatives; hence the term that is, today, associated with slickly run outfits doing much the same. From 1830 onward, many congressmen and congresswomen have spent time talking with lobbyists. Lobbying produced inevitable corruption, which, in turn, prodded lawmakers to find ways of limiting such crookedness. The first law, passed in 1946, stipulated clear regulations for lobbying, which a few years later would be violated, one by one, by AIPAC. The most important of them was the absolute prohibition on representing a foreign country.[21]

In January 1953, it seemed that, for a moment, Eisenhower wanted to renew American activism over the Palestinian refugee issue. He was heard more than once talking about the need to allow their repatriation. Moreover, unlike his predecessor, Truman, Eisenhower distinguished between the American need to provide humanitarian aid to the refugees in their camps and adherence to principled American support for the right of return. His secretary of state, John Foster Dulles, visited the area and reported that allowing the return of refugees was still physically possible. Even in Congress, the possibilities of resettlement on both sides of the River Jordan were discussed in earnest. President Eisenhower judged that the problem of three hundred thousand refugees could be solved in such a way. But the Arab world did not endorse the plan and Israel rejected it, both because of its element of return and, more importantly, because it conflicted with the aim of exploiting the Jordan River for the National Carrier Project of supplying water to Israel. The work on the National Carrier Project led to an angry response by the American president, who suspended aid to Israel, pending an end to the diversion of water from the Jordan River that Israel had begun in September 1953. Israel waited for a friendlier administration.[22]

This somewhat critical stance was maintained by the United States, and the Suez Crisis in 1956 led, yet again, to a threat of sanctions in response to an aggressive Israeli policy. Thus, in a matter of seven years, Israel was thrice threatened with American sanctions. The Americans forced the Israelis out of the Sinai, which was a traumatic lesson for the local leadership. The prospects of such an American position expanding and deepening constituted, in the eyes of the Israeli policy makers, a real existential threat. This was definitely the opinion of Israel's ambassador to the UN, Abba Eban. As part of his efforts to sabotage such a development, he enlisted an official (of Canadian origin) who worked in the UN's public relations office:

Isaiah L. "Si" Kenen. Kenen's first assignment was to write an article alerting the public to the dangers incurred by the anti-Israeli orientation of U.S. policy in the Middle East. The same message was forcefully conveyed in a series of articles Kenen published in a new journal, the *Near East Policy*, which became the pro-Israeli lobby's mouthpiece (funded partly by Israel). Kenen began organizing Jewish support, first in local trade unions and then in communities across the country. The Washington Institute for Near East Policy was founded around the journal as AIPAC's think tank. The first visible result of Kenen's activity was by Jewish members of the dockers' union, who boycotted Arab ships in U.S. harbors in order to prevent U.S. aid reaching Arab states that did not recognize Israel. Then came, around 1960, the first of many Jewish initiatives on Capitol Hill for anti-Arab legislation.[23]

The pro-Israel lobby worked uninterrupted until 1963 when the famous senator, William Fulbright, became intrigued by its activities and demanded a congressional investigation of its financial sources. The three hundred pages produced by the investigating body revealed that, over four years, the lobby had raised $5 million, exempted from tax, from the Jewish community in the United States. This was done by the purchase of bonds clandestinely made over to the State of Israel. American law forbade lobbying for the interests of a foreign country. In order to overcome the legal prohibition, it was stated that the bonds were procured only for welfare purposes in Israel. However, the investigating committee found that none of the money was ever delivered to the deprived citizens of Israel. The money went to the Israeli state and, from there, immediately back to the United States—directly into AIPAC's account. In *Newsweek* (August 12, 1963), it was written that the investigation exposed the AIPAC lobby as "one of the most effective networks of foreign influence."

Fulbright became the pro-Israel lobby's greatest enemy and had to be deposed by all means possible. The campaign against him became an AIPAC model. Everything was done to ensure that he would not be reelected. Anyone standing against him was financed and supported. From that time to this, the road to the Capitol has been scattered with candidates from the elite of American politics whose careers have been similarly torpedoed by AIPAC. In this manner, AIPAC impacted on Congress policy with such successful results that very few have since dared to follow in Fulbright's footsteps.[24]

Kenen was not taken with Eisenhower's successor, John Kennedy, either, but did not dare say so publicly because of the latter's immense popularity. Kennedy "disappointed" because he did not introduce any significant change to his predecessor's policy, but Kennedy's vice president, Lyndon Johnson, was a different story altogether: he was attentive to Israel and its needs. When Kennedy was assassinated and Johnson became president, Kenen said: "We lost a good friend, but we found a better one."[25] By 1969, on the twenty-first anniversary of Israel's founding, the game had come out in the open. Over a huge advertisement published in the *New York Times*, scores of senators and members of the House of Representatives vowed allegiance to Israel's national agenda: Jewish immigration to Israel from the Soviet Union, unlimited arms from the United States, and tough anti-Palestinian policies by the UN.

If Johnson was a true friend, Richard Nixon and his secretary of state, Henry Kissinger, were the pro-Israel lobby's undeniable heroes. When Nixon spelled out his doctrine for safeguarding the American national interest, it included a total reliance on Israel as the main pillar of U.S. policy in the Middle East. AIPAC's mission, on the face of it, had been accomplished. The State Department had been neutralized and it looked as if only the Jewish electoral voice would be heard when crucial decisions were taken pertaining to Israel's fate or even to the future of the Arab world in general. The reality, however, would be somewhat different. During the administrations of Ford, Reagan, and Bush Sr., AIPAC lost out at crucial junctures in the history of the region. The reason was that the well-oiled mechanism, which included a membership of more than thirty thousand, had invested so much effort in terrorizing potential anti-Zionist candidates that it allowed some of the actual policy making in Congress to pass unnoticed. Senators, such as Charles Percy of the Republican Party, who were suspected of being unwilling to provide unconditional support to Israel, were deposed. One can, in fact, pick any year since 1963 and find similar victims of AIPAC's campaign. In 1983, AIPAC succeeded in ending the political career of Paul Findley, a member of the House since 1961 and one of the few critics of Israel's policy in the occupied territories. More recently, the African American members Earl Hilliard and Cynthia McKinney of the Democrats have been targeted.[26]

Other sticks were wedged through the wheels of AIPAC's carriage every now and then, when the lobby was overdoing its business. Some of its members were engaged in real espionage work for Israel. Jonathan Pollard was convicted of doing so in 1986 and, in 2004, the FBI investigated others who were charged with spying inside the Pentagon. Larry Franklin, a former senior analyst on the Pentagon's Iran desk, received a prison sentence of nearly thirteen years for passing top secret information to Steve Rosen and Keith Weissman, who worked for AIPAC at the time.[27]

These debacles have not, as yet, changed the overall picture. The senior members of the Bush administration, who are involved in formulating policy toward Israel and the Middle East, are all, in one way or another, connected to AIPAC and particularly to its think tank, the Institute for Near East Policy. The most conspicuous among them are Donald Rumsfeld and Dick Cheney. They have been present every year at the most glamorous event in the American capital—the AIPAC convention. Each such meeting expresses unconditional support for Israel's policy toward the Palestinians and anyone opposing this policy is immediately considered by AIPAC to be its enemy.[28]

In the United States today, one cannot ignore the level of integration of Jews into the heights of American financial, cultural, and academic power. This has, of course, many positive implications: the Jews in America do not, in Hannah Arendt's words, live "outside the society," as they did in Germany;[29] the anti-Semitism that feeds on, among other things, the alienation of the Jewish experience, did not take root in the United States. On the other hand, the exploitation of the fruits of successful integration into American society for the benefit of a foreign country could itself be the pretext for a new surge of anti-Semitism in the future. Ever since Chaim Weizmann wrote angrily in 1949 of the rich Jews who did not do enough for Zionism, Israel's satisfaction at the affluence of American Jewry testifies that much of its capital is intended to maintain American policy in its pro-Israeli tracks.[30]

THE FIVE SISTERS' LEGACY

There have been those who have argued that, if the principal natural resource of the Middle East had been bananas, the region would not have attracted the interest of various American administrations. But it is oil, not bananas, and this cannot be changed. The Americans began to be interested in the oilfields of the Arab world in the 1920s and four companies (four of the "sisters")—Standard Oil of California, Standard Oil of New Jersey, Standard Oil of New York, and Texaco—won the first concessions to look for oil in Saudi Arabia in the first half of the twentieth century. In 1938, they discovered it there and in

Bahrain. A fifth company, Gulf Oil, found oil a few months later in Kuwait.

Since then, the oil wells have become a principal source for financing the "American way of life"—the electrification and air-conditioning of all life systems at unprecedented and unmatched levels of energy waste. Controlling the oil flow, on the one hand, and extracting earnings from its production, on the other, became the double goal of American policy in the Arab world. The emergence of Arab nationalism in the Middle East foiled the second goal. It was Iranians who first nationalized oil production and even a successful American attempt to topple the Iranian government, with the help of the CIA, did not stop the trend. The next in line was Iraq, which nationalized its oil in 1958. In the Arabian peninsula, oil royalties gushed more into the local banks than the bank accounts of the "five sisters."

But oil flowed to the United States, even if the dividends were now more evenly divided between Arab regimes and owners of the American oil companies. The pro-oil lobby in America lost its impact when, in 1973, the Arab oil-producing states declared their famous embargo. But when it transpired that this step was not, as declared, meant to assist the Palestinians but rather to bring up oil prices, the embargo became a fleeting episode. After all, such aggressive tactics in the world of business are the bread and butter of the capitalist system. And when prices stabilized, to the satisfaction of all concerned, the oil-producing Arab states began formulating a definite pro-American policy. The lesson was clear: American administrations found they could ensure oil flow from Saudi Arabia and, at the same time, categorically reject any sensible peace proposals made by the Saudi crown for solving the Arab-Israeli conflict. (This was the case, for example, in 1981 when King Fahd offered a peace proposal that included recognition of the right of Israel to exist alongside an independent Palestinian state.)

Saddam Hussein, too, seemed to be content with warlike anti-Israeli rhetoric while shipping oil to the United States. Only the Iranian revolution made life difficult for the Americans but, to confront the new regime in Tehran, the Americans did not need Israel. They preferred to have Saddam Hussein as a bulwark, arming and financing him accordingly. Saddam was also led to believe that all his obsessions, including the return of "lost" Kuwait to Iraq, would be supported. In October 1989, after the eight-year-long Iran-Iraq war, April Gillespie, the American ambassador in Baghdad, recommended that Bush Sr. issue a presidential decree ordering a significant improvement in the bilateral trade and oil relationship between the two countries. So, the United States purchased one billion dollars' worth of Iraqi crude oil annually.[31]

In 1990, the Arabist tradition and oil considerations were juxtaposed with pressure from the pro-Israel lobby. In the Arab world, the Iraqi ruler was perceived as a pan-Arabist hero, due to his army's steadfastness against Iranian plans, and Iraqi foreign minister Tariq Aziz took an active role in regional politics. Again, briefly, discrete interests produced a turn in policy. The downfall of the Soviet Union, the Saudi and Iraqi peace initiatives, and the first Palestinian intifada, attracted, in a rare and unique historical moment, Washington's attention to the Palestinian point of view. Israel had, at the time, one of its most right-wing governments. Hence, Bush Sr. engaged in a real dialogue with representatives of two Palestinian power bases: the PLO in Tunis and the Palestinian leadership in East Jerusalem, seated in Orient House. The two bases were perceived as "moderate," not only by Arabists but also by members of the White House.

It was the first time since 1948 that any Palestinian group had been treated in such a way. This was a rare moment of all-Arab consensus on how to solve the conflict—on the basis of the two-state solution—and how to pursue the normalization of the oil supply to the United States. Everyone was happy, apart from Israel and AIPAC. It was, in particular, the pragmatic stance of the Palestinian leadership in Orient House that troubled Israel. Its government reacted with a policy of harassment and the extensive construction of illegal settlements inside East Jerusalem. Official America responded angrily, including a public rebuke from Secretary of State James Baker to the Israeli government.

The pro-Israel lobby reacted on two levels: on Capitol Hill it demonized the Jerusalemite Palestinian leadership and, at the same time, it undermined the alliance with Iraq, aided by its think tank, the Institute for Near East Policy.[32] Iraq's invasion of Kuwait helped enormously on the road to accomplishing the second goal; but it should be noted that the United States had not hesitated to condone such invasions when they served its policy; around that time, its army invaded Grenada and Panama. AIPAC created an anti-Iraq atmosphere long before Saddam Hussein's army invaded Kuwait but the U.S. ambassador in Baghdad concealed this from him, even hinting that the United States would not oppose the invasion. When Iraq did invade Kuwait, the option of sanctions was not even brought forward. The president had been led to this uncompromising policy by a number of experts in the National Security Council and the Pentagon who had known links to the Washington Institute for Near East Policy. The first goal, of demonizing the moderate Palestinians, proved to be tougher. There are always exceptions to the rules of history, and it so happened that George Bush Sr. was ready to tackle Iraq. He accepted Secretary of State James Baker's preference for an Arab coalition as the best means of protecting American interests in the Middle East, even if the price was a peace conference in Madrid that was categorically rejected by Israel.

At the Madrid peace conference, Bush Sr. and his secretary of state were highly impressed by the Palestinian delegation and the leadership evolving around Orient House. Even before Madrid, the beginning of an American dialogue with the PLO in 1988— through the mediation of some American Palestinians, including the late Edward Said and Ibrahim Abu-Lughod—contributed to the continued improvement in the attitude toward the Palestinians, after twelve years of aggressive Republican pro-Israeli policy. In that period, with a continuous license to kill from America, Israel invaded four Arab states and left behind 1,500 dead citizens. Who knows where it would have ended, had not Bush Sr. and, later, Bill Clinton tamed Israel? Thus, for the first time in years, State Department officials were in close contact with a Palestinian group—the teams of the Orient House in Jerusalem—inducing them to believe that the world's superpower was even willing to chastise Israel for its occupation and lack of flexibility. A Palestinian willingness to accept a ministate was to be rewarded with pressure on Israel.

But the Madrid conference and the critical reprimand for Israeli brutality in the occupied territories did not last long. At the end of the day, Bill Clinton proved to be easier prey than AIPAC suspected. A typical Democrat, he was of the opinion that, without the Jewish vote, he could not win presidential elections. The victory of the "peace camp" in the Israeli elections in 1992 enabled Clinton to pursue an explicit pro-Israeli policy that, ostensibly, did not neglect the Palestinian interest. Indeed, Clinton invested much time and energy in the question of Palestine. But the people he appointed to produce a "road map" for peace were mostly Jewish: the remaining Arabists who had a foothold in these issues were pushed out. Without the Arabists, it was easy to advance, on June 30, 1993, a policy paper that stated that Israel should have a free hand in "developing" (read uprooting and colonizing) East

Jerusalem. So the illegal settlements of the past became the integral neighborhoods of the present. The door was opened for the
settlement of two hundred thousand Jews in the eastern part of
the city and the commencement of the transfer of its two hundred
thousand Palestinian inhabitants.[33]

If there were an opposing lobby to AIPAC during Clinton's
years, it came from the Republican camp. It was more of a front
that included not only oil businessmen but also the tycoons who
invested in the arms industry and infrastructure in the Arab world.
This military-industrial nexus had representatives in high positions in the administration: a secretary of state here and a national
security adviser there. Some of the captains of the arms industry,
of course, benefited from military aid to Israel but others did not
fail to see the prospective financial heaven that the Arab world held
for them. It was a formidable and powerful front and yet it failed
totally to redirect American policy. No wonder Mearsheimer and
Walt were so deeply frustrated when they saw such a front, with its
own impressive think tanks and presence in the Ivy League, re-
treating helplessly in the face of AIPAC's charge forward. No wonder they attributed, in their *London Review of Books* piece, such
mystical powers and forces to the Jewish lobby.

This frustration only grew after the election of George Bush Jr.
The Bush family and the influence of the military-industrial complex should have led to a greater say for those who represented oil,
cement, and weapons. At first, indeed, it looked as if these were the
leading considerations. Bush Jr. showed no inclination to be involved where his predecessor had failed. Even the outbreak of the
second intifada was described as the fruit of Clinton's failed policies and did not bother the agenda of the new president. But then
came the 9/11 attacks and Bush's divine Christian and Zionist interventions. The graduates of the Institute for Near East Policy—

Vice President Cheney, Secretary of State Rumsfeld, his deputy Wolfowitz, and Chairman of the Defense Policy Board Advisory Committee Perle—sidelined the more moderate Colin Powell and pressured for a military attack in Iraq. At the same time, a more reasonable assault on al-Qaeda was contemplated in Afghanistan. As Mearsheimer and Walt clearly and convincingly argue, the invasion of Iraq was presented uninhibitedly as, first and foremost, an action to defend Israel against weapons of mass destruction allegedly developed by Saddam Hussein.

Today, this same entourage tries to push for a similar policy toward Iran, a plan that is postponed because of the Iraq quagmire. In 2005, a senior official of the administration testified to one of the senate committees on American policy toward Middle Eastern oil. He enumerated several facts: first, the United States still does not possess an alternative energy source and therefore its policy ought to aim at safeguarding the flow of Middle Eastern oil at all costs; second, an unstable Middle East undermines such a flow; third, global and, in particular, regional trends are anti-American, thus the U.S. economy faces a real danger due to its dependence on Arab oil. There, again, through the prism of "black gold," Israel appears as a liability and not an asset, a message that Arabist policymakers have been trying to convey since 1948. Time will tell if the "five sisters" legacy is eventually successful in balancing the Zionist and Christian lobbies in the United States.[34]

THE MORGENTHAU AND WALTZ LEGACY

In 1943, the German refugee Hans Morgenthau became naturalized as a U.S. citizen. He had arrived in 1937, taught at the University of Kansas, and then moved to the University of Chicago. No other refugee, apart from the Austrian Henry Kissinger, affected American foreign policy as he did.

His book *Politics Among Nations*, published in 1947, provided the clue to his future influence. Morgenthau likened foreign policy to policy in the business world—that is, decision making free of sentiments or values and entirely based on cost/benefit considerations and balances of power. The young state of Israel was one of the first to take up his approach. Throughout October 1948, at the height of Israel's ethnic cleansing of Palestine, Morgenthau advised David Ben-Gurion on a host of political issues. The first prime minister of Israel decided to reward the academic guru by naming a destroyed and evicted Palestinian village after him. The village of Khirbet Beit Far became Tal-Shahar, a translation of Morgenthau to Hebrew.[35] Twenty years later, Kenneth Waltz followed suit. He spent most of his teaching years at Berkeley, California.

He is still today the doyen of international relations as an academic discipline. His claim to fame was a book, *Theory of International Politics*, published in 1979, which challenged some of the basic assumptions of Morgenthau's realist approach; hence, while Morgenthau is referred to as the father of "realism" in international relations, Waltz is the father of "neorealism." Waltz argued that, in the field of international relations, there are no clear patterns of conduct because of the absence of a point of gravity and authority—although he later asserted that U.S. policy could, nevertheless, be based on the cost/benefit considerations that had been sketched by Morgenthau. His is still the ideological infrastructure of most studies in international relations research centers in America. From these centers graduated the American diplomats who were selected to conduct the peace process in the Middle East. The first administration to appoint such a team was that of Richard Nixon, though it was not until the first Bush administration that the existence of such a group became public knowledge. Various experts, some from the State Department and others from the National Security Council and academia, translated the realist and neorealist theories into actual policies. The end result can be summarized as policy based on three principal guidelines. The first and most important is that a peace process has to be based on the local balance of power in the conflictual area.

Thus, when a search begins for the components of a prospective solution, these have to be adapted more to the perception of the stronger party and less to that of the weaker party. We can clearly see, from the very beginnings of the attempt to construct a Pax Americana in Palestine—more or less since 1969—that what the Americans marketed as a peace plan was a formula meant to satisfy the Israeli point of view. The result was a constant and curious disregard of the Palestinian point of view and, more importantly, of what American experts had themselves earlier defined as the heart of the problem: the refugee issue. Today, because the process is in essence an American show, the refugee issue is still written out of the peace script. It is hard to think of a similar concentrated diplomatic effort in modern times that has evaded the root problem of a given conflict. The inevitable collapse of peace efforts at subsequent stages has not altered the basic American position. The second guideline, stemming directly from the first, is that only the stronger party in the conflict should be consulted when the features of a prospective solution are looked for. But within that stronger party, the mediators should seek the "peace camp": its perception is the most flexible element within that stronger party. And its perception has to be imposed on the weaker party.

The essence of peace-making thus became, first, to detect a "peace camp" in Israel in every given historical moment and, then, to attempt to force the view of that camp on the Palestinians. Until 1977, the Israeli Labor Party was that camp. Then, until 1984, the "moderate" wing of the Likud won the title while it was in power.

In the days of Israeli unity governments—which lasted, with a few breaks, until 1992—it was not so much a party as a collection of political figures that, in the eyes of the American experts, represented the political center in Israel. In this century, Ariel Sharon has embodied this camp for the Americans, as today does the party he established—Kadima. The latter is a dream party for any American mediator who wishes to implement the second guideline in peace-making and the "management" of conflicts. "Management," according to the neorealists, means maintaining the conflict as "a low intensity confrontation"—which means the loss of local, human lives, without any damage to the mediating superpower.

The debate inside Israel over the future of the areas it occupied in 1967 helped, of course, to consolidate this guideline: it created the false impression of a genuine debate between a "peace camp" (willing to withdraw fully from the occupied areas) and a "war camp" (favoring a Greater Israel). Since the realist approach did not allow engagements with marginal groups, it focused on the Israeli Labor Party. So, when the latter selected the Jordanians as the only partners for negotiations over the future of the West Bank and the Gaza Strip, the American peace plan was exclusively based on the "Jordanian option." Henry Kissinger was sent to convince the Jordanians to accept the Israeli peace plans, but these offered too little space for the Hashemite leader to be induced to take part in the process. Yet these plans, which offered to leave a sizeable part of the West Bank in Israel and enclave the Gaza Strip as an open-air prison, have remained the basis of any peace plan conceived by successive Israeli peace camps or American "road maps" to peace.

As long as the PLO was too weak to prevent a Jordanian monopoly over the peace plan, American diplomats followed Kissinger and tried to build an Israeli-Hashemite alliance, at the expense of the Palestinians. But, in 1976, the people of the West Bank and the

Gaza Strip deposed the pro-Hashemite leadership in democratic elections and replaced it with one that identified with the PLO. The Americans still refused to include the PLO as a legitimate partner in peace and accepted Israel's image of the organization as a terrorist outfit in the service of the USSR, rather than a liberation movement. Thus, the realist approach connected with the perceptions of the American Christian right; Israel's image as the frontline fighter in the holy war against the Soviet Antichrist continued to dominate American policy in the area. Later, the Antichrist was substituted and became "the Muslim," but Israel retained its special position defending the realm at the very front of the battlefield. This approach distanced the Americans even further from the Palestinian point of view and from the historical UN attempt to solve the conflict.

The Palestinians insisted that the conflict with Israel did not break out in 1967 but stemmed from the ethnic cleansing that Israel committed in 1948. They also tried, with little success, to convey to the Americans a different narrative of the PLO's origins and essence: an organization built by the refugees in order to facilitate their return. There seemed also little point in highlighting for American policy makers the transformation of Fatah's position in 1974. This was when the movement consented to the creation of a Palestinian ministate on the territories Israel occupied in 1967 (22 percent of historical Palestine), provided the right of return would be retained and peace would reign. The basic misunderstanding of Palestinian conditions surrounding the two-state solution led to the fatal course taken later within the framework of the Oslo Accord and the shaky peace proposals that followed in the wake of its demise.

The third guideline is that the peace process has no history. Every attempt begins afresh from a starting point that assumes that there have never been such attempts in the past. Such an approach disables a process of learning—crucial for anyone facing complex human problems of ethnic and national conflicts.

This approach fit well with the interests of those who led the Zionist peace camp in Israel. Thus, when the United States returned to the politics of Palestine in 1969, the Zionist peace camp's understanding—that 1967 was the day the conflict broke out—became rooted in the American conscience and, due to the second guideline, their position became seen as the outline for the whole peace process. Therefore, the peace process became an effort to find a solution to the question of the areas Israel occupied in 1967. The year 1948 was excluded from the peace agenda and, with it, the Palestinians were pushed out as claimants, to be replaced by the Hashemites of Jordan. Only in 1988, when the Hashemite dynasty seemed to have had enough of waiting for a deal and had probably also noticed the strengthening of a collective Palestinian identity in the occupied territories (which unequivocally supported the PLO), was a new realist approach called for. Thus in 1988, when King Hussein declared the cession of the West Bank from Jordan, a new Israeli—and, in turn, new American—approach developed.

The collapse of the Soviet Union weakened, in any case, the image of the PLO as a Soviet agent and eased the onset of PLO-American negotiations. These started in Tunis that year. The Israeli peace movement declared that it was now willing to enter negotiations with the PLO. Again, there was a fusion of discrete historical processes, which matured during the Clinton administration. Never before had international relations academics been given such a free hand in engineering a peace process as Dennis Ross and his friends during the Clinton days. The disastrous fruits of the theoretical games they played with our lives, here in Palestine and Israel, are still with us. The three guidelines were put to the test. The peace camp was now the Rabin Labor government.

The bargain was the same—Israel was willing to withdraw from only part of the occupied territories. The sole change was a new "weak" recipient: the PLO. It was asked to accept, not only part of the territories, but also only part of the authority in them. In addition, it was asked to give up the refugees' right of return or a claim to Jerusalem.

Meanwhile, the reality in the occupied territories changed as well—the settlement project expanded to such proportions that it simply accentuated the humiliating nature of the new Israeli proposal for peace. It is true that, in the very same period, the 1980s and 1990s, American peacemakers could have listed a number of achievements in the realm of Israeli bilateral relations with Jordan and Egypt. Ironically, these peace treaties were concluded because of minimal American involvement in the negotiations. The formula for their success—if the "cold peace" between Israel and its two neighbors can be described as such—was that the treaties did not relate to the Palestine question. The Oslo Accord, although it began in a similar way—namely with minimal American involvement—did become an American show. In fact, for the troubled President Clinton, it was the only show in town. And, at first, it looked likely to work, since the Israelis and the Americans found a Palestinian leader who was willing to succumb to pressure, so completing the process: a plan for peace conceived in the Israeli peace camp, dictated to and accepted by the Palestinians.

As we know now, it was possible because the Palestinian leader Yasser Arafat believed that this state of affairs was temporary; he believed that the Israeli peace camp would dominate the scene for five years before the commencement of final status negotiations, which would bring into consideration the basic Palestinian position. When did Arafat realize he was cheated? We do not know. Was it in Cairo in 1994 when he had to be almost physically coerced by President Hosni Mubarak to sign the Oslo B agreement and when the vague ideas of the September 1993 Declaration of Principles were being translated by Israeli generals into an impossible reality? The expansion of Israeli settlements, the enclaving of Palestinian "autonomous" areas within the settlements, military bases, and highways were not combined with any solution for Jerusalem or the refugee problem. Or did he feel it during the grotesque show Clinton staged much later, in 2000, when he was again physically pushed into a hut in Camp David to sign the Palestinian letter of submission to neorealist logic? The submission text included a final solution that consisted of a Palestinian bantustan in part of the occupied territories and peace for Israel. Even for the fragile Arafat, this was too much. He resisted and the rest, as we know, is indeed history. A sterile version of this outline was repeated after the second intifada broke out. American mediators attempted in vain to revive their mechanism in the framework of the "road map"—that led to nowhere.

The Zionist colonization deepened and produced a particularly desperate resistance, which, in turn, produced the barbaric "retaliation" so familiar to us today. And thus—instead of Dennis Ross and his team asking themselves, as a possible explanation for the lack of progress, who in Israel benefits economically from the occupation—came 9/11. The ensuing narrative was easily plotted: "primitive Islamic fanaticism" explained the inability of the Palestinians to take part in a reasonable and sensible Pax Americana. Ariel Sharon and, after him, Ehud Olmert composed another Israeli version of peace: disengagement from Gaza, while leaving the Palestinians even less territory than was promised to them in Oslo in 1993 and Camp David in 2000. The new prescription was a lasting peace based on a Palestinian state stretching over 12 percent of historical Palestine, with no real sovereignty or economic independence and, of course, with no solution to the fate of Jerusalem or the refugee problem. Again, the developing reality on the ground was grimmer than the words on the pages. Gaza became a huge prison camp, bombarded and starved, with American official and civil society alike blindly standing by. But, who knows, they may still find a Palestinian who will call it an acceptable solution.

CONCLUSION

Of all these historical clusters, it is the bottom line that is definitive—displayed in great strength at the AIPAC annual convention of 2005. In the Washington Congress Center, 26,000 kosher meals were prepared, decorated with 32,640 hors d'oeuvres, 5 tons of salmon, 2.5 tons of turkey, 1 ton of poultry, and 1 ton of hummos. It was enough to feed the 5,000 participants. This culinary feast is only matched by one other event in Washington—the annual joint meeting of the two houses of Congress. The list of guests is similar at both events. Another bottom line can be shown not in tons but in dollars. Since 1949, the United States has passed to Israel more than $100 billion in grants and $10 billion in special loans.[36] Other bodies not part of the administration annually transfer to Israel $1 billion. This is larger than the amount of money transferred by the United States to North Africa, South America, and the Caribbean put together. Their joint population amounts to over one billion people; Israel's population is seven million. Over the last twenty years, $5.5 billion has been given to Israel for military purchases.[37] There is no precedent for such bilateral relations and one does not have to overstate the implications of such a policy for the Palestinians and for the chances of peace in the Middle East. But in this historical narrative, there are also rays of hope. In the complex reality that formulates the American policy, there are factors and processes that, in the past, directed it on a more positive track. And it may be that history, as Michel Foucault tried to convince us, is a list of discrete, disconnected processes whose joint impact is not linked to any one of them but to their fusion into one big explosion. In that case, history is not just a linear movement of endless American support for Israel against, and at the expense of, the Palestinian cause but a more distorted, curved line of ups and downs that indicate possible changes in the future. Moreover, a concerted effort to bring about such a change is a worthy goal—inside and outside the United States. But what we have this year is the ominous call at the 2006 AIPAC convention for the United States to attack and invade Iran.[38]

THREE

STATE OF DENIAL: THE *NAKBAH* IN ISRAELI HISTORY AND TODAY

For Israelis, 1948 is a year in which two things happened that contradict each other: On one hand, Zionism, the Jewish national movement, claimed it fulfilled an ancient dream of returning to a homeland after two thousand years of exile. From this perspective, 1948 was "a miraculous event" in the collective Israeli Jewish memory. It constitutes a chapter in history that not only proclaims triumph and the realization of dreams but also carries associations with moral purity and absolute justice. This is why anything that happened in that year is wedded to the most basic values of present Israeli society. Hence, the military conduct of the Jewish soldiers on the battlefield in 1948 became a model for generations to come, and the leadership's statesmanship in those years is still a paragon for future political elites. The leaders are described as people devoted to the Zionist ideals and as men who disregarded their private interests and good for the sake of the common cause. Nineteen forty-eight, then, is a sacred year, revered in more than one way as the formative source of all that is good in the Jewish society of Israel.

On the other hand, 1948 also marked the worst chapter in Jewish history. In that year, Jews did in Palestine what Jews had not done anywhere else in the previous two thousand years. Even if one puts aside the historical debate about why what happened in 1948 in fact transpired, no one seems to question the enormity of the tragedy that befell the indigenous population of Palestine as a result of the emergence and success of the Zionist movement. Jews expelled, massacred, destroyed, and raped in that year, and generally behaved like all the other colonialist movements operating in the Middle East and Africa since the beginning of the nineteenth century.

In normal circumstances, as Edward Said recommended in his seminal *Culture and Imperialism*,[1] painful dialogue with the past should enable a given society to digest both the most evil and the most glorious moments of its nation's history. But this could not work in a case where a moral self-image is considered to be the principal asset in the battle for public opinion, and thus the best means of surviving in a hostile environment. The way out for the Jewish society in the newly founded state was to erase in the collective memory the unpleasant chapters of the past, and leave intact the gratifying ones. It was a conscious mechanism put in place and motion in order to solve the impossible tension arising from the two contradictory messages of the past.

Moreover, the fact that so many of the people in Israel today lived through the 1948 period has made the task all the more difficult. Nineteen forty-eight is not a distant memory, and the crimes committed then are still visible in the landscape around for the present generation of Israelis to behold and comprehend. On the Palestinian side there are still victims living, who can tell their story; and when they are gone, their descendents—who have heard the tales of the 1948 horrors over and over again—are likely to represent their point of view for generations to come. And, of course, there are people in Israel who know exactly what they did, and there are even more who know what others did.

Nevertheless, the Israeli authorities continue to succeed in eliminating these deeds totally from the society's collective memory, while struggling vigorously against anyone trying to shed light on the repulsive chapters of the 1948 history, whether inside or outside Israel. When one examines Israeli textbooks, curricula, media, and political discourse one notices that this chapter in Jewish history—the chapter of expulsion, colonization, massacres, rape, and the burning of villages—is totally absent. In its stead one finds chapters of heroism, glorious campaigns, and amazing tales of moral courage and military competence, unheard of in any other history of a people's liberation in the twentieth century.

Let us, then, begin with a brief overview of the denied chapters of the history of 1948. Some of these chapters are also missing thus far from the Palestinian collective memory. The two forms of amnesia stem, of course, from two very different ways of dealing with the past: Jewish Israelis are unwilling to acknowledge, or be accountable for, what happened in 1948, whereas the Palestinians, as a community of victims, have little appetite to revisit the traumas of the past. For such distinct reasons, popular memory on both sides, and the failure or unwillingness of professional historians to provide a true representation of the past, have left us without a clear picture of the events of 1948.

THE ERASED CHAPTERS OF EVIL

The 1948 war's diplomatic maneuvers and military campaigns are well engraved in Israeli Jewish historiography. What is missing is the chapter on the ethnic cleansing carried out by the Jews in 1948. As a result of that campaign, five hundred Palestinian villages and eleven urban neighborhoods were destroyed, seven hundred thousand Palestinians were expelled, and several thousand were massacred.[2] Even today, it is hard to find a succinct summary of the planning, execution, and repercussions of these tragic results.

In November 1947, the UN proposed to partition Palestine into a Jewish and an Arab state as the best solution to the conflict. That scheme was very problematic from its inception, for two major reasons. First, it was presented to the two contending parties, not as a basis for negotiation but as a fait accompli, even though the total Palestinian rejection of the principles underpinning the plan was well known to the UN. The alternative course, as proposed by a number of UN member states and later recognized by the American State Department as the better option, was to begin, in 1948, negotiations under the auspices of the UN that would last for several years. The scheme proposed by the UN, in contrast, faithfully represented the Zionist strategy and policy. Imposing the will of one side through the agencies of the UN could not have been a recipe for peace, but rather for war. The Palestinian side viewed the Zionist movement much as the Algerians did the French colonialists. Just as it was unthinkable for the Algerians to agree to share their land with the French settlers, it was unacceptable for the Palestinians to divide Palestine with the Zionist movement. The Palestinians recognized, however, that the cases were different, and consequently a longer period of negotiations was needed, but was not granted.

Second, the Jewish minority (660,000 out of two million) was offered the larger portion of the land (56 percent). The imposed partition, then, would begin with an unjust proposal. Thirdly, because of the demographic distributions of the two communities—the Palestinians and the Jews—the 56 percent of the land offered to the Jews as a state included an equal number of Jews and Palestinians living there. All the Zionist leaders, from left to right, concurred on the need to maintain a considerable Jewish majority in Palestine; in fact, the absence of such a solid majority was regarded as heralding the demise of Zionism. Even a cursory knowledge of Zionist ideology and strategy should have indicated to the UN peace architects that this demographic reality would lead to the near total cleansing of the local population from the future Jewish state.

On March 10, 1948, the Haganah, the main Jewish underground in Palestine, issued a military blueprint preparing the community for the expected British evacuation of Palestine, scheduled for May 15, 1948. The total Arab and Palestinian rejection had led the Jewish leadership to declare the UN resolution dead for all intents and purposes. Already in May 1947, the Jewish Agency had drawn up a map that designated most of Palestine as a Jewish state, apart from the West Bank of today, which was granted to the Transjordanians. Thus, a plan was devised on March 10, 1948, to take over Palestine, apart from those areas promised to Transjordan. The plan was called Plan D (plans A, B, and C had been similar blueprints in the past formulating Zionist strategy vis-à-vis an unfolding and changing reality). Plan D (or *Dalet* in Hebrew) instructed the Jewish forces to cleanse the Palestinian areas falling under their control. The Haganah had several brigades at its disposal, and each one of them received a list of villages it had to occupy and destroy. Most of the villages were destined to be destroyed and only in very exceptional cases were the forces ordered to leave them intact.[3]

The ethnic cleansing operation, beginning in December 1947, continued well into the 1950s. Villages were surrounded on three flanks, and the fourth one was left open for flight and evacuation. In some cases the tactic did not work, and many villagers remained in their houses—it was then that the massacres took place. This was the principal strategy of the Judaization of Palestine.

Ethnic cleansing took place in three stages. The first one was from December 1947 until the end of the summer of 1948, when the coastal and inner plains were destroyed and their population evicted by force. The second one took place in the autumn and winter of 1948–49 and included the Galilee and the Naqab (Negev).

By the winter of 1949, the guns in the land of Palestine were silent. The second phase of the war had ended, and with it the second stage of the cleansing had terminated. Nevertheless, the expulsion continued long after the noise of war had subsided. The third phase of the ethnic cleansing would extend beyond the war, until 1954 in fact, when dozens of additional villages were destroyed and their inhabitants expelled. Of the approximately nine hundred thousand Palestinians living in the territories designated by the UN as a Jewish state only one hundred thousand remained on or near their lands and homes. Those who remained became the Palestinian minority in Israel. The rest were expelled, or fled under the threat of expulsion, and a few thousand died in massacres.

The landscape of the countryside, the rural heartland of Palestine with its thousand colorful and picturesque villages, was ruined. Half the villages were erased from the face of the earth, run over by Israeli bulldozers that set to work in August 1948 when the government decided either to convert the villages into cultivated land or to build new Jewish settlements on their ruins. A special committee was established to give Hebraized versions of the original Arab names to the new settlements—thus, Lubya became Lavi and Safuria was turned into Zipori. David Ben-Gurion, the first prime minister of Israel, explained that this was part of an attempt to prevent future claims to these villages. This process was supported also by the Israeli archeologists who authorized the names, not so much as a takeover of a title, but rather as a form of poetic justice that restored to "ancient Israel" its ancestral map.

Place names were taken from the Bible and attached to the destroyed villages.

Urban Palestine was torn apart and crushed in a similar way. The Palestinian neighborhoods in mixed towns were wrecked, apart from a few quarters that were left empty, waiting to be populated later by incoming Jewish immigrants from Arab countries.

The Palestinian refugees spent the winter of 1948 in tent camps provided by volunteer agencies. Most of these locations were to become their permanent residences. The tents were replaced by clay huts that became a familiar feature of Palestinian existence in the Middle East. The only hope for these refugees at the time was the one offered by UN Resolution 194 (December 11, 1948), promising them a speedy return to their homes. This is one of many pledges made by the international community to the Palestinians that remains unfulfilled to this day.

The catastrophe that befell the Palestinians would be remembered in the collective national memory as the Nakbah (the disaster), kindling the fire that would restore the Palestinians as a national movement. The self-image of this national movement would be that of an indigenous population led by a guerrilla movement striving to turn the clock back, with, as it transpired, very little success.

The Israelis' collective memory, on the other hand, would depict the war as an act of a national liberation movement, fighting both British colonialism and Arab hostility, and ultimately triumphing against all the odds. The loss of 1 percent of the Jewish population, of course, would cast a cloud over the joy of having achieved independence, but would not deter the will and determination of the Zionists to Judaize Palestine and turn it into the future haven for world Jewry. In any event, Israel would turn out to be the most dangerous place for Jews to live in the second half of the twentieth century. Moreover, most Jews have preferred to live outside Israel, and quite a few did not identify with the Jewish project in Palestine, and did not wish to be associated with its dire consequences. Nevertheless, a vociferous minority of Jews in the United States continues to give the impression that world Jewry in general condones the uprooting of the Palestinians and the other events of 1948. The illusion that the majority of Jews have legitimized whatever Israel did in 1948 and thereafter has dangerously compromised the relationship between Jewish minorities and the rest of society in the Western world; particularly in places where public opinion since 1987 has become increasingly hostile to Israel's policies toward the Palestinians.

PROFESSIONAL *REMEMBERING* AND THE NAKBAH

Until very recently, the Israeli-Zionist representation of the 1948 war has dominated the academic world, and probably because of that also, the more general public's perception of the Nakbah. A consequence of this is that the events of 1948 have been consistently portrayed as primarily a war between two armies. Such an assumption calls on the expertise of military historians, who can analyze the military strategy and tactics of both sides. In such a manner, all activities, including even atrocities, are portrayed as part of the theater of war, wherein things are judged on a moral basis in a manner very different from the way they would be treated in a noncombat situation. For instance, it is within this context that the death of civilians during a battle is accepted as an integral part of the battle, and condoned as an action deemed necessary as part of the overall attempt to win a war—although even within a war, of course, there are exceptional atrocities that are not accepted, but rather treated as illegitimate in the military historiography.

Portraying a conflict as a "war" entails also the presumption of parity in questions of moral responsibility for the unfolding events on the ground, including in our case the massive expulsion of an indigenous population. In such a fashion, the paradigm of balancing between the two sides was deemed to be "academic" and "objective," while any Palestinian narrative claiming that there were in 1948 not two equally equipped armies, but rather an expeller and an expelled, an offender and its victims, was dismissed as sheer propaganda.

I suggest, however, that the events that unfolded after May 1948 in Israel and Palestine should be reviewed from within the paradigm of ethnic cleansing, rather than as part of military history. Historiographically, this would mean then that the deeds perpetrated were part of the domestic policies implemented by a regime vis-à-vis civilians—in many cases, given the fact that the ethnic cleansing took place within the designated UN Jewish state, these were operations conducted by a regime against its own citizens.

A Palestinian resident of the village of Tantura has described this new reality better than any historian. His village, situated thirty kilometers south of Haifa, on the coast, became, on May 15, 1948, part of the Jewish state, by virtue of UN partition resolution 181 (November 29, 1947). On May 23 this person, like many others, found himself in a prison camp in Um Khaled (thirty kilometers to the south of his village), and after being there for a year and half, was expelled to the West Bank. "A few days after my new state occupied my village, I became a prisoner of war rather than a citizen." He was a young boy—not an "enemy soldier"—at the time. He was, however, luckier than others of his age who were massacred in his village. Indeed his village Tantura was not a battlefield between two armies, but rather a civilian space invaded by military troops. Ethnic ideology, settlement policy, and demographic strategy were the decisive factors here, not military plans. Massacres, whether premeditated or not, were an integral, not exceptional, part of the ethnic cleansing, even though history has taught us that, in most cases, expulsion was preferred to killing.

For historians the evidence in the archive of the regime committing the ethnic cleansing prevents a clear picture from emerging, since the aim of the regime from the beginning was to obscure its intentions, and this is manifested in the language of the orders and that of the post-event reports. This is why evidence of victims and victimizers is so vital. In the case of the Tantura venture, for example, it was possible to reconstruct what happened mainly through the "bridging" of the evidence provided by the collective and individual memories of victim and victimizer alike.

The ethnic cleansing paradigm also explains why expulsions rather than massacres were of the essence of such crimes. As emerges from the evidence of the Balkan wars of the 1990s, within the general pattern of ethnic cleansing the sporadic massacres perpetrated were more motivated by revenge than the acting out of a clear-cut plan. However, the scheme to create new ethnic realities was facilitated by these massacres, no less than if they had been the result of a policy of systematic expulsion.

The Jewish operation in 1948 fits the definitions of ethnic cleansing contained in the UN reports on the Balkan wars of the 1990s. The UN council for human rights linked the wish to impose ethnic rule on a mixed area—the making of Greater Serbia—with acts of expulsion and with other violent mechanisms. The report defines acts of ethnic cleansing as including the separation of men from women, the detention of men, and the destruction of houses and their repopulation by another ethnic group later on. This was precisely the repertoire of the Jewish soldiers in the 1948 war.

NAKBAH MEMORY IN THE PUBLIC EYE

Ethnic cleansing was perpetrated in 1948 and later altogether denied both in and by Israel. The mechanism of denial is so forceful in Israel, and among its ardent supporters in the United States, that the perspective in this essay provokes much deeper questions. The most important question is the relevance of the Zionist ideology in general to the crimes committed in 1948. Others have shown already that the massive expulsion was the inevitable outcome of a strategy dating back to the late nineteenth century.[4]

The ideology of "transfer" emerged the moment the leaders of the Zionist movement realized that the making of a Jewish state in Palestine could not be achieved as long as the indigenous people of Palestine remained on the land. The presence of a local society and culture had been known to the founding fathers of Zionism even before the first settlers set foot on the land. Theodor Herzl, the founding father of Zionism, already predicted that his dream of a Jewish homeland in Palestine would necessitate expulsion of the indigenous population, as evidenced in one of his diary entries for June 12, 1895. Moving on from his comments on constituting a Jewish society in the land, he got down to the question of forming a state for Jews. He wrote that, having occupied the land and expropriated the private property, "We shall endeavour to expel the poor population across the border unnoticed, procuring employment for it in the transit countries, but denying it any employment in our own country." Herzl added that both "the process of expropriation and the removal of the poor must be carried out discreetly and circumspectly."[5] Ethnic cleansing was also on the minds of the leaders of the second aliya, a kind of a Zionist Mayflower generation.[6]

Two means were used to alter the demographic and "ethnic" reality of Palestine, and impose the Zionist program on the local reality: the dispossession of the indigenous population from the land, and its repopulation with newcomers—i.e., expulsion and settlement. The colonization effort was pushed forward by a movement that had not yet won regional or international legitimacy, and therefore had to buy land and create enclaves within the indigenous population.

The British Empire was very helpful in bringing this scheme into reality. Yet, from the very beginning of the Zionist strategy, the leaders of Zionism knew that settlement was a very long and measured process, which might not be sufficient to realize the revolutionary dreams of the movement and its desire to alter the realities on the ground, and to impose its own interpretation on the land's past, present, and future. To achieve that, the movement needed to resort to more telling means, such as ethnic cleansing and transfer.

As means of Judaizing Palestine, transfer and ethnic cleansing—which would be possible to achieve as suitable "historical opportunities" presented themselves—had been closely associated in Zionist thought and practice. Appropriate circumstances could include the indifference of the international community or the presence of such "revolutionary conditions" as war would provide. The link between purpose and timing was elucidated very clearly in a letter David Ben-Gurion wrote to his son Amos on October 5, 1937: "We must expel Arabs and take their places...and if we have to use force—not to dispossess the Arabs of the Negev and Transjordan, but to guarantee our own right to settle in those places—then we have force at our disposal."[7]

This notion reappeared ever after in Ben-Gurion's addresses to his Mapai party members throughout the mandatory period,[8] right up to the moment when such an opportune moment arose—in 1948.

It is not surprising to read in the Israeli press today, then, that Ariel Sharon considers himself to be the new Ben-Gurion, about to settle the Palestine question once and for all. While the media in the West may be misled into believing that this is part of a newly adopted discourse of peace on the part of a past warmonger, it is, in fact, an ever-loyal contemporary representation of a Ben-Gurionist's search for yet another revolutionary moment that would enable him to further, if not to complete, the process, which had already begun in 1882, of de-Arabizing Palestine and Judaizing it.

THE STRUGGLE AGAINST NAKBAH DENIAL

Nakbah denial in Israel and the West was helped by the overall negation of the Palestinians as a people—the by now infamous denial of the Palestinian people by Israeli prime minister Golda Meir in 1970 epitomized this attitude. Toward the end of the 1980s, as a result of the first intifada, the situation improved somewhat, with the humanization of the Palestinians in the Western media and the result that they could be introduced into the field of Middle Eastern Studies as a legitimate subject matter. In Israel itself, even in those years, Palestinian affairs, academically or publicly, were discussed only by academics who were former intelligence experts on the subject, and who still had close ties with the security services and the IDF (Israeli Defense Forces). This Israeli academic perspective effectively erased the Nakbah as a historical event, and prevented local scholars and academics from challenging the overall denial and suppression of the catastrophe in the world outside the ivory towers of the universities.

The mechanisms of denial in Israel are very effective, because they are a comprehensive means of indoctrination, covering the whole of a citizen's life from the cradle to the grave. It ensures the state that its people do not get confused by facts and reality, or, at least, that they view reality in such a way that it does not create any moral problems.

Nevertheless, already in the 1980s, cracks were beginning to appear in the wall of denial. Even in Israel and the West, the wide exposure in the world media of Israeli war crimes since 1982 raised troubling questions about Israel's self-image as "the only democracy in the Middle East," or as a community belonging to the world of human and civil rights and universal values. But it was the

emergence of critical historiography in Israel in the early 1990s—
the so-called new history—which relocated the Nakbah at the center of the academic and public debate about the conflict. This "new
history" in effect legitimized the Palestinian narrative, after it had
been portrayed for years as sheer propaganda by Western journalists, politicians, and academics.

The challenge to the hitherto hegemonic Zionist presentation of
the 1948 war appeared in various areas of cultural expression—in the
media, academia, and popular arts. It affected the discourse both in
the United States and Israel, but it never entered the political arena.
The celebrated "new history," in fact, was no more than a few books
on 1948 written in English by professionals—e.g., Flapan in 1979 and
1987; Kimmerling in 1983; Masalha in 1992; Morris in 1987, 1990,
and 1993; Pappé in 1988 and 1992; Segev in 1986 and 1993; Shahak in
1975; Shapira in 1992; Shlaim in 1988—only some of which were
translated into Hebrew.[9] These, nevertheless, made it possible, for
anyone wishing to do so, to learn how the Jewish State had been built
on the ruins of the indigenous people of Palestine, whose livelihood,
houses, culture, and land had been systematically destroyed.

Public response in Israel at the time moved between indifference
and the total rejection of the findings of the "new historians." It was
only through elements of the media and the educational system
that people were stimulated, somewhat hesitantly, to take a new
look at the past. Meanwhile, however, from above, the establishment did everything it could to quash these early buds of Israeli
self-awareness and recognition of Israel's role in the Palestinian
catastrophe—a recognition in any event, that would, have helped
Israelis considerably to understand better the continued deadlock
in the peace process.

Outside the academic world, in the West in general, and in the
United States and Israel in particular, this shift in academic percep-

tion had very little impact on the mainstream media and the political scene. In both America and in Jewish Israel, terms such as "ethnic cleansing" and "expulsion" are still today totally alien to politicians, journalists, and common people alike. The relevant chapters of the past that would justify categorically the application of such terms to Israeli origins are either distorted in the recollection of people or are totally absent.

A brief look at Western public opinion is illuminating. One notes that new initiatives were taken in several European countries in the course of the 1990s to relocate the historic and future refugees. It is too early yet to judge how much such efforts—undertaken in the main by pro-Palestinian NGOs—would affect the policies of the various governments. Even in the United States there were signs of movement in a similar direction, when, in April 2000, the first ever American "Right of Return" conference was convened, with about a thousand representatives from all over the country in attendance.[10] But, before September 11, 2001, such efforts failed to impinge upon Capitol Hill, the *New York Times*, or the White House, irrespective of who was in office over the last fifteen years. However, the events of September 11, 2001, have put an end to the new trend, and have promoted the revival of anti-Palestinianism in the United States.

NAKBAH DENIAL AND THE PALESTINE-ISRAEL PEACE PROCESS

Even before the U-turn in American public opinion after September 11, 2001, the movement of academic critique in Israel and the West, with its fresh view on the 1948 ethnic cleansing, was not a particularly impressive player on the stage. It made no impact whatsoever on the Palestine-Israel peace agenda, even though Palestine was the focus of peace efforts precisely at the time when the fresh voices were heard. At the center of these peace efforts was the Oslo Accord that began to roll forward in September 1993. The concept behind this process, as in all previous peace endeavors in Palestine, was a Zionist one. Hence, the Oslo Accord was conducted according to the Israeli perception of peace, from which, of course, the Nakbah was totally absent. The Oslo formula was designed by Israeli thinkers from the Jewish peace camp, people who since 1967 had played an important role in the Israeli public scene. They were institutionalized in an extra-parliamentary movement, Peace Now, and had several parties on their side in the Israeli parliament. In all their previous discourses and plans these Peace Now people had totally evaded the 1948 issue, and had sidelined the refugee question. They did the same in 1993, and this time with the dire consequences of raising hopes of peace, as they seemed to find a Palestinian partner to embrace a concept of peace that altogether buried 1948 and its victims.

With the final stages approaching, the Palestinians realized that, in addition to the absence of a genuine Israeli withdrawal from the occupied West Bank and Gaza Strip, there was no proposed solution to the refugee question on offer. In frustration they rebelled. The climax of the Oslo negotiations at Camp David—the summit meeting between then prime minister of Israel, Ehud Barak, and Yasser Arafat in the summer of 2000—gave the false impression that nothing less than the end of the conflict was on offer. The somewhat naive Palestinian negotiators put the Nakbah, and Israel's responsibility for it, at the top of the Palestinian list of demands. This, of course, was totally rejected by the Israeli team, which succeeded in enforcing its point of view on the summit. But to the Palestinian side's credit, we can acknowledge that, at least for a while, the catastrophe of 1948 was brought to the attention of a local, regional, and, to a certain extent, global audience. Yet, it is clear that the continued denial of the Nakbah in the peace process was the main explanation for the failure of the Camp David summit, the consequence of which was the second uprising in the occupied territories.

Clearly, it was necessary to remind those concerned with the Palestine question, not only in Israel but also in the United States and even in Europe, that the Palestine-Israel conflict involved more than the future of the occupied territories. It also had to contend with the fate of the Palestinian refugees, who had been forced from their homes in 1948. The Israelis had succeeded earlier in sidelining the issue of the refugees' rights from the Oslo Accord, an aim facilitated by ill-managed Palestinian diplomacy and strategy.

Indeed, the Nakbah had been so efficiently kept off the agenda of the peace process that when it suddenly appeared on it, the Israelis felt as if a Pandora's box had been pried open in front of them. The worst fear of the Israeli negotiators was that there was a possibility that Israel's responsibility for the 1948 catastrophe would now become a negotiable issue, and this "danger" was, accordingly, immediately confronted. In the Israeli media and parliament (Knesset), a consensual position was formulated: no Israeli negotiator would be allowed even to discuss the right of return of the Palestinian refugees to the homes they had occupied before 1948. The Knesset passed a law to this effect, and Barak made a public commitment to it on the stairs of the plane taking him to Camp David.

It can be seen, then, that a public debate on the issue of the Nakbah, whether conducted in Israel itself or in the United States, its imperial protector, could open up questions concerning the moral legitimacy of the Zionist project as a whole. The mechanism of denial, therefore, was crucial, not only for defeating the counter-claims made by Palestinians in the peace process, but, far more importantly, for disallowing any significant debate on the very essence and moral foundations of Zionism.

But after the horrid events of September 11, 2001, and the outbreak of the second intifada, with its waves of suicide bombers, the cracks that had already appeared in academia and were beginning to break into public discourse began immediately to close up. Soon the practice of past denials reemerged in Israel with added strength and conviction.

In the United States, an unholy coalition of neoconservatives, Christian Zionists, and AIPAC have had, since 2001 in particular, a firm hold over the American media's presentation of the conflict in Palestine. That coalition's portrayal of the conflict—an altogether innocent, civilized society under siege by terrorists—enables Israel to get away with both its past behavior and its present policies, which, if perpetrated by any other state would surely merit for it the designation "pariah state."

FUTURE PROSPECTS

As I review the attempts I have made—I have been involved personally in the struggle against Nakbah denial in Israel, and, together with others, have attempted to bring the Nakbah onto the Israeli public agenda—a very mixed picture emerges. I detect serious cracks in the wall of denial and repression that surrounds the issue of the Nakbah in Israel, which have come about as a result of the debate on the "new history" in Israel, and of the new political agenda of the Palestinians in Israel. The new atmosphere has also been helped by a clarification of the Palestinian position on the refugee issue toward the end of the Oslo peace process. As a result, notwithstanding more than fifty years of systemic government suppression, it is becoming more and more difficult in Israel to deny the expulsion and destruction of the

Palestinians in 1948. However, this relative success has also brought with it two negative reactions, which were formulated after the outbreak of the Al-Aqsa Intifada.

The Israeli political establishment was the first to react. The Sharon government, through its minister of education, has undertaken the systematic removal of any textbook or school syllabus that refers to the Nakbah, even marginally. Similar instructions have been given to the public broadcasting authorities. The second reaction has been even more disturbing, and has encompassed wider sections of the public. Although a very considerable number of Israeli politicians, journalists, and academics have ceased to deny what happened in 1948, they have nonetheless also been willing to justify it publicly, not only in retrospect, but also as a prescription for the future. Thus, the idea of "transfer" has entered Israeli political discourse openly for the first time, portraying "population transfer" as legitimate, being the most effective means of dealing with the Palestinian "problem."

Indeed, if I were asked to sum up what best characterizes the current Israeli response to the Nakbah, I would stress the growing popularity of the transfer option in the Israeli public mood and thought. The Nakbah—the expulsion of the Palestinians from Palestine—now seems to many in the center of the political map as an inevitable and justifiable consequence of the Zionist project in Palestine. If there is any lament, it is that the expulsion was not completed. The fact that even an Israeli "new historian" such as Benny Morris now subscribes to the view that the expulsion was inevitable, and should have been more comprehensive in 1948, helps to legitimize future Israeli plans for further ethnic cleansing.

"Population transfer" is now the official, "moral" option recommended by one of Israel's most prestigious academic centers, the Centre for Interdisciplinary Studies in Herzliya, which advises the government. It has appeared as a policy proposal in papers presented to their government by senior Labor Party ministers. It is openly advocated by university professors and media commentators, and very few now dare to condemn it (such as the Beer Sheba historian, Professor Benny Morris, and the Haifa historian, Professor Yoav Gelber, and Haifa University geography professor Arnon Sofer in a direct manner, and in an indirect manner by Professor Shlomo Avineri of the Hebrew University and Ephraim Sneh of the Labor Party, who suggest the annexation of the Palestinian parts of Israel to a Palestinian state). And, lately, even the leader of the majority in the U.S. House of Representatives has openly endorsed it.[11]

As this book is written there is a new president in the White House. So far the American policy has not produced any changes in previous approaches. The political scene in Israel has also remained much the same: transferists such as Avigdor Liberman hold key positions such as foreign minister, and frequent censuses indicate a growing support for transfer of Arabs from any part deemed Jewish.

Thus, the circle is being closed, almost before our very eyes. When Israel took almost 80 percent of Palestine in 1948, it did so through settlement and the ethnic cleansing of the original Palestinian population. The country now has a consensual government that enjoys wide public support, and wants to determine by force the future of the remaining 20 percent. It has, as have all its predecessors, from Labor and Likud alike, resorted to settlement as the best means for doing this. This entails the destruction of an independent Palestinian infrastructure. These politicians sense—and they may not be wrong in this—that the public mood in Israel would allow them to go even further, should they wish to do so. They could emulate the ethnic cleansing of 1948, this time not only by driving the Palestinians out of the occupied territories, but, if necessary, also driving out the one million Palestinians living within the pre-1967 borders of Israel.

In such an atmosphere, then, the Nakbah is not so much denied in Israel as cherished. Nevertheless, the full story of 1948 needs to be told to the Israelis, as there may still be some among that state's population who are sensitive about their country's past and present conduct. This segment of the population should be alerted to the fact that horrific deeds were concealed from them about Israeli actions in 1948, and they should be told, too, that such deeds could easily now be repeated, if they, and others, do not act to stop them before it is too late.

The struggle against the denial of the Nakbah in Israel is now the focus of the agenda of certain Palestinian groups, both inside and outside Israel. They are joined by the committed and impressive Jewish NGO, Zochrot, struggling against Nakbah denial in Israel. Since the fortieth anniversary of the Nakbah in 1988, the Palestinian minority in Israel has associated, in a way that it never did previously, its collective and individual memories of the catastrophe with the general Palestinian situation, and with their predicament in particular. This association has been manifested through an array of symbolic gestures, such as memorial services during Nakbah commemoration day, organized tours to deserted or formerly Palestinian villages in Israel, seminars on the past, and extensive interviews with Nakbah survivors in the press.

In Israel itself, through its political leaders, NGOs, and the media, the Palestinian minority has been able to force the wider public to take notice of the Nakbah. This reemergence of the Nakbah as a topic for public debate will also disable any future peace plans that will be built on Nakbah denial, including, of course, the various plans and initiatives that have emerged since 2003.

FOUR

"EXTERMINATE ALL THE BRUTES": GAZA 2009

On Saturday December 27, 2008, the latest U.S.-Israeli attack on helpless Palestinians was launched. The attack had been meticulously planned, for over six months according to the Israeli press. The planning had two components: military and propaganda. It was based on the lessons of Israel's 2006 invasion of Lebanon, which was considered to be poorly planned and badly advertised. We may, therefore, be fairly confident that most of what has been done and said was pre-planned and intended.

That surely includes the timing of the assault: shortly before noon, when children were returning from school and crowds were milling in the streets of densely populated Gaza City. It took only a few minutes to kill over two hundred people and wound seven hundred, an auspicious opening to the mass slaughter of defenseless civilians trapped in a tiny cage with nowhere to flee.[1]

The attack specifically targeted the closing ceremony of a police academy, killing dozens of policemen. The international law division of the Israeli Army (IDF, Israeli Defense Forces) had criticized the plans for months, but under army pressure, its director, Colonel

Pnina Sharvit-Baruch, gave the department's approval. "Also under pressure," *Haaretz* reports, "Sharvit-Baruch and the division also legitimized the attack on Hamas government buildings and the relaxing of the rules of engagement, resulting in numerous Palestinian casualties." The international law division adopts "permissive positions" so as "to remain relevant and influential," the article continues. Sharvit-Baruch then joined the law faculty at Tel Aviv University, over protests by the director of the university's human rights center and other faculty.

The legal division's decision was based on the army's categorization of the police "as a resistance force in the event of an Israeli incursion into the Gaza Strip," Hebrew University law professor Yuval Shany observed, adding that the principle scarcely "differentiates them from [Israeli] reservists or even from 16-year-olds who will be drafted in two years"—hence takes much of Israel's population to be legitimate targets of terror.[2] To take a different analogy, the IDF rules of engagement justify the terrorist attack on police cadets in Lahore in March 2009, killing at least eight, rightly condemned as "barbaric"; Pakistani elite forces could, however, respond in this case, killing or capturing the terrorists, an option not available to Gazans. The narrow scope of the IDF concept of "protected civilian" is explained further by a senior figure in its international law division: "The people who go into a house despite a warning do not have to be taken into account in terms of injury to civilians, because they are voluntary human shields. From the legal point of view, I do not have to show consideration for them. In the case of people who return to their home in order to protect it, they are taking part in the fighting."[3]

In his retrospective analysis entitled "Parsing Gains of Gaza War," *New York Times* correspondent Ethan Bronner cited the first day's achievement as one of the most significant of the war's gains.

Israel calculated that it would be advantageous to appear to "go crazy," causing vastly disproportionate terror, a doctrine that traces back to the 1950s. "The Palestinians in Gaza got the message on the first day," Bronner wrote, "when Israeli warplanes struck numerous targets simultaneously in the middle of a Saturday morning. Some 200 were killed instantly, shocking Hamas and indeed all of Gaza." The tactic of "going crazy" appears to have been successful, Bronner concluded: there are "limited indications that the people of Gaza felt such pain from this war that they will seek to rein in Hamas," the elected government.[4] Inflicting pain on civilians for political ends is another long-standing doctrine of state terror, in fact its guiding principle. I do not, incidentally, recall the *Times* retrospective "Parsing Gains of Chechnya War," though the gains were great.

The meticulous planning also presumably included the termination of the assault. It ended just before the inauguration, thus minimizing the (remote) threat that President Obama might have to say some words critical of these vicious U.S.-supported crimes.

Two weeks after the Sabbath opening of the assault, with much of Gaza already pounded to rubble and the death toll approaching a thousand, the UN agency UNRWA (the United Nations Relief and Works Agency for Palestine Refugees in the Near East), on which most Gazans depend for survival, announced that the Israeli military refused to allow aid shipments to Gaza, saying that the crossings were closed for the Sabbath.[5] To honor the holy day, Palestinians at the edge of survival must be denied food and medicine, while hundreds can be slaughtered on the Sabbath by U.S. jet bombers and helicopters.

The rigorous observance of the Sabbath in this dual fashion attracted little if any notice. That makes sense. In the annals of U.S.-Israeli criminality, such cruelty and cynicism scarcely merit more than a footnote. They are too familiar. To cite one relevant parallel, in June 1982 the U.S.-backed Israeli invasion of Lebanon opened with the bombing of the Palestinian refugee camps of Sabra and Shatila, later to become famous as the site of terrible massacres supervised by the IDF. The bombing hit the local hospital—the Gaza hospital—and killed over two hundred people, according to the eyewitness account of an American Middle East academic specialist. The massacre was the opening act in an invasion that slaughtered some fifteen thousand to twenty thousand people and destroyed much of southern Lebanon and Beirut, proceeding with crucial U.S. military and diplomatic support. That included vetoes of Security Council resolutions seeking to halt the criminal aggression that was undertaken, scarcely concealed, to defend Israel from the threat of peaceful political settlement. This was contrary to useful fabrications about Israelis suffering under intense rocketing, a fantasy of apologists.[6]

All of this is normal, and quite frankly discussed by high Israeli officials. Thirty years ago Chief of Staff Mordechai Gur observed that since 1948, "we have been fighting against a population that lives in villages and cities."[7] As Israel's most prominent military analyst, Zeev Schiff, summarized his remarks, "the Israeli Army has always struck civilian populations, purposely and consciously...The Army," he said, "has never distinguished civilian [from military] targets...[but] purposely attacked civilian targets."[8] The reasons were explained by the distinguished statesman Abba Eban: "there was a rational prospect, ultimately fulfilled, that affected populations would exert pressure for the cessation of hostilities." The effect, as Eban well understood, would be to allow Israel to implement, undisturbed, its programs of illegal expansion and harsh repression. Eban was commenting on a review of Labor government attacks against civilians by Prime Minister Begin, presenting a picture, Eban said, "of an Israel wantonly inflicting every possible measure of death and anguish on civilian populations in a mood reminiscent of regimes which neither Mr. Begin nor I would dare to mention by name."[9] Eban did not contest the facts that Begin reviewed, but criticized him for stating them publicly. Nor did it concern Eban, or his admirers, that his advocacy of massive state terror is also reminiscent of regimes he would not dare to mention by name.

Eban's justification for state terror is regarded as persuasive by respected authorities. As the current U.S.-Israel assault raged, *New York Times* columnist Thomas Friedman explained that Israel's tactics in the current attack, as in its invasion of Lebanon in 2006, are based on the sound principle of "trying to 'educate' Hamas, by inflicting a heavy death toll on Hamas militants and heavy pain on the Gaza population." That makes sense on pragmatic grounds, as it did in Lebanon, where "the only long-term source of deterrence was to exact enough pain on the civilians—the families and employers of the militants—to restrain Hezbollah in the future."[10] And by similar logic, bin Laden's effort to "educate" Americans on 9/11 was highly praiseworthy, as were the Nazi attacks on Lidice and Oradour, Putin's destruction of Grozny, and other notable educational exercises.

New York Times correspondent Steven Erlanger reports that Israeli human rights groups are "troubled by Israel's strikes on buildings they believe should be classified as civilian, like the parliament, police stations and the presidential palace"—and, we may add, villages, homes, densely populated refugee camps, water and sewage systems, hospitals, schools and universities, mosques, UN relief facilities, ambulances, and indeed anything that might relieve the pain of the unworthy victims. A senior Israeli intelligence officer explained that the IDF attacked "both aspects of Hamas—its resistance or military wing and its dawa, or social wing," the latter a euphemism for the civilian society. "He argued that Hamas was all of a piece," Erlanger continues, "and in a war, its instruments of political and social control were as legitimate a target as its rocket caches." Erlanger and his editors add no comment about the open advocacy, and practice, of massive terrorism targeting civilians, though correspondents and columnists signal their tolerance or even explicit advocacy of such crimes, as noted. But keeping to the norm, Erlanger does not fail to stress that unlike U.S.-Israeli actions, Hamas rocketing is "an obvious violation of the principle of discrimination and fits the classic definition of terrorism."[11]

Like others familiar with the region, Middle East specialist Fawaz Gerges observes, "What Israeli officials and their American allies do not appreciate is that Hamas is not merely an armed militia but a social movement with a large popular base that is deeply entrenched in society." Hence when they carry out their plans to destroy Hamas's "social wing," they are aiming to destroy Palestinian society.[12]

Gerges may be too generous. It is highly unlikely that Israeli and American officials—or the media and other commentators—do not appreciate these facts. Rather, they implicitly adopt the traditional perspective of those who virtually monopolize the means of violence: our mailed fist can crush any opposition, and if our furious assault has a heavy civilian toll, that's all to the good—perhaps the remnants will be properly educated.

IDF officers clearly understand that they are crushing the civilian society. Ethan Bronner quotes an Israeli colonel who says that he and his men are not much "impressed with the Hamas fighters." "They are villagers with guns," said a gunner on an armored personnel carrier. They resemble the victims of the murderous IDF Iron Fist operations in occupied southern Lebanon in 1985, directed by Shimon Peres, one of the great terrorist commanders of the era of Reagan's "war on terror." During these operations, Is-

raeli commanders and strategic analysts explained that the victims were "terrorist villagers," difficult to eradicate because "these
terrorists operate with the support of most of the local population." An Israeli commander complained that "the terrorist...has
many eyes here, because he lives here," while the military correspondent of the *Jerusalem Post* described the problems Israeli
forces faced in combating the "terrorist mercenary" "fanatics, all
of whom are sufficiently dedicated to their causes to go on running the risk of being killed while operating against the IDF,"
which must "maintain order and security" in occupied southern
Lebanon despite "the price the inhabitants will have to pay." The
problem has been familiar to Americans in South Vietnam, Russians in Afghanistan, Germans in occupied Europe, and others
who find themselves righteously implementing the Gur-Eban-
Friedman doctrine.[13]

Gerges believes that U.S.-Israeli state terror will fail: Hamas, he
writes, "cannot be wiped out without massacring half a million
Palestinians. If Israel succeeds in killing Hamas's senior leaders, a
new generation, more radical than the present, will swiftly replace
them. Hamas is a fact of life. It is not going away, and it will not
raise the white flag regardless of how many casualties it suffers."[14]

Perhaps, but there is often a tendency to underestimate the effi-
cacy of violence. It is particularly odd that such a belief should be
held in the United States. Why are we here?

Hamas is regularly described as "Iranian-backed Hamas, which
is dedicated to the destruction of Israel." One will be hard put to
find something like "democratically elected Hamas, which has
long been calling for a two-state settlement in accord with the international consensus"—blocked for more than thirty years by the
United States and Israel. All true, but not a useful contribution to
the Party Line, hence dispensable.

Such details as those mentioned earlier, though minor in context, nevertheless teach us something about ourselves and our clients. So do others. To mention another one, as the latest U.S.-Israeli assault on Gaza began, a small boat, the *Dignity*, was on its way from Cyprus to Gaza. The doctors and human rights activists aboard intended to violate Israel's criminal blockade and to bring medical supplies to the trapped population. The ship was intercepted in international waters by Israeli naval vessels, which rammed it severely, almost sinking it, though it managed to limp to Lebanon. Israel issued the routine lies, refuted by the journalists and passengers aboard, including CNN correspondent Karl Penhaul and former U.S. representative and Green Party presidential candidate Cynthia McKinney.[15] That is a serious crime—much worse, for example, than hijacking boats off the coast of Somalia. It passed with little notice. The tacit acceptance of such crimes reflects the understanding that Gaza is occupied territory, and that Israel is entitled to maintain its siege, and is even authorized by the guardians of international order to carry out crimes on the high seas to implement its programs of punishing the civilian population for disobedience to its commands—under pretexts to which we return, almost universally accepted but clearly untenable.

The lack of attention again makes sense. For decades, Israel had been hijacking boats in international waters between Cyprus and Lebanon, killing or kidnapping passengers, sometimes bringing them to prisons in Israel, including secret prison/torture chambers, to hold as hostages for many years.[16] Since the practices are routine, why treat the new crime with more than a yawn? Cyprus and Lebanon reacted quite differently, but who are they in the scheme of things?

Who cares, for example, if the editors of Lebanon's *Daily Star*, generally pro-Western, write,

Some 1.5 million people in Gaza are being subjected to the murder-ous ministrations of one of the world's most technologically ad-vanced but morally regressive military machines. It is often suggested that the Palestinians have become to the Arab world what the Jews were to pre-World War II Europe, and there is some truth to this in-terpretation. How sickeningly appropriate, then, that just as Euro-peans and North Americans looked the other way when the Nazis were perpetrating the Holocaust, the Arabs are finding a way to do nothing as the Israelis slaughter Palestinian children.[17]

Perhaps the most shameful of the Arab regimes is the brutal Egyptian dictatorship, the beneficiary of the most U.S. military aid, apart from Israel.

According to Lebanese scholar Amal Saad-Ghorayeb, Israel still "routinely abducts Lebanese civilians from the Lebanese side of the Blue Line [the international border], most recently in De-cember 2008." And of course "Israeli planes violate Lebanese air-space on a daily basis in violation of UN Resolution 1701." That too has been happening for a long time. In condemning Israel's double standards after its invasion of Lebanon in 2006, Israeli strategic analyst Zeev Maoz wrote that "Israel has violated Lebanese airspace by carrying out aerial reconnaissance missions virtually every day since its withdrawal from Southern Lebanon six years ago. True, these aerial overflights did not cause any Lebanese casualties, but a border violation is a border violation. Here too, Israel does not hold a higher moral ground." And in general, there is no basis for the "wall-to-wall consensus in Israel that the war against the Hezbollah in Lebanon is a just and moral war," a consensus "based on selective and short-term memory, on an introvert world view, and on double standards. This is not a just war, the use of force is excessive and indiscriminate, and its ultimate aim is extortion."[18]

Maoz also reminds his Israeli readers that overflights with sonic booms to terrorize Lebanese are the least of Israeli crimes in Lebanon, even apart from its five invasions since 1978:

On July 28, 1988 Israeli Special Forces abducted Sheikh Obeid, and on May 21, 1994 Israel abducted Mustafa Dirani, who was responsible for capturing the Israeli pilot Ron Arad [when he was bombing Lebanon in 1986]. Israel held these and 20 other Lebanese who were captured under undisclosed circumstances in prison for prolonged periods without trial. They were held as human "bargaining chips." Apparently, abduction of Israelis for the purpose of prisoners' exchange is morally reprehensible, and militarily punishable when it is the Hezbollah who does the abducting, but not if Israel is doing the very same thing.[19]

And on a far grander scale and over many years.

Israel's regular practices are significant even apart from what they reveal about Israeli criminality and Western support for it. As Maoz indicates, these practices underscore the utter hypocrisy of the standard claim that Israel had the right to invade Lebanon once again in 2006 when Israeli soldiers were captured at the border, the first cross-border action by Hezbollah in the six years since Israel's withdrawal from southern Lebanon, which it occupied in violation of Security Council orders going back twenty-two years. Yet during these six years after withdrawal Israel violated the border almost daily with impunity, and is met only with silence here.

The hypocrisy is, again, routine. Thus Thomas Friedman, while instructing us on how the lesser breeds are to be "educated" by terrorist violence, writes that Israel's invasion of Lebanon in 2006, once again destroying much of southern Lebanon and Beirut while killing another thousand civilians, was a just act of self-defense, responding to Hezbollah's crime of "launching an unprovoked war across the U.N.-recognized Israel-Lebanon border, after Israel had unilaterally withdrawn from Lebanon." Similarly, Senate Foreign Relations Committee Chair John Kerry, speaking at the Brookings Institution, laments "the failure of Israel's unilateral disengagements from Southern Lebanon and Gaza to bring peace" (we will return to its "disengagement" from Gaza). Putting aside the deceit, by the same logic, terrorist attacks against Israelis that are far more destructive and murderous than any that have taken place would be fully justified in response to Israel's criminal practices in Lebanon and on the high seas, which vastly exceed Hezbollah's crime of capturing two soldiers at the border. The veteran Middle East specialist of the *New York Times* surely knows about these crimes, at least if he reads his own newspaper. For example, the eighteenth paragraph of a story on prisoner exchange observes, casually, that thirty-seven of the Arab prisoners "had been seized recently by the Israeli Navy as they tried to make their way from Cyprus to Tripoli," north of Beirut.[20]

Of course all such conclusions about appropriate actions against the rich and powerful are based on a fundamental flaw: This is *us*, and that is *them*. This crucial principle, deeply embedded in Western culture, suffices to undermine even the most precise analogy and the most impeccable reasoning.

The new crimes that the United States and Israel were committing in Gaza as 2009 opened do not fit easily into any standard category—except for the category of familiarity; I have just mentioned several examples, and will return to others. Literally, the crimes fall under the official U.S. government definition of "terrorism," but that designation does not capture their enormity. They cannot be called "aggression," because they are being conducted in occupied territory, as the United States tacitly concedes, and as serious scholarship recognizes. In their comprehensive history of Israeli settlement in the occupied territories, Idith Zertal and Akiva Eldar point out that after Israel withdrew its forces from Gaza in August 2005, the ruined territory was not released "for even a single day from Israel's military grip or from the price of the occupation that the inhabitants pay every day." They write, "Israel left behind scorched earth, devastated services, and people with neither a present nor a future. The settlements were destroyed in an ungenerous move by an unenlightened occupier, which in fact continues to control the territory and kill and harass its inhabitants by means of its formidable military might"[21]—which can be exercised with extreme savagery, thanks to firm U.S. support and participation.

The U.S.-Israeli assault on Gaza escalated in January 2006, a few months after the formal withdrawal, when Palestinians committed a truly heinous crime: they voted "the wrong way" in a free election. Like others, Palestinians learned that one does not disobey with impunity the commands of the master, who never ceases to orate about his "yearning for democracy" without eliciting ridicule from the educated classes, another impressive achievement.

Since the terms "aggression" and "terrorism" are inadequate, some new term is needed for the sadistic and cowardly torture of people caged with no possibility of escape, while they are being pounded to dust by the most sophisticated products of U.S. military technology. That technology is used in violation of international and even U.S. law, but for self-declared outlaw states that is just another minor technicality.

Also a minor technicality is the fact that on December 31, 2008, while terrorized Gazans were desperately seeking shelter from the ruthless assault, Washington hired a German merchant ship to transport from Greece to Israel three thousand tons of unidentified "ammunition." The new shipment "follows the hiring of a commercial ship to carry a much larger consignment of ordnance in December from the United States to Israel ahead of air strikes in the Gaza Strip," Reuters reported.[22] "Israel's intervention in the Gaza Strip has been fueled largely by U.S. supplied weapons paid for with U.S. tax dollars," said a briefing by the New America Foundation, which monitors the arms trade.[23] The new shipment was hampered by the decision of the Greek government to bar the use of any port in Greece "for the supplying of the Israeli army."[24]

All of this is separate from the more than $21 billion in U.S. military aid provided by the Bush administration to Israel, almost all grants. Obama intends to ensure that the largesse extends far into the future, whatever circumstances might be down the road. He calls for "sending up to $30 billion in unconditional military aid to Israel over the next 10 years," foreign policy analyst Stephen Zunes reports, a 25 percent increase over the Bush administration, and "a bonanza for U.S. arms manufacturers," who contribute to candidates "several times what the 'pro-Israel' PACs contribute," and tirelessly "promote massive arms transfers to the Middle East and elsewhere."[25]

Greece's response to U.S.-backed Israeli crimes is rather different from the craven performance of the leaders of most of Europe. The distinction reveals that Washington may have been quite realistic in regarding Greece as part of the Near East, not Europe, until 1974. Perhaps Greece is just too civilized to be part of Europe.

For anyone who might find the timing of the new arms deliveries to Israel curious, the Pentagon has an answer: the shipment would arrive too late to escalate the Gaza attack, and the military equipment, whatever it may be, is to be pre-positioned in Israel for eventual use by the U.S. military.[26] That is quite plausible. One of the many services that Israel performs for its patron is to provide it with a valuable military base at the periphery of the world's major energy resources. It can therefore serve as a forward base for U.S.

aggression—or to use the technical terms, to "defend the Gulf" and "ensure stability."

The huge flow of arms to Israel serves many subsidiary purposes. Middle East policy analyst Mouin Rabbani observes that Israel can test newly developed weapons systems against defenseless targets. This is of value to Israel and the United States "twice over, in fact, because less effective versions of these same weapons systems are subsequently sold at hugely inflated prices to Arab states, which effectively subsidizes the U.S. weapons industry and U.S. military grants to Israel."[27] These are additional functions of Israel in the U.S.-dominated Middle East system, and among the reasons why Israel is so favored by the state authorities, along with a wide range of U.S. high-tech corporations, and of course military industry and intelligence.

Apart from Israel, the United States is by far the world's major arms supplier. The recent New America Foundation report concludes that "U.S. arms and military training played a role in 20 of the world's 27 major wars in 2007," earning the United States $23 billion in receipts, increasing to $32 billion in 2008. Small wonder that among the numerous UN resolutions that the United States opposed in the December 2008 UN session was one calling for regulation of the arms trade. In 2006, the United States was alone in voting against the treaty, but in November 2008 it was joined by a partner: Zimbabwe.[28]

There were other notable votes at the December UN session. A resolution on "the right of the Palestinian people to self-determination" was adopted by 173 to 5 (United States, Israel, Pacific Island dependencies; the United States and Israel added evasive pretexts). The vote reaffirms U.S.-Israeli rejectionism, in international isolation. Similarly a resolution on "universal freedom of travel and the vital importance of family reunification" was adopted over the opposition of the

United States, Israel, and Pacific Island dependencies, presumably with Palestinians in mind: Israel bars entry to Palestinians from the occupied territories who wish to join their Israeli spouses.

In voting against the right to development the United States lost Israel but gained Ukraine. In voting against the "right to food," the United States was alone, a particularly striking fact in the face of the enormous global food crisis, dwarfing the financial crisis that threatens Western economies.

It is easy to understand why the UN voting record is consistently unreported and dispatched deep into the memory hole by the media and conformist intellectuals. It would not be wise to reveal to the public what the record implies about their elected representatives.

One of the heroic volunteers in Gaza, Norwegian doctor Mads Gilbert, described the scene of horror as an "all-out war against the civilian population of Gaza." He estimated that half the casualties were women and children. Gilbert reported that he had scarcely seen a military casualty among the hundreds of bodies. That is not too surprising. Hamas "made a point of fighting at a distance—or not at all," Ethan Bronner reports while "parsing the gains" of the U.S.-Israeli assault. So Hamas's manpower remains intact, and it was mostly civilians who suffered pain: a positive outcome, according to widely held doctrine.[29]

These estimates were confirmed by UN humanitarian chief John Holmes, who informed reporters that it is "a fair presumption" that most of the civilians killed were women and children in a humanitarian crisis that is "worsening day by day as the violence continues." But we could be comforted by the words of Israeli foreign minister Tzipi Livni, the leading dove in the ongoing electoral campaign, who assured the world that there is no "humanitarian crisis" in Gaza, thanks to Israeli benevolence.[30]

Like others who care about human beings and their fate, Gilbert and Holmes pleaded for a cease-fire—but not yet. "At the United Nations, the United States blocked the Security Council from issuing a formal statement on Saturday night calling for an immediate cease-fire," the *New York Times* mentioned in passing. The official reason was that "there was no indication Hamas would abide by any agreement."[31] In the annals of justifications for slaughter, this pretext must rank among the more cynical. That of course was Bush and Rice, soon to be displaced by Obama, who compassionately repeated, "if somebody was sending rockets into my house, where my two daughters sleep at night, I'm going to do everything in my power to stop that." He was referring to Israeli children, not the many hundreds being torn to shreds in Gaza by U.S. arms. Beyond that Obama maintained his silence.[32]

A few days later, on January 8, the Security Council passed a resolution calling for a "durable cease-fire." The vote was 14 to 0, United States abstaining. Israel and U.S. hawks were angered that the United States did not veto the resolution, as usual. The abstention, however, sufficed to give Israel at least a yellow light to escalate the violence, as it did virtually right up to the moment of the inauguration, as had been predicted.

As the cease-fire (theoretically) went into effect, the Palestinian Center for Human Rights released its figures for the final day of the assault: 54 Palestinians killed, including 43 unarmed civilians, 17 of them children, while the IDF continued to bombard civilian homes and UN schools. The death toll, they estimated, mounted to 1,184, including 844 civilians, 281 of them children. The IDF continued to use incendiary bombs across the Gaza Strip, and to destroy houses and agricultural land, forcing civilians to flee their homes. A few hours later, Reuters reported more than 1,300 killed. The staff of the Al Mezan Center, which carefully monitors casualties and destruction, visited areas that had previously been inaccessible because of incessant heavy bombardment. They discovered dozens of civilian corpses decomposing under the rubble of destroyed houses or rubble removed by Israeli bulldozers. Entire urban blocks had disappeared.[33]

The figures for killed and wounded are surely an underestimate. And it is unlikely that there will be any serious investigation of these atrocities, despite calls for an inquiry into war crimes by Amnesty International, Human Rights Watch, and the Israeli human rights organization B'Tselem. Crimes of official enemies are subjected to rigorous investigation, but our own are systematically ignored. General practice, again, and understandable on the part of the masters, who rigorously adhere to a variant of the "too big to fail" insurance policy granted to major financial institutions by Washington, which provides them with great competitive advantages in a form of protectionism that is protected from the usage of the unfavourable term *protectionism*. The United States is just "too big to hold to account," whether by judicial inquiry, boycott and sanctions, or other means.

The January 8 Security Council resolution called for stopping the flow of arms into Gaza. The United States and Israel (Rice-Livni) soon reached an agreement on measures to ensure this result, concentrating on Iranian arms. There is no need to stop smuggling of U.S. arms into Israel, because there is no smuggling: the huge flow of arms is quite public, even when not reported, as in the case of the arms shipment announced as the slaughter in Gaza was proceeding. It was later learned that shortly after the end of its military attack on Gaza, Israel apparently also bombed Sudan, killing dozens of people, also sinking a ship in the Red Sea.[34] The targets were suspected to be arms shipments intended for Gaza, so there was no reaction. An Iranian effort to impede the flow of U.S.

arms to the aggressor would have been regarded as a horrendous terrorist atrocity, which might well have led to nuclear war.

The resolution also called for "ensur[ing] the sustained reopening of the crossing points on the basis of the 2005 Agreement on Movement and Access between the Palestinian Authority and Israel"; that agreement determined that crossings to Gaza would be operated on a continuous basis and that Israel would also allow the crossing of goods and people between the West Bank and the Gaza Strip.

The Rice-Livni agreement had nothing to say about this aspect of the Security Council Resolution. The United States and Israel had abandoned the 2005 agreement as part of their punishment of Palestinians for voting the wrong way in the January 2006 election. Rice's press conference after the 2009 Rice-Livni agreement emphasized Washington's continuing efforts to undermine the results of the one free election in the Arab world: "There is much that can be done," she said, "to bring Gaza out of the dark of Hamas's reign and into the light of the very good governance the Palestinian Authority can bring"—at least, that it can bring as long as it remains a loyal client, rife with corruption and willing to carry out harsh repression, but obedient.[35]

Returning from a visit to the Arab world, Fawaz Gerges strongly affirmed what others on the scene had reported. The effect of the U.S.-Israeli offensive in Gaza has been to infuriate the populations and to arouse bitter hatred of the aggressors and their collaborators. "Suffice it to say that the so-called moderate Arab states [that is, those that take their orders from Washington] are on the defensive, and that the resistance front led by Iran and Syria is the main beneficiary. Once again, Israel and the Bush administration have handed the Iranian leadership a sweet victory." Furthermore, "Hamas will likely emerge as a more powerful political force than before and will likely top Fatah, the ruling apparatus of President Mahmoud Abbas's Palestinian Authority,"[36] Washington's current favorite. That conclusion was reinforced by a poll by the independent Jerusalem Media and Communications Center (JMCC), which found that support for Hamas in the West Bank rose from 19 percent the preceding April to 29 percent after the Gaza attack, while support for Fatah dropped from 34 percent to 30 percent. Far from weakening militant Islamist groups and their sponsors, JMCC concluded, "the war weakened and undermined to a very large extent the moderates—not only in Palestine but also in the region." Fifty-three percent of West Bank Palestinians felt that Hamas had won the war; only 10 percent overall saw it as an Israeli victory.[37]

It is worth bearing in mind that the Arab world was not scrupulously protected from the only regular live TV coverage of what was happening in Gaza, namely the "calm and balanced analysis of the chaos and destruction" provided by the outstanding correspondents of Al Jazeera, offering "a stark alternative to terrestrial Israeli channels," as reported by the London *Financial Times*. In the 105 countries lacking our efficient modalities of self-censorship, people could see what was happening hourly, and the impact is said to be very great. In the United States, the *New York Times* reports, "the near-total blackout…is no doubt related to the sharp criticism Al Jazeera received from the United States government during the initial stages of the war in Iraq for its coverage of the American invasion." Cheney and Rumsfeld objected, so, obviously, the independent media could only obey.[38]

There is much sober debate about what the attackers hoped to achieve. Some of objectives are commonly discussed, among them, restoring what is called "the deterrent capacity" that Israel lost as a result of its failures in Lebanon in 2006—that is, the capacity to terrorize any potential opponent into submission. There are, however, more fundamental objectives that tend to be ignored, though they seem fairly obvious when we take a look at recent history.

Israel abandoned Gaza in September 2005. Rational Israeli hardliners, like Ariel Sharon, the patron saint of the settlers' movement, understood that it was senseless to subsidize a few thousand illegal Israeli settlers in the ruins of Gaza, protected by a large part of the IDF while they used much of the land and scarce resources. It made more sense to turn all of Gaza into the world's largest prison and to transfer settlers to the West Bank, much more valuable territory, where Israel is quite explicit about its intentions, in word and more importantly in deed. One goal is to annex the arable land, water supplies, and pleasant suburbs of Jerusalem and Tel Aviv that lie within the separation wall, irrelevantly declared illegal by the World Court. That includes a vastly expanded Jerusalem, in violation of Security Council orders that go back forty years, also irrelevant. Israel has also been taking over the Jordan Valley, about one-third of the West Bank. What remains is therefore imprisoned, and, furthermore, broken into fragments by salients of Jewish settlement that trisect the territory: one to the east of Greater Jerusalem through the town of Ma'aleh Adumim, developed through the Clinton years to split the West Bank; and two to the north, through the towns of Ariel and Kedumim. What remains to Palestinians is segregated by hundreds of mostly arbitrary checkpoints.

The checkpoints have no relation to security of Israel, nor does the wall, and if intended to safeguard settlers, they are flatly illegal, as the World Court ruled definitively.[39] In reality, their major goal is to harass the Palestinian population and to fortify what Israeli peace activist Jeff Halper calls the "matrix of control," designed to make life unbearable for the "drugged roaches scurrying around in a bottle" who seek to remain in their homes and land. All of that is fair enough, because they are "like grasshoppers compared to us" so that their heads can be "smashed against the boulders and walls." The terminology is from the highest Israeli political and military leaders, in this case the revered "princes" (Chief of Staff Rafael Eitan and Prime Minister Yitzhak Shamir). And similar attitudes, even if more discreetly expressed, shape policies.[40]

The racist rhetoric of political and military leaders is mild as compared to the preaching of rabbinical authorities. They are not marginal figures. On the contrary, they are highly influential in the army and in the settler movement, which Zertal and Eldar describe for good reason as the "lords of the land," with enormous impact on policy. One of the memorable photographs from the Gaza war showed three orthodox Jews in traditional black garb with the caption "Israelis, like these men, have come to hills near Gaza to watch their forces pound the Palestinian enclave in an attempt to stop Hamas rocket attacks" (an attempt to which we return). The story in the *Wall Street Journal* describes how Israelis, orthodox and secular, come to the hilltops that have "become the war's peanut gallery…some with sack lunches and portable radios tuned to the latest reports of the battle raging in front of them…[some]…to egg on friends and family members in the fight," some shouting "Bravo! Bravo!" as they watch the exploding bombs, hardly able to contain their glee, some with their binoculars and lawn chairs criticizing the Israeli attackers for hitting the wrong targets, much like fans at sporting events who criticize the coach.[41]

Soldiers fighting in northern Gaza were afforded an "inspirational" visit from two leading rabbis, who explained to them that there are no "innocents" in Gaza, so everyone there is a legitimate target, quoting a famous passage from Psalms calling on the Lord to seize the infants of Israel's oppressors and dash them against the rocks. The rabbis were breaking no new ground. A year earlier, the former chief Sephardic rabbi wrote to Prime Minister Olmert, informing him that all civilians in Gaza are collectively guilty for rocket attacks, so that there is "absolutely no moral prohibition against the indiscriminate killing of civilians during a potential massive military offensive on Gaza aimed at stopping the rocket launchings," as the *Jerusalem Post* reported his ruling. His son, chief rabbi of Safed, elaborated: "If they don't stop after we kill 100, then we must kill a thousand, and if they do not stop after 1,000 then we must kill 10,000. If they still don't stop we must kill 100,000, even a million. Whatever it takes to make them stop."[42]

Similar views are expressed by prominent American intellectuals. When Israel invaded Lebanon in 2006, Harvard Law School professor Alan Dershowitz explained in the liberal online journal Huffington Post that all Lebanese are legitimate targets of Israeli violence. Lebanon's citizens "pay the price" for supporting "terrorism"—that is, for supporting resistance to Israel's invasion. Accordingly, the vast majority of Lebanese civilians are no more immune to attack than Austrians who supported the Nazis. The fatwa of the Sephardic rabbi applies to them. In a video on the *Jerusalem Post* website, Dershowitz went on to ridicule talk of excessive kill ratios of Palestinians to Israelis: they should be increased to 1,000 to 1, he said, or even 1,000 to 0, meaning that the brutes should be completely exterminated. Of course, he is referring to "terrorists," a broad category that includes the victims of Israeli power, since "Israel never targets civilians," he emphatically declared. It follows that Palestinians, Lebanese, Tunisians, in fact anyone who gets in the way of the ruthless armies of the Holy State is a terrorist, or an accidental victim of their just crimes.[43]

It is not easy to find historical counterparts to these performances. It is perhaps of some interest that they elicit virtually no censure and are thus apparently considered entirely appropriate in the reigning intellectual and moral culture—when they are produced on "our side," that is. From the mouths of official enemies such words would elicit righteous outrage and calls for massive preemptive violence to punish the villains.

The claim that "our side" never targets civilians is familiar doctrine in violent states. And there is some truth to it. Powerful states, like the United States, do not generally try to kill particular civilians. Rather, they carry out murderous actions that they and their educated classes know will slaughter many civilians, but without specific intent to kill particular ones. In law, the routine practices might fall under the category of depraved indifference, but that is not an adequate designation for standard imperial practice and doctrine. It is more similar to walking down a street knowing that we might kill ants, but without intent to do so, because they rank so low that it just doesn't matter. Thus Clinton's bombing of the main pharmaceutical plant in a poor African country (Sudan) might be expected to lead to the deaths of tens of thousands of people, as it apparently did. But since we did not aim at particular ones, there is no guilt, Western moralists assure us. And the same holds in much more extreme cases, which are all too easy to enumerate. The same is true when Israel carries out actions that it knows will kill the "grasshoppers" and "drugged roaches" who happen to infest the lands it "liberates." There is no good term for this form of moral depravity—arguably worse than deliberate slaughter and all too familiar.

In the former Palestine, the rightful owners (by divine decree, according to the "lords of the land") may decide to grant the drugged roaches a few scattered parcels. Not by right, however: "I believed, and to this day still believe, in our people's eternal and historic right to this entire land," Prime Minister Olmert informed a joint session of Congress in May 2006 to rousing applause.[44] At the same time he announced his "convergence" program for taking over what is valuable in the West Bank, as outlined earlier, leaving the Palestinians to rot in isolated cantons. He was not specific about the borders of the "entire land," but then, the Zionist enterprise never has been, for good reasons: permanent expansion is an important internal dynamic. If Olmert was still faithful to his origins in Likud, he might have meant both sides of the Jordan, including the current state of Jordan, at least valuable parts of it, though the 1999 Likud electoral platform—the program of current Prime Minister Binyamin Netanyahu—is ambiguous. It declares, "the Jordan Valley and the territories that dominate it shall be under Israeli sovereignty." What "dominates" the Jordan Valley is not defined, but it certainly includes everything to the west of the Jordan, the former Palestine, to remain under Israeli sovereignty. Within that territory there can never be a Palestinian state and settlement must be unconstrained, the platform declares, since "settlement of the land is a clear expression of the unassailable right of the Jewish people to the Land of Israel."[45]

For Olmert and his Likud successor, our people's "eternal and historic right to this entire land" contrasts dramatically with the lack of any right of self-determination for the temporary visitors, the Palestinians. As noted earlier, the lack of any such right was reiterated by Israel and its patron in Washington in December 2008, in their usual isolation and accompanied by the usual resounding silence.[46]

The plans that Olmert sketched in 2006 were later abandoned as not sufficiently extreme. But what replaces the convergence program, and the actions that proceed daily to implement it, are approximately the same in general conception. In 2008, West Bank settlement construction rose by 60 percent, according to a report by Peace Now, which monitors settlement. Housing starts in West Bank settlements rose by 46 percent over the previous year, while they declined in Tel Aviv by 29 percent and in Jerusalem by 14 percent. Peace Now reported further that some 6,000 new units had been approved with

58,000 waiting approval: "If all the plans are realized," the report said, "the number of settlers in the territories will be doubled." There are many ways to expand the settlement project without eliciting protest from the paymasters in Washington, for example, setting up an "outpost" that is later linked to the national electricity and water grids and over time slowly becomes a settlement or a town. Or simply by expanding the "rings of land" around a settlement for alleged security reasons, seizing Palestinian lands, all processes that continue.[47]

These devices, which have roots in the pre-state period, trace back to the earliest days of the occupation, when the basic idea was formulated poetically by Defense Minister Moshe Dayan, who was in charge of the occupied territories: "the situation today resembles the complex relationship between a Bedouin man and the girl he kidnaps against his will...You Palestinians, as a nation, don't want us today, but we'll change your attitude by forcing our presence on you." You will "live like dogs, and whoever will leave, will leave," while we take what we want.[48]

That these programs are criminal has never been in doubt. Immediately after the 1967 war, the Israeli government was informed by its highest legal authority, Teodor Meron, that "civilian settlement in the administered territories contravenes the explicit provisions of the Fourth Geneva Convention," the foundation of international humanitarian law. Israel's justice minister concurred. Dayan conceded that "settling Israelis in occupied territories contravenes, as is known, international conventions, but there is nothing essentially new in that," so the issue can be dismissed. The World Court unanimously endorsed Meron's conclusion in 2004, and the Israeli High Court technically agreed while disagreeing in practice, in its usual style.[49]

In the West Bank, Israel can pursue its criminal programs with U.S. support and no disturbance, thanks to its effective military control and by now the cooperation of the collaborationist Palestinian security forces armed and trained by the United States and allied dictatorships. It can also carry out regular assassinations and other crimes, while settlers rampage under IDF protection. But while the West Bank has been effectively subdued by terror, there is still resistance in the other half of Palestine, the Gaza Strip. That too must be quelled for the U.S.-Israeli programs of annexation and destruction of Palestine to proceed undisturbed.

Hence the invasion of Gaza.

The timing of the invasion was widely assumed to be influenced by the coming Israeli election. Defense Minister Ehud Barak of the centrist Labor Party, who was lagging badly in the polls, gained one parliamentary seat for every forty Arabs killed in the early days of the slaughter, Israeli commentator Ran HaCohen calculated.[50]

That changed, however. The Israeli far right gained substantially from the invasion, though as the crimes passed beyond what the carefully honed Israeli propaganda campaign was able to suppress, even confirmed supporters of the invasion became concerned about the way the outside world was perceiving Israel's just war. The highly regarded political scientist and historian Shlomo Avineri offered an analysis of these "critical differences of opinion" between Israel and outsiders. Among the causes, he explained, were "the harsh images—a consequence of the firepower Israel used, as magnified by the media—as well as disinformation and, undoubtedly, plain old hatred of Israel." But he discerned a deeper reason: "The name given to the operation, which greatly affects the way in which it will be perceived. Israelis associate the Hebrew for Cast Lead, as the operation was called, with a line written by poet Haim Nahman Bialik that is part of a Hanukkah song typically sung by cute little children. The fact that the operation began around Hanukkah sharpened that association. Abroad, however, it was seen differently. In English, not to mention German, Cast Lead has a whole other association. Lead is cast into bullets, bombs and mortar shells. When the world reported on Cast Lead it sounded militaristic, brutal and aggressive; it was associated with death and destruction rather than spinning dreidels. Even before the first shot was fired or the first speech explaining Israel's case was made, the operation had already acquired an image of belligerence," a terrible failure of Israeli *hasbara*. Perhaps it should have been called something more gentle, Avineri felt, "like the Gates of Gaza, which also has a historical ring to it."[51]

Other war supporters warned that the carnage is "Destroying [Israel's] soul and its image. Destroying it on world television screens, in the living rooms of the international community and most importantly, in Obama's America" (Ari Shavit). Shavit was particularly concerned about Israel's "shelling a United Nations facility...on the day when the UN secretary general is visiting Jerusalem," an act that is "beyond lunacy," he felt.[52]

Adding a few details, the "facility" was the UN compound in Gaza City, which contained the UNRWA warehouse. The shelling destroyed "hundreds of tons of emergency food and medicines set for distribution today to shelters, hospitals and feeding centres," according to UNRWA director John Ging. Military strikes at the same time destroyed two floors of the al-Quds hospital, setting it ablaze, and also a second warehouse run by the Palestinian Red Crescent society. The hospital in the densely populated Tal-Hawa neighborhood was destroyed by Israeli tanks "after hundreds of frightened Gazans had taken shelter inside as Israeli ground forces pushed into the neighbourhood," Al Jazeera reported.

There was nothing left to salvage inside the smoldering ruins of the hospital. "They shelled the building, the hospital building," paramedic Ahmad Al-Haz told the Associated Press. "It caught fire. We tried to evacuate the sick people and the injured and the people who were there. Firefighters arrived and put out the fire, which burst into flames again and they put it out again and it came back for the third time." It was suspected that the blaze might have been set by white phosphorus, also suspected in numerous other fires and serious burn injuries.[53]

The suspicions were confirmed by Amnesty International (AI) after the cessation of the intense bombardment made inquiry possible. Israel had sensibly barred all journalists, even Israeli, while its crimes were proceeding in full fury. Israel's use of white phosphorus against Gaza civilians is "clear and undeniable," AI reported, condemning its repeated use in densely populated civilian areas as "a war crime." AI investigators found white phosphorus edges scattered around residential buildings, still burning, "further endangering the residents and their property," particularly children "drawn to the detritus of war and often unaware of the danger." Primary targets, they report, were the UNRWA compound, where the Israeli "white phosphorus landed next to some fuel trucks and caused a large fire which destroyed tons of humanitarian aid" after Israeli authorities "had given assurance that no further strikes would be launched on the compound." On the same day, "a white phosphorus shell landed in the al-Quds hospital in Gaza City also causing a fire which forced hospital staff to evacuate the patients…White phosphorus landing on skin can burn deep through muscle and into the bone, continuing to burn unless deprived of oxygen." Whether purposely intended or beyond depraved indifference, such crimes are inevitable when the weapon is used in attacks on civilians.[54]

The white phosphorus shells were U.S.-made, AI reported. In a report reviewing use of weapons in Gaza, AI concluded that Israel used U.S.-supplied weapons in "serious violations of international humanitarian law," and called on "the U.N. Security Council to impose an immediate and comprehensive arms embargo on the

Jewish state."⁵⁵ Though conscious U.S. complicity is hardly in doubt, it is excluded from the call for punishment by the analogue of the "too big to fail" doctrine.

It is, however, a mistake to concentrate too much on Israel's severe violations of *jus in bello*, the laws designed to bar wartime practices that are too savage. The invasion itself is a far more serious crime. And if Israel had inflicted horrendous damage by bows and arrows, it would still be a criminal act of extreme depravity.

It is also a mistake to focus attention on specific targets. The campaign was far more ambitious in scope. Its goal was "the destruction of all means of life," officials warned. A large part of the agricultural land was destroyed, some perhaps permanently, along with poultry, livestock, greenhouses, and orchards, creating a major food crisis, the World Food Program reported. The IDF also targeted the Ministry of Agriculture and "the offices of the Palestinian Agricultural Relief Committees in Zaitoun—which provides cheap food for the poor—ransacked and vandalised by soldiers who left abusive graffiti." Large areas were flattened by bulldozers. Beyond "the physical damage done by Israeli bulldozers, bombing and shelling, land has been contaminated by munitions, including white phosphorus, burst sewerage pipes, animal carcasses and even asbestos used in roofing. In many places, the damage is extreme. In Jabal al-Rayas, once a thriving farming community, every building has been knocked down, and even the cattle killed and left to lie rotting in the fields." Leaders of Gaza's business community, generally apolitical, "say that much of the 3 per cent of industry still operating after the 18-month shutdown caused by Israel's economic siege has now been destroyed" by Israeli forces using "aerial bombing, tank shelling and armoured bulldozers to eliminate the productive capacity of some of Gaza's most important manufacturing plants," destroying or severely damaging 219 factories, according to Palestinian industrialists.⁵⁶

To impede potential recovery, the IDF attacked universities, largely destroying the agriculture faculty at al-Azhar University (considered pro-Fatah, Washington's favored faction), al-Da'wa College for Humanities in Rafah, and the Gaza College for Security Sciences. Six university buildings in Gaza were razed to the ground and sixteen damaged. Two of those destroyed housed the science and engineering laboratories of the Islamic University in Gaza.[57] The pretext was that they contributed to Hamas military activities. By the same principle, Israeli (and U.S.) universities are legitimate targets of large-scale terror.

There were occasional reports of the Israeli navy firing on fishing boats, but these conceal what appears to be a systematic campaign in recent years to drive the fishing industry toward shore—thereby destroying it, because the vast pollution caused by Israel's destruction of power stations and sewage facilities makes fishing impossible near shore. Citing recent incidents, the Al Mezan Center for Human Rights in Gaza, which has been a highly reliable source, "strongly condemn[ed] the continuous escalation of the IOF [Israeli Occupation Forces] offensive against Palestinian civilians, including fishermen." International human rights observers report regular attacks on fishing vessels in Gazan territorial waters. Accompanying Palestinian fishers, they report having "witnessed countless acts of Israeli military aggression against them whilst in Gazan territorial waters, despite a six-month cease-fire agreement holding at the time," and now again after the January cease-fire. "Gaza's 40,000 fishermen have been deprived of their livelihood" by Israel naval attacks, Gideon Levy reported from the bedside of a nineteen-year-old Gaza fisherman, severely wounded by Israeli gunboats who attacked his boat without warning near the Gaza shore on October 5, a month before the cease-fire was broken by Israel's invasion of Gaza, events to which we return. "Every few days the International

Solidarity Movement (ISM) publishes reports from its volunteers in Gaza about attacks on fishermen. Sometimes the naval boats ram the wretched craft, sometimes the sailors use high-pressure water hoses on the fishermen, hurtling them into the sea, and sometimes they open lethal fire on them," Levy reported.[58]

The international observers report that attacks on fishing boats began after the discovery of quite promising natural gas fields by the BG Group in 2000, in Gaza's territorial waters. The regular attacks gradually drove fishing boats toward shore, not by official order but by threat and violence. Oil industry journals and the Israeli business press report that Israel's state-owned Israel Electric Corp. is negotiating "for as much as 1.5 billion cubic meters of natural gas from the Marine field located off the Mediterranean coast of the Palestinian controlled Gaza Strip." It is hard to suppress the thought that the Gaza invasion may be related to the project of stealing these valuable resources from Palestine, which cannot take part in the negotiations.[59]

Aggression always has a pretext: in this case, that Israel's patience had "run out" in the face of Hamas rocket attacks, as Ehud Barak put it. The mantra that is endlessly repeated is that Israel has the right to use force to defend itself. The thesis is partially defensible. The rocketing is criminal, and it is true that a state has the right to defend itself against criminal attacks. But it does not follow that it has a right to defend itself by force. That goes far beyond any principle that we would or should accept. Putin had no right to use force in response to Chechen terror—and his resort to force is not justified by the fact that he achieved results so far beyond what the United States achieved in Iraq that if General Petraeus had approached them, he might have been crowned king.[60] Nazi Germany had no right to use force to defend itself against the terrorism of the partisans. Kristallnacht was not justified by Herschel Grynszpan's assassination of a German Embassy official in Paris. The British were not justified in using force to defend themselves against the (very real) terror of the American colonists seeking independence, or to terrorize Irish Catholics in response to IRA terror—and when they finally turned to the sensible policy of addressing legitimate grievances, the terror virtually ended. It is not a matter of "proportionality," but of choice of action in the first place: Is there an alternative to violence? In all these cases, there plainly was, so the resort to force had no justification whatsoever.

Any resort to force carries a heavy burden of proof, and we have to ask whether it can be met in the case of Israel's effort to quell any resistance to its daily criminal actions in Gaza and in the West Bank, where they still continue relentlessly after more than forty years. Perhaps I may quote myself in an interview in the Israeli press on the legitimacy of Palestinian resistance: "We should recall that Gaza and the West Bank are recognized to be a unit, so that if resistance to Israel's destructive and illegal programs is legitimate within the West Bank (and it would be interesting to see a rational argument to the contrary), then it is legitimate in Gaza as well."[61]

Palestinian-American journalist Ali Abunimah observed that "there are no rockets launched at Israel from the West Bank, and yet Israel's extrajudicial killings, land theft, settler pogroms and kidnappings never stopped for a day during the truce. The western-backed Palestinian Authority of Mahmoud Abbas has acceded to all Israel's demands. Under the proud eye of United States military advisors, Abbas has assembled 'security forces' to fight the resistance on Israel's behalf. None of that has spared a single Palestinian in the West Bank from Israel's relentless colonization"—thanks to firm U.S. backing. The respected Palestinian parliamentarian Dr. Mustapha Barghouti adds that after Bush's Annapolis extravaganza in November 2007, with much uplifting rhetoric about dedication to peace and justice, Israeli attacks on Palestinians escalated in the West Bank, along with a sharp increase in settlements and Israeli checkpoints. Obviously these criminal actions are not a response to rockets from Gaza, though the converse may well be the case.[62]

The actions of people resisting brutal occupation can be condemned as criminal and politically foolish, but those who offer no alternative have no moral standing to issue such judgments. The conclusion holds with particular force for Americans who choose to be directly implicated in Israel's ongoing crimes—by their words, their actions, or their silence. All the more so because there are very clear nonviolent alternatives—which, however, have the disadvantage that they bar the programs of illegal expansion that the United States strongly supports in practice, while occasionally issuing a mild admonition that they are "unhelpful."[63]

Israel has straightforward means to defend itself: put an end to its criminal actions in occupied territories, and accept the long-standing international consensus on a two-state settlement that has been blocked by the United States and Israel for over thirty years, since the United States first vetoed a Security Council resolution calling for a political settlement in these terms in 1976. I will not once again run through the inglorious record, but it is important to be aware that U.S.-Israeli rejectionism today is even more blatant than in the past. The Arab League has gone even beyond the consensus, calling for full normalization of relations with Israel. Hamas has repeatedly called for a two-state settlement in terms of the international consensus. Iran and Hezbollah have made it clear that they will abide by any agreement that Palestinians accept.[64]

One can seek ambiguities and incompleteness, but not in the case of the United States and Israel, which remain in splendid isolation, not only in words.

The more detailed record is informative. The Palestinian National Council formally accepted the international consensus in 1988. The response of the Shamir-Peres coalition government, affirmed by James Baker's State Department, was that there cannot be an "additional Palestinian state" between Israel and Jordan—the latter already a Palestinian state by U.S.-Israeli dictate. The Oslo Accord that followed explicitly put to the side potential Palestinian national rights: the Declaration of Principles signed with much fanfare on the White House lawn in September 1993 referred only to UN 242, which grants nothing to the Palestinians, while pointedly ignoring subsequent UN declarations, all blocked by Washington, which respect Palestinian national rights. The threat that these rights might be realized in some meaningful form was systematically undermined throughout the Oslo years by Israel's steady expansion of illegal settlements, with U.S. support. Settlement accelerated in 2000, President Clinton's and Prime Minister Barak's final year, when negotiations took place at Camp David against that background.

After blaming Yasser Arafat for the breakdown of the Camp David negotiations, Clinton backtracked and recognized that the U.S.-Israeli proposals were too extreme to be acceptable to any Palestinian. In December 2000, he presented his "parameters," vague but more forthcoming. He then announced that both sides had accepted the parameters, while both expressed reservations. The two sides met in Taba, Egypt, in January 2001—four months after the outbreak of the intifada—and came very close to an agreement. They would have been able to do so in a few more days, they said in their final press conference. But the negotiations were canceled prematurely by Israeli prime minister Ehud Barak. That week in Taba is the one break in over thirty years of U.S.-Israeli rejectionism. There is no reason why that one break in the record cannot be resumed.[65]

The preferred version, reiterated by Ethan Bronner, is that "many abroad recall Mr. Barak as the prime minister who in 2000 went further than any Israeli leader in peace offers to the Palestinians, only to see the deal fail and explode in a violent Palestinian uprising [the intifada] that drove him from power." It is quite true that "many abroad" believe this deceitful fairy tale, thanks to what Bronner and too many of his colleagues call "journalism."[66]

It is commonly claimed that a two-state solution is now unattainable because if the IDF tried to remove settlers, it would lead to a civil war. That may be true, but much more argument is needed. Without resorting to force to expel illegal settlers, the IDF could simply withdraw to whatever boundaries are established by negotiations. The settlers beyond those boundaries would have the choice of leaving their subsidized homes to return to subsidized homes in Israel or to remain under Palestinian authority. The same was true of the carefully staged "national trauma" in Gaza in 2005, so transparently fraudulent that it was ridiculed by Israeli commentators. It would have sufficed for Israel to announce that the IDF would withdraw, and the settlers who were subsidized to enjoy their life in Gaza would have quietly climbed into the lorries provided to them and traveled to their new subsidized residences in the other occupied territories. But that would not have produced tragic photos of agonized children and passionate calls of "never again," thus providing a welcome propaganda cover for the real purpose of the partial "disengagement": expansion of illegal settlement in the rest of the occupied territories.[67]

To summarize, contrary to the claim that is constantly reiterated, Israel has no right to use force to defend itself against rockets from Gaza, even if they are regarded as terrorist crimes. Furthermore, the reasons are transparent. The pretext for launching the attack is without merit.

There is also a narrower question. Does Israel have peaceful short-term alternatives to the use of force in response to rockets from Gaza? One such alternative would be to accept a cease-fire. Sometimes Israel has formally done so, while quickly violating it. The most recent and currently relevant case is June 2008. The cease-fire called for opening the border crossings to "allow the transfer of all goods that were banned and restricted to go into Gaza." Israel formally agreed, but immediately announced that it would not abide by the agreement and open the borders until Hamas released Gilad Shalit, an Israeli soldier captured by Hamas in June 2006.[68]

After the Gaza invasion, Israel continued to reject Hamas proposals of a long-term truce, again citing the capture of Shalit. Partly on the same grounds, it refused to permit any reconstruction, even the import of macaroni, crayons, tomato paste, lentils, soap, toilet paper, and other such weapons of mass destruction—eliciting some polite queries from Washington.[69]

The steady drumbeat of accusations about the capture of Shalit is, again, blatant hypocrisy, even putting aside Israel's long history of kidnapping. In this case, the hypocrisy could not be more glaring. One day before Hamas captured Shalit, Israeli soldiers entered Gaza City and kidnapped two civilians, the Muamar brothers, bringing them to Israel to join the thousands of other prisoners held there, hundreds reportedly without charge. Kidnapping civilians is a far more serious crime than capturing a soldier of an attacking army, but as is the norm, it was barely reported in contrast to the furor over Shalit. And all that remains in memory, blocking peace, is the capture of Shalit, another illustration of the depth of imperial mentality in the West. Shalit should be returned—in a fair prisoner exchange.[70]

It was after the capture of Shalit that Israel's unrelenting military attack against Gaza passed from merely vicious to truly sadistic.

But it is well to recall that even before his capture, Israel had fired more than 7,700 shells at northern Gaza after its September withdrawal, eliciting virtually no comment.[71]

After immediately rejecting the June 2008 cease-fire it had formally accepted, Israel maintained its siege. We may recall that a siege is an act of war. In fact, Israel has always insisted on an even stronger principle: hampering access to the outside world, even well short of a siege, is an act of war, justifying massive violence in response. Interference with Israel's passage through the Straits of Tiran was a large part of the justification offered for Israel's invasion of Egypt (with France and England) in 1956, and for its launching of the June 1967 war. The siege of Gaza is total, not partial, apart from occasional willingness of the occupiers to relax it slightly. And it is vastly more harmful to Gazans than closing the Straits of Tiran was to Israel. Supporters of Israeli doctrines and actions should therefore have no problem justifying rocket attacks on Israeli territory from the Gaza Strip.

Of course, again we run into the nullifying principle: This is *us*, that is *them*.

Israel not only maintained the siege after June 2008, but did so with extreme rigor. It even prevented UNRWA from replenishing its stores, "so when the ceasefire broke down, we ran out of food for the 750,000 who depend on us," UNRWA director John Ging informed the BBC.[72]

Despite the Israeli siege, rocketing sharply reduced. According to the spokesperson for the prime minister, Mark Regev, there was not a single Hamas rocket among the few that were launched from the onset of the June 2008 cease-fire until November 4, when Israel violated it still more egregiously with a raid into Gaza, leading to the death of six Palestinians and a retaliatory barrage of rockets (with no injuries). The raid was on the evening of the U.S. presidential elections, when attention was focused elsewhere. The pretext for the raid was that Israel had detected a tunnel in Gaza that might have been intended for use to capture another Israeli soldier; a "ticking tunnel" in official communiques. The pretext was transparently absurd, as a number of commentators noted. If such a tunnel existed, and reached the border, Israel could easily have barred it right there. But as usual, the ludicrous Israeli pretext was deemed credible, and the timing was overlooked.[73]

What was the reason for the Israeli raid? We have no internal evidence about Israeli planning, but we do know that the raid came shortly before scheduled Hamas-Fatah talks in Cairo aimed at "reconciling their differences and creating a single, unified government," British correspondent Rory McCarthy reported. That was to be the first Fatah-Hamas meeting since the June 2007 civil war that left Hamas in control of Gaza, and would have been a significant step toward advancing diplomatic efforts. There is a long history of Israel provocations to deter the threat of diplomacy, some already mentioned. This may have been another one.[74]

The civil war that left Hamas in control of Gaza is commonly described as a Hamas military coup, demonstrating again their evil nature. The real world was a little different. The civil war was incited by the United States and Israel, in a crude attempt at a military coup to overturn the free elections that brought Hamas to power. That has been public knowledge at least since April 2008, when David Rose published a detailed and documented account of how Bush, Rice, and Deputy National Security Adviser Elliott Abrams "backed an armed force under Fatah strongman Muhammad Dahlan, touching off a bloody civil war in Gaza and leaving Hamas stronger than ever." The account was corroborated by Norman Olsen, who served for twenty-six years in the Foreign Service, including four years working in the Gaza Strip and four years at the U.S. Embassy in Tel Aviv, and then moved on to become associate coordinator for counterterrorism at the Department of State. Olsen and his son detail the State Department shenanigans intended to ensure that their candidate, Abbas, would win in the January 2006 elections—in which case it would have been hailed as a triumph of democracy. After the election-fixing failed, the United States and Israel turned to the punishment of Palestinians for voting the wrong way, and began arming a militia run by Dahlan. But "Dahlan's thugs moved too soon," the Olsens write, and a Hamas pre-emptive strike undermined the coup attempt.[75]

The Party Line is more convenient.

The U.S.-Israel responded to the failed coup attempt by introducing far harsher measures to punish the people of Gaza, and to ensure that the plague of disobedience would not spread to the rest of Palestine. Together with Jordan, the United States undertook to arm and train a more efficient Palestinian "security force" to maintain order in the West Bank, under the direction of U.S. general Keith Dayton. Israeli military officers participate as well, Ethan Bronner reported in the *New York Times*, describing how "an Israeli officer inaugurated the firing range here, shooting a Palestinian weapon to test it and give his seal of approval." The major achievement of the new paramilitary force, Bronner elaborated, was to have "maintained tight order" to prevent any kind of "uprising"—that is, significant show of sympathy and support—while Israel slaughtered Palestinians in Gaza and reduced much of it to rubble.

The effective performance of these forces also impressed Senate Foreign Relations Committee chair John Kerry. In his address to the Brookings Institution, he spoke eloquently of "the need to give the Israelis a legitimate partner for peace," which they evidently lacked during the decades of unilateral U.S.-Israeli rejection of the international consensus on a peace settlement, which the Palestine Liberation Organization supported, along with the Arab states (and the world, outside the U.S.-Israel). We must overcome this failure, Kerry explained, suggesting several ways to weaken the elected government and strengthen our man Mahmoud Abbas. "Most importantly," Kerry went on, "this means strengthening General Dayton's efforts to train Palestinian security forces that can keep order and fight terror…Recent developments have been extremely encouraging: During the invasion of Gaza, Palestinian Security Forces largely succeeded in maintaining calm in the West Bank amidst widespread expectations of civil unrest. Obviously, more remains to be done, but we can help do it."[76]

So we can. The United States has had a century of rich experience in developing paramilitary and police forces to pacify conquered populations and to impose the structure of a long-lasting coercive security state that undermines nationalist and popular aspirations and sustains obedience to the wealthy classes and their foreign associates.[77]

After Israel broke the June 2008 cease-fire (such as it was) in November, the siege was tightened further, with even more disastrous consequences for the population. According to Sara Roy, the leading academic specialist on Gaza, "On Nov. 5, Israel sealed all crossing points into Gaza, vastly reducing and at times denying food supplies, medicines, fuel, cooking gas, and parts for water and sanitation systems…During November, an average of 4.6 trucks of food per day entered Gaza from Israel compared with an average of 123 trucks per day in October. Spare parts for the repair and maintenance of water-related equipment have been denied entry for over a year. The World Health Organization just reported that half of Gaza's ambulances are now out of order"—and the rest soon became targets for Israeli attack. Gaza's only power station was forced to suspend operation for lack of fuel, and could not be started up again because it needed spare parts, which had been sitting in the Israeli port of Ashdod for eight months. Shortage of electricity led to a 300 percent increase in burn cases at Shifaa' hospital in the Gaza Strip, resulting from efforts to light wood fires. Israel barred shipment of chlorine, so that by mid-December in Gaza City and the north access to water was limited to six hours every three days. The human consequences are not counted among Palestinian victims of Israeli terror.[78]

After the November 4 Israeli attack, both sides escalated violence (all deaths were Palestinian) until the cease-fire formally ended on December 19, and Prime Minister Olmert authorized the full-scale invasion.

A few days earlier Hamas had proposed to return to the original July cease-fire agreement, which Israel had not observed. Historian and former Carter administration high official Robert Pastor passed the proposal to a "senior official" in the IDF, but Israel did not respond. The head of Shin Bet, Israel's internal security agency, was quoted in Israeli sources on December 21 as saying that Hamas is interested in continuing the "calm" with Israel, while its military wing is continuing preparations for conflict.

"There clearly was an alternative to the military approach to stopping the rockets," Pastor said, keeping to the narrow issue of Gaza. There was also a more far-reaching alternative, which is rarely discussed: namely, accepting a political settlement including all of the occupied territories.[79]

Israeli senior diplomatic correspondent Akiva Eldar reports that shortly before Israel launched its full-scale invasion on Saturday, December 27, "Hamas politburo chief Khaled Meshal announced on the Iz al-Din al-Qassam Web site that he was prepared not only for a 'cessation of aggression'—he proposed going back to the arrangement at the Rafah crossing as of 2005, before Hamas won the elections and later took over the region. That arrangement was for the crossing to be managed jointly by Egypt, the European Union, the Palestinian Authority presidency and Hamas," and as noted earlier, called for opening of the crossings to desperately needed supplies.[80]

A standard claim of the more vulgar apologists for Israeli violence is that in the case of the current assault, "as in so many instances in the past half century—the Lebanon War of 1982, the 'Iron Fist' response to the 1988 intifada, the Lebanon War of 2006—the Israelis have reacted to intolerable acts of terror with a determination to inflict terrible pain, to teach the enemy a lesson. The civilian suffering and deaths are inevitable; the lessons less so" (*New Yorker* editor David Remnick).[81] The 2006 invasion can be justified only on the grounds of appalling cynicism, as already discussed. The reference to the vicious response to the 1988 intifada is too depraved even to discuss; a sympathetic interpretation might be that it reflects astonishing ignorance. But Remnick's claim about the 1982 invasion is quite common, a remarkable feat of incessant propaganda, which merits a few reminders. The lessons, particularly about American intellectuals, are all too easy to recognize, though hardly "inevitable."

Uncontroversially, the Israel-Lebanon border was quiet for a year before the Israeli invasion, at least from Lebanon to Israel, north to south. Through the year, the PLO scrupulously observed a U.S.-initiated cease-fire, despite constant Israeli provocations, including bombing with many civilian casualties, presumably intended to elicit some reaction that could be used to justify Israel's planned invasion. The best Israel could achieve was two light symbolic responses. It then invaded with a pretext too absurd to be taken seriously.

The invasion had nothing to do with "intolerable acts of terror," though it did have to do with intolerable acts: of diplomacy. That has never been obscure. Shortly after the U.S.-backed invasion began, Israel's leading academic specialist on the Palestinians, Yehoshua Porath—no dove—wrote that Arafat's success in maintaining the cease-fire constituted "a veritable catastrophe in the eyes of the Israeli government," since it opened the way to a political settlement. The government hoped that the PLO would resort to terrorism, undermining the threat that it would be "a legitimate negotiating partner for future political accommodations."

The facts were well understood in Israel, and not concealed. Prime Minister Yitzhak Shamir stated that Israel went to war because there was "a terrible danger.... Not so much a military one as a political one," prompting the fine Israeli satirist B. Michael to write that "the lame excuse of a military danger or a danger to the Galilee is dead." We "have removed the political danger" by striking first, in time; now, "Thank God, there is no one to talk to." Historian Benny Morris recognized that the PLO had observed the cease-fire, and explained that "the war's inevitability rested on the PLO as a political threat to Israel and to Israel's hold on the occupied territories." Others have frankly acknowledged the unchallenged facts.[82]

In a front-page think piece on the latest Gaza invasion, *New York Times* correspondent Steven Lee Meyers writes that "in some ways, the Gaza attacks were reminiscent of the gamble Israel took, and largely lost, in Lebanon in 1982 [when] it invaded to eliminate the threat of Yasser Arafat's forces." Correct, but not in the sense he has in mind. In 1982, as in 2008, it was necessary to eliminate the threat of political settlement.[83]

The hope of Israeli propagandists has been that Western intellectuals and media would buy the tale that Israel reacted to rockets raining on the Galilee, "intolerable acts of terror." And they have not been disappointed.

It is not that Israel does not want peace: everyone wants peace, even Hitler. The question is: on what terms? From its origins, the Zionist movement has understood that to achieve its goals, the best strategy would be to delay political settlement, meanwhile slowly building facts on the ground. Even the occasional agreements, as in 1947, were regarded by the leadership as temporary steps toward further expansion.[84] The 1982 Lebanon war was a dramatic example of the desperate fear of diplomacy. It was followed by Israeli support for Hamas so as to undermine the secular PLO and its irritating peace initiatives. Another case that should be familiar is Israeli provocations before the 1967 war, designed to elicit a Syrian response that could be used as a pretext for violence and takeover of more land—at least 80 percent of the incidents, according to Defense Minister Moshe Dayan.[85]

The story goes far back. The official history of the Haganah, the pre-state Jewish military force, describes the assassination of the religious Jewish poet Jacob de Haan in 1924, accused of conspiring for an accommodation between the traditional Jewish community (the Old Yishuv) and the Arab Higher Committee. And there have been numerous examples since.[86]

The effort to delay political accommodation has always made perfect sense, as do the accompanying lies about how "there is no partner for peace." It is hard to think of another way to take over land where you are not wanted.

Similar reasons underlie Israel's preference for expansion over security. Its violation of the cease-fire on November 4, 2008, is one of many recent examples.

When Israel broke the June 2008 cease-fire on November 4, Amnesty International reported that the June 2008 cease-fire

> has brought enormous improvements in the quality of life in Sderot and other Israeli villages near Gaza, where before the

ceasefire residents lived in fear of the next Palestinian rocket strike. However, nearby in the Gaza Strip the Israeli blockade remains in place and the population has so far seen few dividends from the cease-fire. Since June 2007, the entire population of 1.5 million Palestinians has been trapped in Gaza, with dwindling resources and an economy in ruins. Some 80 percent of the population now depend on the trickle of international aid that the Israeli army allows in.[87]

But the gains in security for Israeli towns near Gaza were evidently outweighed by the felt need to deter diplomatic moves that might impede West Bank expansion, and to crush any remaining resistance within Palestine.

The preference for expansion over security has been particularly evident since Israel's fateful decision in 1971, backed by Henry Kissinger, to reject the offer of a full peace treaty by President Sadat of Egypt, offering nothing to the Palestinians—an agreement that the United States and Israel were compelled to accept at Camp David eight years later, after a major war that was a near disaster for Israel. A peace treaty with Egypt would have ended any significant security threat, but there was an unacceptable quid pro quo: Israel would have had to abandon its extensive settlement programs in the northeastern Sinai. Security was a lower priority than expansion, as it still is.[88]

Today, Israel could have security, normalization of relations, and integration into the region. But it very clearly prefers illegal expansion, conflict, and repeated exercise of violence, actions that are not only criminal, murderous, and destructive but are also eroding its own long-term security. U.S. military and Middle East specialist Andrew Cordesman writes that while Israel military force can surely crush defenseless Gaza, "neither Israel nor the US can gain from a war that produces [a bitter] reaction from one of the wisest and most moderate voices in the Arab world, Prince Turki al-Faisal of

Saudi Arabia, who said on January 6 that 'The Bush administration has left [Obama] a disgusting legacy and a reckless position towards the massacres and bloodshed of innocents in Gaza.... Enough is enough, today we are all Palestinians and we seek martyrdom for God and for Palestine, following those who died in Gaza.'"[89]

One of the wisest voices in Israel, Uri Avnery, writes that after an Israeli military victory, "What will be seared into the consciousness of the world will be the image of Israel as a blood-stained monster, ready at any moment to commit war crimes and not prepared to abide by any moral restraints. This will have severe consequences for our long-term future, our standing in the world, our chance of achieving peace and quiet. In the end, this war is a crime against ourselves too, a crime against the State of Israel."[90]

There is good reason to believe that he is right. Israel is deliberately turning itself into one of the most hated countries in the world, and is also losing the allegiance of the population of the West, including younger American Jews, who are unlikely to tolerate its persistent shocking crimes for long. Decades ago, I wrote that those who call themselves "supporters of Israel" are in reality supporters of its moral degeneration and probable ultimate destruction. Regrettably, that judgment looks more and more plausible.

Meanwhile we are quietly observing a rare event in history, what the late Israeli sociologist Baruch Kimmerling called "politicide," the murder of a nation—at our hands.[91]

FIVE

BLUEPRINT FOR A ONE-STATE MOVEMENT:
A TROUBLED HISTORY

The demise of the Oslo Accord at the very beginning of the twenty-first century gave special impetus to the old/new idea of a one-state solution. It seems to be with us again and the interest in it grows by the day. And yet it does not appear as an item on the agenda of any actor of significance on the Palestine chessboard. Neither major powers nor small political factions endorse it as a vision or strategy let alone as a tactic for the future. Its attractiveness, however, is undeniable given the failure of the alternative solutions. This seems to be the appropriate moment to ponder its past history and its future trajectory.

This essay does not wish to recap the faults of the two-state solution, nor does it strive to argue for the advantages of the one-state solution. The purpose here is first to remind readers that although the idea today is hypothetical, theoretical, and quite abstract, it used be a concrete plan, strategy, and vision. Second, based on this historical recognition, this chapter argues that it is time to transform the idea once more into a real political plan that would be carried out by a popular movement for change in Israel and Palestine. One cannot doubt

that there is a new impulse inside and outside of Palestine for a regime
change: there is now a constant quest to change the realities in the present republic of Israel, which is a one-state solution by itself (ethnically
and racially oppressive toward its Palestinian citizens and subjects). It
is by and large a nonviolent impulse for equality and a craving for nor-
mality that should be translated into a powerful agent of change for the
sake of Palestinians and Israelis alike.

A TROUBLED HISTORY

The one-state solution has a troubled history. It began as a soft
Zionist concept of Jewish settlers, some of whom were leading
intellectuals in their community, who wished to reconcile colonialism and humanism. They were looking for a way that would
not require the settlers either to return to their homelands or to
give up the idea of a new Jewish life in the "redeemed" ancient
homeland. They were also moved by more practical considerations, such as the relatively small number of Jewish settlers
within a solid Palestinian majority. They offered binationalism
within one modern state. They found some Palestinian partners
when the settlers arrived in the 1920s but were soon manipulated
by the Zionist leadership to serve that movement's strategy and
then disappeared into the margins of history. In the 1930s, notable members among them, such as Yehuda Magnes, were appointed as emissaries by the Zionist leadership for talks with the
Arab Higher Committee. Magnes and his colleagues genuinely
believed, then and in retrospect, that they served as harbingers of
peace, but in fact they were sent to gauge the impulses and aspirations on the other side, so as to defeat it in due course.[1] They
existed in one form or another until the end of the Mandate.
Their only potential ally, the Palestine Communist Party, for a
while endorsed their idea of binationalism, but in the crucial

final years of the Mandate, adopted the principle of partition as the only solution (admittedly due to orders from Moscow rather than out of a natural growth of its ideology). So by 1947, there was no significant support for the idea on either the Zionist or Palestinian side. Moreover, it seems that there was no genuine desire locally or regionally to look for a local solution and it was left to the international community to propose one.

The appearance in 1947 of the one-state solution as an international option is a chapter of history very few know about or bother to revisit. The scope of this article does not allow me to expand on it. But it is worth remembering that at one given point during the discussions and deliberations of UNSCOP (the United Nations Special Committee on Palestine, February to November 1947), those members of the UN who were not under the influence of either the United States or the USSR—and they were not many—regarded the idea of one state in Palestine as the best solution for the conflict. They defined it as a democratic unitary state, where citizenship would be equal and not determined on the basis of ethnicity or nationality. The indigenous population was defined as those who were in Palestine at that time, nearly two million people who were mostly Palestinians. When their idea was put in a minority report of UNSCOP (the majority report was the basis for the famous [or infamous] Resolution 181 of November 29, 1947), half of the then members of the UN General Assembly supported it, before succumbing to pressure by the superpowers to vote in favor of the partition resolution.[2] It is not surprising in hindsight that people around the world, who did not feel, like the Western powers did, that the creation of a Jewish state at the expense of the Palestinians was the best compensation for the horrors of the Holocaust, would support the unitary state. After all the Jewish community in Palestine was made of newcomers and settlers, and were only one-third of the overall population. But common decency and sense were not allowed to play a role where Palestine was concerned.[3]

So Palestine was partitioned between Israel, Jordan, and Egypt. But the idea was kept alive when the Palestine Liberation Organization (PLO) came into being. Its version of one state was a secular and democratic one (although unsympathetic toward the possible presence of Jewish settlers who arrived after 1948) and was attractive enough even to inspire a small anti-Zionist group in Israel—Matzpen—to accept it for a while. The Arab world, in words and through the Arab League, seemed to stand behind the idea. This was the vision of the liberation movement until the 1970s, when lack of success, pragmatism, and a growing realization of how powerful Israel had become due to unconditional American support—which was not equaled by the limited aid the USSR gave the PLO—led to new ideas about the future. Thus came to the world Fatah's Stages Program. This was a willingness to consider a two-state solution. Initially, the plan was presented as a temporary means for bringing peace and justice to Palestine, but later on it was portrayed as a strategy, and perhaps even a vision.

The idea of a two-state solution, however, did not germinate on the Palestinian side. It was always the preferred solution of pragmatic Zionism. Pragmatic Zionism, or mainstream Zionism, led the Jewish community in Palestine since the late nineteenth century and its basic ideas still guide the Israeli political system today. The power of the two-state solution depends largely on the power of pragmatic Zionism. Those who are presently regarded as pragmatic Zionists are defined as such due to their support for the two-state solution. Since the support only has to be verbal and noncommittal, even right-wing parties in Israel, despite their declared ideology of a Greater Israel (a one-state solution with exclusive Jewish presence and rights) can endorse it. This was recently demonstrated by Binyamin Netanyahu's pledge to such a solution made only in order to allow the continued strategic alliance between an allegedly more critical American administration and a more hawkish Israeli government.

But because the two-state solution is so closely connected to the fortunes of pragmatic Zionism, it is important to recap the historical record of this mainstream Zionist force. The leaders and movements who represented pragmatic Zionism were responsible for the 1948 ethnic cleansing of Palestine, the military rule imposed on the Palestinians inside Israel for almost twenty years, the colonization of the West Bank in the last forty years, and the repertoire of oppressive and brutal policies against the people of Gaza in the last eight years. And the list of course is longer and new chapters of oppression and dispossession are added to it by the day. And yet the total identification of pragmatic Zionism with the two-state solution, and before it with territorial compromise with Jordan (the Jordanian option) equated it in the eyes of the world with "peace" and "reconciliation." As transpired clearly during the days of the Oslo Accord, the discourse of two states and peace provided a shield that enabled the pragmatic Zionist governments to expand the settlement project in the West Bank and escalate the oppressive policies against the Gaza Strip.

Looked at from a different angle, pragmatic Zionism was the only actor on the ground that gave substance to the idea of two states; whereas the PLO, even when it endorsed the idea, had to accept the Zionist interpretation of it. The relevant international actors and the United States in particular followed this Zionist interpretation as they still do today. This interpretation meant that the two-state solution is based on total Israeli control of the whole of what used to be Mandatory Palestine: its airspace, territorial waters, and external borders. It includes a limited measure of Palestinian sovereignty within those parts of Palestine that Israel is not interested in (the Gaza Strip and less than half of the West Bank). This sovereignty would also be limited in essence: a demilitarized government would have little say in defense, foreign, and financial policies.

It seems that even a fragile Yasser Arafat realized twice what this hegemonic interpretation of the two-state solution meant. This occurred first before the signing in Cairo of the Oslo B agreement and then for the second time during the Camp David summit of 2000. In the first instance, it was too late, literally minutes before the ceremony, and there was no way out. On the second occasion he had time to ponder more profoundly and refused to accept this Israeli dictate that at the end of the day probably cost him his life. One would think that this fate is partly behind his successor's consent, hesitant as it is, to continue with this idea and accept the pragmatic Zionist interpretation as long as he can.

But the potency of this Zionist interpretation of the two-state solution, which remains to this very moment the only interpretation, is waning. This is the main reason for the reemergence of the one-state solution. The latter was kept alive by those who always believed in it as the only moral, not just political, settlement that contains, and answers, all the outstanding problems involved in the ongoing conflict. Issues such as the refugees' right of return, the colonialist nature of Zionism, and the need to accommodate the multireligious and multicultural fabric of society seem to have no room in the two-state solution. The first group of one-state supporters were joined by the "desperadoes," those who reluctantly endorse the one-state solution since they despair of any hope of implementing a two-state solution. They regard the new geopolitical realities Israel created on the ground as irreversible and they recognize there is no will on the Israeli side to accept a truly independent and sovereign Palestinian state alongside Israel.

Thus, despite its troubled history, the one-state idea is still with us today. And yet it remains on the margins and attributed to naive daydreamers. From this very brief, and admittedly somewhat esoteric description, it is clear that only a significant erosion of the validity of the two-state solution can revert attention to the concept of a one-state solution, in whatever form. However, it is important to stress early on that the idea was kept alive not by those who despaired of the possibilities of a two-state solution, but rather by those who did not lose faith in the moral validity of the concept and its political feasibility. These very few feel vindicated in the last decade by the many that joined them as "new converts," as the demise of the two-state solution becomes clearer by the day.

As these words are being written, it is mainly a large number of individuals, and not even NGOs, who stand firmly behind the idea. They are visible and have advanced the case of the one-state solution significantly in recent years by structuring the discussion and airing the outstanding issues beyond slogans and ideals. The final boost to this intellectual and public activity was the appearance of several coherent books, whose authors along with other writers joined efforts to disseminate the concept and root it deeply in the public discourse and mind.[4] But as mentioned, there are no political parties upholding this idea and although an intuitive survey of the scores of NGOs working on the ground in Israel, Palestine, and the exilic communities indicates wide support in Palestinian civil society for this idea, none of the present governmental and non-governmental actors have officially taken a stance of support.

A political movement has first and foremost to clarify its position vis-à-vis those in power; or, put differently, decide whether it wishes to substitute for the powers that be or to influence them. In the former case, the one-state movement can only act by becoming a party, a faction, or whatever term one uses these days in the abnormal reality on the ground in Palestine where a sovereign state exists alongside an occupied, stateless enclaved and imprisoned community.

But there is another option that may be a necessary and preliminary stage before a clearer decision on strategy is taken. For this one has to adopt a more fluid definition of the concept of a movement than the one usually appearing in the professional literature. The movement we are looking for is a vehicle that represents certain impulses and hopes, and a vision. As such its main task is to translate popular, or bottom-up, demands in the political realm that are ignored by the political and media elites in a given society. In our particular case, it wants those in power to urgently examine new options for salvaging an escalating catastrophe.

There are two paradoxes that would have to be dealt with early on. One is that it takes a long time to build a movement, and the reality on the ground demands from every activist urgency and immediate activism to thwart the continued oppression. The second is that quite often the popular demand from the political elite is engendered and propelled by growing suspicion of, and total lack of confidence in, that very political elite, without necessarily showing enthusiasm for replacing it.

These are given constraints and I do not suggest that we can reconcile the paradoxes, just be aware of them. There is a way around it as another similar effort to create a movement has shown us. This is the BDS (Boycott, Divestment, and Sanctions) for Palestine movement. It is a call for using very drastic nonviolent action against Israel in order to stop the present criminal policies on the ground (such as the Gaza massacre in January 2009), but also at the same time engender a general discussion about the nature of the regime and its international legitimacy. It also relates to the second paradox

I mentioned by not wishing to play a role in the political elite, but forcing that same elite to take a stance on the issue given the failure of all the other strategies of the struggle. It began a few years ago as the brainchild of a small number of individuals and grew into significant proportions when it was fully endorsed by the civil society in the occupied territories, and thence supported widely by Palestinians around the world and inside Israel.[5]

Before remarking further on the two options for the one-state movement, whether to build a political movement per se or to engage in establishing a broad following for the one-state idea, there is a preliminary issue that has to be addressed. This refers to the problems arising from the formation of the new coalition that now pushes the idea forward. As mentioned, it is made of longtime believers in the idea and "desperadoes" joining late in the day due to their frustration regarding the inability to implement the two-state solution. This is not the healthiest of coalitions to advance a concept that is still utopian and rejected by the political elites and mainstream media. Motivation and inspiration are not likely to be found among the "desperadoes." This was very clear for instance in the contribution to the March 2009 conference of Meron Benvenisti.[6] But his valuable deconstruction and explication, and others like it, of what is wrong with the two-state solution and their engagements with realpolitik, can benefit the one-state movement enormously.

If a minimal basis for cooperation can be found, and again judging from the evidence so far, this is not something one can take for granted, the next stage is to direct the efforts of persuasion toward "state skeptics," who although not oblivious to the chaotic reality produced by a constant adherence of the international community to the two-state solution, still do not find the courage to support the one-state solution.

It is really a question of how to enlarge both the core group of the movement and its base of support. The effort should be to elasticize the concept so as to increase its attraction to its maximal optimum.

I think we are more or less there, at that stage, after the Boston March 2009 conference. As noted before, it is from here that we should weigh the two possible options: playing by the rules the political elites set or working through the popular networks to change public discourse and the political elites' orientations.

The nature of politics, especially in the West, has been since the Second World War evolutionary and not revolutionary. Sticking to formulas is thus in the nature of such political systems and unless catastrophe proves such formulas to be dead for all intents and purposes, political elites are not likely to deviate from them. Let alone when the issue is not the highest on their agenda; even when it is prominent among their concerns, it is so only for a very short span of time. Thus, even very visible indicators of the impossibility of implementing a two-state solution of any kind, or one that can only be unilaterally accepted by Israel, are not likely to produce a dramatic change of orientation or policy. This means that the first option explored above, of impacting a change of policy toward a one-state solution from among the political elites, is premature and is likely to result at this stage in total disappointment and a dangerous transformation of the one-state movement into a quixotic voyage into oblivion.

Therefore, the more viable option is the one that does not play a part yet in the political elite game, but prepares the ground for the inevitable earthquake that would also force the politicians and principal actors to take a different stance. A movement in this respect is literally an attempt to move people's mindsets, attentions, and recognitions. This can be seen as a three-pronged effort: reintroduce the past into the equation, deconstruct the essence of the present peace process, and prepare projects that translate the concept of one state into a tangible reality in the future.

RESELLING THE PAST

The struggle over memory in the case of Palestine seems to be the most important task in this century for anyone committed to the Palestine cause. The convergence of industrious Palestinian historiography with the new revelations made by revisionist historians in Israel transformed not only the research agenda of academia but also the public discourse among activists. It was in many ways the exposure to the full picture of what occurred in 1948 that expanded the spectrum of peace activists, and members of Palestinian solidarity committees, so that it included the 1948 Nakbah. Even President Obama in his June 2009 Cairo speech acknowledged a Palestinian suffering that spans over sixty years.

The struggle over historic memory is highly relevant to the debate about a one-state solution. Only the historical perspective reveals the reductionist nature of the two-state solution: the fact that "Palestine" refers to only one-fifth of the land and about one-third of the Palestinians.

A deeper historical recognition exposes the colonialist nature of the Zionist movement. It does not only show that Palestinians were ethnically cleansed in 1948 and were never allowed to return, but also that the ideology that produced that policy is still operative today.

A brave Italian journalist and writer compared the narrative employed hitherto as the raison d'être of a two-state solution to a historical narrative that explains the French Revolution as a violent juncture that has no origins or any background information.[7]

The unified Palestinian experience from the late nineteenth century up to 1948 has been replaced by discrete experiences due to the fragmentation of the people and the bisection of the land. But these new disjointed experiences all without exception relate to what happened in 1948: in other words whether you live in Ramallah, London, Yarmouk, or Nazareth, your present predicament is a direct result of what occurred in 1948.

Moreover, the ideology that produced the 1948 ethnic cleansing is the one that keeps refugees in their camps today, discriminates against Palestinians inside Israel, and oppresses those under occupation in the West Bank and imprisonment in the Gaza Strip.

Seen from that perspective, a two-state solution is a small lid trying to cover a huge boiling pot and whenever it is put on, it drowns. The resolution of a conflict can only occur when such a lid can be put firmly on the past and bring its horrors and evils to a close.

At the academic and civil society level this realization is solid and has created fertile ground for the discussion about a one-state solution. However, this is unfortunately not the case with the mainstream media and political arena in the West or in the Arab world. There is a better chance to debate the historical narrative that to propagate the one-state solution at this stage in the struggle. Mainstream media and politicians reject out of hand the one-state solution, but may be willing to accept that their historical narrative so far was distorted and wrong and that they should view the conflict as a process that began in 1948, even in 1882, and not in 1967.

In other words what should be hammered in is that what the "desperadoes" call the facts on the ground that gradually made the desired two-state solution impossible were not an accident. They are the outcome of a strategy aiming at granting the State of Israel control over all of Mandatory Palestine. This strategy was and is the cornerstone of pragmatic Zionism and it divided the land into two territories: the one that Israel rules directly and in it wishes to implement what Shimon Peres coined "maximum territory and minimum Arabs."[8] And the other territory is the one that Israel controls indirectly of through proxies such as a collaborationist Palestinian Authority. What was and still is presented by Western journalists and politicians as a fundamental debate inside Israel about peace and war, of retaining the territories or withdrawing from them, is in effect a debate about what "maximum territory" is and what are the means of achieving it, as well as how one attains the target of minimum Arabs.

Unmasking the paradigm of parity, the charade of a genuine debate in the Israeli society, and revealing the strategy behind Israeli policy in the last forty years is a task the one-state movement should take upon itself in the near future.

DECONSTRUCTING THE PEACE PROCESS

The biggest contemporary obstacle for putting forward the one-state solution as a viable option is that the raison d'être of the "peace process" of the last forty years is firmly based on the vision of two states. It is so powerful that even some of the bravest and most committed colleagues in the struggle for Palestine endorse it in the name of realpolitik.

In order to confront it successfully with the modest means that a one-state movement has and will have, it is important to recognize the premises that underlie the raison d'être of the peace process, as today they are still governing the Obama administration, the Palestine Authority, the so-called peace camp in Israel, and large sections of the political and media elite in the West.

The peace process began immediately after the June 1967 war ended, and while the early initiators were French, British, and Russians, it soon became an attempt to impose a Pax Americana. The basic American assumption underlying the "peace" effort was an absolute reliance on the balance of power as the principal prism through which the possibility of solutions should be examined. As Israeli superiority was unquestioned after the war it meant that whatever Israeli politicians and generals devised as a peace plan soon became the basis for the process as a whole.

Thus, the Israeli political elite constantly produced the common wisdom of the peace process and formulated its guidelines according to its own concerns. These American-Israeli guidelines were drafted in the first years after the 1967 occupation and crystallized as a vision for a new geopolitical map for historical Palestine. Pragmatic Zionism dictated that the country would roughly be divided into two spheres: one that Israel controls directly as a sovereign state and the other that Israel rules indirectly while giving Palestinians limited autonomy.

The principal American role was to present to the world these dictates in a positive manner as "Israeli concessions," "reasonable behavior," and "flexible positions."[9] To this day, either out of ignorance or interest, successive American administrations adopted a perception of the conflict that caters solely to the internal Israeli scene and one that disregards totally the Palestinian perspective of whatever nature or inclination.

This hegemonic American-Israeli presence produced five guidelines that so far have not been challenged politically and diplomatically by the Quartet and whoever manages the peace process and all the histrionics around it.

The first guideline relates directly to the struggle over historic memory mentioned above. It states that the "conflict" began in 1967 and hence the essence of its solution is an agreement that would determine only the future status of the West Bank and the Gaza Strip. Such a perspective confines a settlement to 78 percent of Palestine.

The second guideline is that everything visible in those areas is divisible and that such divisibility is the key for peace. So even the remaining 22 percent of Palestine has to be divided for the sake of peace. Moreover, the peace agenda meant that not only the 1967 occupied areas should be divided, but also its people and natural resources.

The third guideline is that anything that happened until 1967, including the consequences of the Nakbah and its ethnic cleansing, are not negotiable. This pushed the refugee issue off the agenda, where it remains to this very day.

The fourth guideline is an equation between the end of the Israeli occupation and the end of the conflict. Namely, once some kind of eviction or control were agreed upon, the conflict would be resolved for all intents and purposes.

The last guideline is that Israel is not committed to any concession until the Palestinian armed struggle ends.

In 1993, these five guidelines were translated into the Oslo Accord, when a Palestinian partner seemed to accept them in principle. They were repackaged again in Camp David 2000 and in both cases after trials and tribulations rejected by the PLO and the Palestinian Authority (PA). But these are still the agreed upon principles for the peace process.

The task here is twofold. The first is to associate in the public mind the present reality, which is accepted by international observers as representing a human catastrophe of unimaginable dimensions, as the inevitable outcome of this peace process and its principles. Thus, exposing it as a political act that provides international immunity for a policy of colonization and dispossession. It is true that this policy has escalated dramatically since 2000, but it is not true that the escalation is the result of the collapse of the peace process—it is the result of the process's raison d'être.

The one-state movement has the academics, journalists, and activists who possess the means of disseminating this knowledge through books, journals, and public meetings whenever the current affairs of Palestine and Israel are discussed. A media monitor of sorts is already working, but not in a professional or systematic way. Although one has to admit that it is much more timidity than ignorance that prevents intelligent and knowledgeable journalists and politicians from exposing the "peace process," shielding a well-structured Israeli plan, devised already in 1967, to enclave the Palestinians in bantustans. Pragmatic Zionism did not wish to directly control the populated Palestinian areas in the West Bank and the Gaza Strip, did not dare to expel them, and did not wish to give them more than limited autonomy.

The second task is to bring to the fore the Palestinian voices that were directly victimized by this Israeli policy in the last forty years within a paradigm of analysis that highlights the connection between their sufferings and the charade of peace. In other words, the debate is not only about the question whether the road taken so far was right, but an accusation of those who led us on that road as contributing directly to the continued oppression of the Palestinians in the occupied territories. This would mean challenging the very agenda of the Palestinian Authority that claims that peace with Israel under the old premises will bring an end to the suffering of the occupied people, while the counterargument should be that it is having precisely the opposite effect: deepening the occupation and perpetuating the oppression.

This deconstruction of the peace process should not remain an academic exercise. It should have some immediate practical implications. The first was already mentioned, a systematic challenge of the media coverage of the peace process in the West. Second, it should help to transform the nature of the peace activity in Western civil societies, and for that matter among the peace groups still active in Israel as well. These activists until recently were loyal to both the paradigm of parity and the logic of the two-state solution as the vision of peace. Thus, peace activity for years was based, as was the peace process itself, on the paradigm of two equal narratives that needed mediation and bridging. Hence both the EU and the major funding bodies in the West were financing and encouraging the phenomenon of "kissing cousins" meetings. Similarly, Western activists believed their main mission was to bring the two sides together on a neutral, namely Western, ground. This noble impulse gave unintentional support for the official peace process and presented it as a reflection of a wider desire among Western societies.

The one-state movement can be the pinnacle of a new orientation and effort of this impulse of Western civil societies to transform the reality in Palestine. Instead of facilitating futile encounters—unnecessary at any rate as they can take place at any given moment on the ground—they can provide venues for strategizing around the campaign for changing the policies of Western governments and for pondering a more genuine and comprehensive solution for the conflict.

Desegregating the activity of civil society in the West, as well as inside Israel, illustrates the very essence of a one-state solution when the one-state movement is still in its embryonic stage. An activity around themes, and not according to national, religious, or ethnic identity, can be the unique contribution of the one-state movement. But again themes can sound too abstract and fluid for a movement that seeks desperately to change the public mind after years of being conditioned by a distorted historical narrative, manipulated media coverage, and a lethal futuristic vision. Thus the themes should be closely connected to tangible results. The last part of this essay explores some of these themes and results.

PREPARING FOR THE FUTURE: THE MODULAR MODEL

In its present form the one-state movement is made of individuals from all walks of life who can bring to the fore their activism and professionalism before the vision is taken up more systematically by NGOs and political parties. It is time to expand the activity beyond the big conferences that have so far successfully heralded the idea and exposed the fallacies of the two-state solution model. There are more areas of investigation that the one-state movement can focus on.

The first is a survey of attitudes toward the one-state idea. So far no one has attempted such a survey and despite the obvious weakness of such an instrument this is a precondition for any future campaign of disseminating the idea and recruiting others for it.

The second is the formation of working teams, very much on the basis of the Tawaqim (professional teams) that were preparing, in earnest but in vain, for the creation of an independent state in the Orient House during the Madrid conference days. These teams should prepare the practical products emanating from a future political outfit for Palestine and Israel in whatever form it will appear: a constitution, an educational system, curricula and textbooks, basic guidelines for an economic system, the practical implications within a state of a multicultural and multireligious society, and so on. For some of these aspects of statehood there is no need to reinvent the wheel, as the Tawaqim were quite good in covering them; for others inspiration should be found elsewhere in history, other geographies, and human thought.

A particular project that would have to be considered is a serious contemplation about the future of the Israeli Jewish colonies. For the Tawaqim it was clear that a future Palestinian state meant one without these colonies. In the case of the one-state solution this is a different matter. I do not propose here a solution, but only point out to the need to discuss it now and not later.

Constructing, in the most practical way, these end products—such as a prototype constitution, an educational curriculum, laws of citizenships for all (indigenous, returnees, and new immigrants), land and property ownership regulations (including compensations and absentee properties), and similar projects—can give substance to the idea of one state beyond slogans and the deconstruction of the two-state solution.

The last project for the one-state movement before it hopefully becomes a potent, popular, and political movement is to focus on small teams and later in front of larger audiences—on how to disseminate the idea and educate people about it. Palestinian NGOs domestic and abroad, the few NGOs in Israel that are still engaged in the struggle against the occupation, the Palestine solidarity campaigns and committees, and all the other NGOs in Western societies and around the Arab and Muslim worlds can be all recruited to take a firmer stand on the issue.

The struggle for one state cannot be had without close cooperation with official PLO, Hamas, and PA representatives, nor without adoption of the discourse or dictionary of these groups on the ground. This would allow the one-state movement to envision peace and reconciliation in a less limited, more inclusive way. One doubts whether Arab regimes would help, apart from heads of state who are already openly in support of the idea. On the other hand, the South African government and NGOs have already shown greater enthusiasm for the idea than any other state actor on the international scene. With these limitations in mind, and with these potential partners, the voice of the one-state movement should be heard at all times.

This can be accomplished, despite the profound knowledge that

popular support for the idea depends crucially on a total disinte-
gration of the two-state solution and this scenario in turn is beyond the influence of the one-state movement. While waiting for
developments beyond our control and influence, we should prepare as if this moment is around the corner and assume that millions of desperate Palestinians, Israelis, and whoever cares about
them in the world would quickly seek an alternative to the paradigm that so disastrously informed the peace process in Palestine
and Israel. Activism, scholarship, dissemination of information,
persuasion, protest, and solidarity are the most powerful weapons
powerless people have. Let us use them wisely.

SIX

THE GHETTOIZATION OF PALESTINE: A DIALOGUE WITH ILAN PAPPÉ AND NOAM CHOMSKY

First, are you working on something at the moment that you would like to let us know about?

Ilan Pappé: I am completing several books. The first is a concise history of the Israeli occupation of the West Bank and the Gaza Strip, with a particular focus on the key Israeli decisions taken in the early years, which I claim have not been deviated from until today. The other is on the Palestinian minority in Israel and one on the Arab Jews. I am also completing an edited volume comparing the South African situation to that of Palestine.

Noam Chomsky: The usual range of articles, talks, et cetera. No time for major projects right now.

A British MP recently said that he had felt a change in the last five years regarding Israel. British MPs nowadays sign EDMs (Early Day Motions) condemning Israel in bigger numbers than ever before and he told me that it was now easier to express criticism toward Israel even when speaking on U.S.

This interview took place on several occasions in 2009 and 2010.

campuses. Also, in the last few weeks, John Dugard, independent investigator on the Israeli-Palestinian conflict for the UN Human Rights Council said that "Palestinian terror is an 'inevitable' result of occupation," the European parliament adopted a resolution saying that the "policy of isolation of the Gaza Strip has failed at both the political and humanitarian level" and the UN has condemned Israel's use of excessive and disproportionate force in the Gaza Strip.[1] Could we interpret that as a general shift in attitude toward Israel?

Pappé: The two examples indicate a significant shift in public opinion and in the civil society. However, the problem remains what it has been in the last sixty years: these impulses and energies are not translated, and are not likely to be translated in the near future, into actual policies on the ground. And thus, the only way of enhancing this transition from support from below to actual policies is by developing the idea of sanctions and boycott. This can give a clear orientation and direction to the many individuals and NGOs that have for years shown solidarity with the Palestine cause.

Chomsky: There has been a very clear shift in recent years—on U.S. campuses and with general audiences as well. It was not long ago that police protection was a standard feature of talks at all critical of Israeli policies—meetings were broken up, audiences very hostile and abusive. Now it is sharply different, with scattered exceptions. Apologists for Israeli violence now tend often to be defensive and desperate, rather than arrogant and overbearing. But the critique of Israeli actions is thin, because the basic facts are systematically suppressed. That is particularly true of the decisive U.S. role in barring diplomatic options, undermining democracy, and supporting Israel's systematic program of undermining the possibility for an eventual political settlement. But portrayal of the United States as an "honest broker," somehow unable to pursue its benign objectives, is characteristic, not only in this domain.

The word *apartheid* is more and more often used by NGOs to describe Israel's actions toward the Palestinians (in Gaza, the occupied Palestinian territories [OPT], and also in Israel itself). Is the situation in Palestine and Israel comparable to apartheid South Africa?

Pappé: There are similarities and dissimilarities. The colonialist history has many chapters in common and some of the features of the apartheid system can be found in the Israeli policies toward its own Palestinian minority and toward those in the OPT. Some aspects of the occupation, however, are worse than the apartheid reality of South Africa and some aspects in the lives of Palestinian citizens in Israel are not as bad as they were in the heyday of apartheid. The main point of comparison to my mind is political inspiration. The anti-apartheid movement, the ANC, the solidarity networks developed throughout the years in the West, should inspire a more focused and effective pro-Palestinian campaign. This is why there is a need to learn the history of the struggle against apartheid, much more than dwell too long on comparing the Zionist and apartheid systems. An additional point, which is both historical and ideological, is the critical analysis of many of us today who realize change will not come from within Israel.

Chomsky: There can be no definite answer to such questions. There are similarities and differences. Within Israel itself, there is serious discrimination, but it's very far from South African apartheid. Within the occupied territories, it's a different story. In 1997, I gave the keynote address at Ben-Gurion University for a conference on the anniversary of the 1967 war. I read a paragraph from a standard history of South Africa. No comment was necessary.

Looking more closely, the situation in the OPT differs in many ways from apartheid. In some respects, South African apartheid was more vicious than Israeli practices, and in some respects the opposite is true. To mention one example, White South Africa depended on Black labor. The large majority of the population could not be expelled. At one time Israel relied on cheap and easily exploited Palestinian laborers, but they have long ago been replaced by the miserable of the earth from Asia, Eastern Europe, and elsewhere. Israelis would mostly breathe a sigh of relief if Palestinians were to disappear. And it is no secret that the policies that have taken shape accord well with the recommendations of Moshe Dayan right after the 1967 war: Palestinians will "continue to live like dogs, and whoever wishes, may leave."[2] More extreme recommendations have been made by highly regarded left humanists in the United States. For example, Michael Walzer of the Institute for Advanced Studies in Princeton and editor of the democratic socialist journal *Dissent*, advised thirty-five years ago that since Palestinians are "marginal to the nation," they should be "helped" to leave.[3] He was referring to Palestinian citizens of Israel itself, a position made familiar more recently by the ultra-right Avigdor Liberman, and now being picked up in the Israeli mainstream. I put aside the real fanatics, like Harvard Law professor Alan Dershowitz, who declares that Israel never kills civilians, only terrorists, so that the definition of "terrorist" is "killed by Israel"; and Israel should aim for a kill ratio of 1,000 to 0,[4] which means "exterminate the brutes" completely. It is of no small significance that advocates of these views are regarded with respect in enlightened circles in the United States, indeed the West. One can imagine the reaction if such comments were made about Jews.

On the query, to repeat, there can be no clear answer as to whether the analogy is appropriate.

Israel has recently said that it will boycott the UN conference on human rights in Durban because "it will be impossible to prevent the conference

from turning into a festival of anti-Israeli attacks"[5] and has also canceled a meeting with Costa Rican officials over the Central American nation's decision to formally recognize a Palestinian state.[6] Is Israel's refusal to accept any sort of criticism toward its policies likely to eventually backfire?

Pappé: One hopes it will backfire one day. However, this depends on the global and regional balances of power, not only on the Israelis "overreacting." The two, namely the balance of power and Israel intransigence, may be interconnected in the future. If there is a change in America's policy, or in its hegemonic role in the politics of the region, then a continued Israeli inflexibility can encourage the international community to adopt a more critical position against Israel and exert pressure on the Jewish state to end the occupation and dispossession of Palestine.

Chomsky: Israel's refusal to accept criticism is already backfiring. In a recent international poll—taken before the invasion of Gaza—nineteen out of twenty-one countries regarded Israel as having a negative influence in the world; the exceptions were the United States, where slightly more were positive, and Russia, where opinion was divided.[7] Israel ranked last along with Iran and Pakistan. After the invasion of Gaza attitudes are surely more sharply negative. That has been increasing over time.

How can Israel reach a settlement with an organization that declares it will never recognize Israel and whose charter calls for the destruction of the Jewish state? If Hamas really wants a settlement, why won't it recognize Israel?

Pappé: Peace is made between enemies not lovers. The end result of the peace process can be a political Islamic recognition of the place of the Jews in Palestine and in the Middle East as a whole, whether in a separate state or a joint state. The PLO entered negotiations with

Israel without changing its charter, which is not that different as far as the attitude to Israel is concerned. So the search should be for a text, solution, and political structure that is inclusive—enabling all the national, ethnic, religious, and ideological groups to coexist.

Chomsky: Hamas cannot recognize Israel any more than Kadima can recognize Palestine, or than the Democratic Party in the United States can recognize England. One could ask whether a government led by Hamas should recognize Israel, or whether a government led by Kadima or the Democratic Party should recognize Palestine. So far they have all refused to do so, though Hamas has at least called for a two-state settlement in accord with the long-standing international consensus, while Kadima and the Democratic Party refuse to go that far, keeping to the rejectionist stance that the United States and Israel have maintained for over thirty years in international isolation. As for words, when Prime Minister Olmert declares to a joint session of the U.S. Congress that he believes "in our people's eternal and historic right to this entire land," to rousing applause, he is denying any meaningful rights to Palestinians.[8] Often that rejection is explicit government policy, as in 1989, in response to formal Palestinian acceptance of a two-state settlement, when the coalition Peres-Shamir government declared that there can be no "additional Palestinian state" between Jordan and Israel, Jordan already being a Palestinian state by Israeli decision—backed explicitly by the United States. But far more important than words are actions. Israel's settlement and development programs in the occupied territories—all illegal, as Israel was informed in 1967 by its highest legal authorities and affirmed recently by the World Court—are designed to undermine the possibility of a viable Palestinian state. By providing decisive support for these policies throughout, the United States is taking the same stand. In comparison to this rejection of Palestinian rights, words are insignificant.

On Hamas, I think it should abandon those provisions of its charter, and should move from acceptance of a two-state settlement to mutual recognition, though we must bear in mind that its positions are more forthcoming than those of the United States and Israel.

During the last few months, Israel has accentuated its attacks on Gaza and is talking of an imminent ground invasion. There is also a strong possibility that it is involved in the killing of the Hezbollah leader Imad Mughniyeh and it is pushing for stronger sanctions (including military) on Iran. Do you believe that Israel's appetite for war could eventually lead to its self-destruction?

Pappé: Yes, I think that the aggressiveness is increasing and Israel antagonizes not only the Palestinian world, but also the Arab and Islamic ones. The military balance of power, at present, is in Israel's favor, but this can change at any given moment, especially if the United States were to withdraw its support.

Chomsky: I wrote decades ago that those who call themselves "supporters of Israel" are in reality supporters of its moral degeneration and probable ultimate destruction. I have also believed for many years that Israel's very clear choice of expansion over security, ever since it turned down Sadat's offer of a full peace treaty in 1971, may well lead to that consequence.

Does it also mean that the only language Israel understands from its enemy is force?

Pappé: It does in many ways. Although successful military operations, such as the ones conducted by Hezbollah, beget even fiercer and more callous military responses from Israel, so we are better off believing that nonviolent pressure such as BDS (boycott, divestment, and sanctions) is more effective, while building on the ground, on both sides, a peace movement of reconciliation.

Chomsky: What Israel understands most clearly is orders from Washington—"the boss-man called 'partner,'" as Israeli analyst Amir Oren wrote.[9] When the United States insists that Israel abandon programs and policies, as has happened repeatedly, Israel regularly obeys. It has no real choice.

What would it take for the United States to withdraw its unconditional support to Israel?

Pappé: Externally, a collapse of its Middle East policy, mainly through the downfall of one of its allies. Alternatively, but less likely, the emergence of a counter, European policy. Internally, a major economic crisis and the success of the present coalition of forces working within the civil society to impact such a change.

Two additional points should be made: first, that historically the American position was not always embarrassingly pro-Israel. Until Kennedy's term in office, which is also the time of the emergence of an effective AIPAC (American Israel Public Affairs Committee, the pro-Israel lobbying group), the two previous administrations, that of Truman and particularly that of Eisenhower, were seriously considering decisions that were in Palestine's favor, although of course they eventually retracted under pressure. Truman considered retreat from the partition plan in March 1948 and Eisenhower seriously contemplated a peace plan that included the return of the refugees. So we should not take a teleological stance on this. Second, the triangle of the U.S.-Israeli relationship has three equal legs—AIPAC, the military-industrial complex, and the Christian Zionists—and if one of them collapses, the whole structure crumbles.

Chomsky: To answer that, we have to consider the sources of the support. The corporate sector in the United States, which dominates policy formation, appears to be quite satisfied with the current situation. One indication is the increasing flow of investment to Israel by Intel, Hewlett-Packard, Microsoft, and other leading elements of the high-tech economy. Military and intelligence relations remain very strong. Since 1967, U.S. intellectuals have had a virtual love affair with Israel, for reasons that relate more to the United States than to Israel, in my opinion. That strongly affects portrayal of events and history in media and journals. Palestinians are weak, dispersed, friendless, and offer nothing to concentrations of power in the United States. A large majority of Americans supports the international consensus on a two-state settlement, and even calls for equalizing aid to Israel and the Palestinians. In this as in many other respects, both political parties are well to the right of the population. Ninety-five percent of the U.S. population thinks that the government should pay attention to the views of the population, a position rejected across the elite spectrum (sometimes quite explicitly, at other times tacitly). Hence one step toward a more evenhanded stance would be "democracy promotion" within the United States. Apart from that eventuality, what it would take is events that lead to a recalculation of interests among elite sectors.

Could the current economic crisis be this "major crisis"?

Pappé: The current crisis is working in a different direction than implied in your question. It stresses the marginality of the Palestine issue in the overall global view of the new administration. The Gaza operation created the illusion that Palestine is on Obama's top priority list, but when George Mitchell (the American special envoy to the Middle East for the Obama administration) comes back empty-handed, as it seems most likely, the economic crisis would marginalize the Palestine issue.

However, there is one scenario in which the crisis is so deep and taxpayer expenses incurred in maintaining Israel so high and both are interconnected in the public mind so as to limit American commitment to the Jewish state. But this could be rather a long-term process.

Chomsky: The economic crisis is very severe, and its outcome cannot be predicted with confidence. But there is no indication that it is influencing policies toward Israel-Palestine, and no particular reason to expect that.

During the last U.S. presidential election something telling happened. It seemed that the winning candidate would be the one showing that he and only he was Israel's best friend. Both Obama and McCain went to AIPAC's annual dinner and gave amazing speeches in support of Israel. Does this show that the pro-Israel lobby in the States now has more power than ever?

Pappé: I think it does. It was very clear that at least at the campaign level no one dare take AIPAC head on and there is a known ritual and discourse one has to adhere to. But the important issue is what happens after elections. It is important to remember that Obama's first thank-you speech was to AIPAC. I think there is a misunderstanding not only about the power of AIPAC, but also about its aims. What it demands from a new administration is not necessarily to toe the line of a current Israeli government, say the Netanyahu one. The demand is not to deviate from the Israeli Zionist consensus; namely not to adopt policies that run contrary to those of either the Likud, the Labor Party, or Kadima. In many ways the direction Obama's policy took since his election testify to this "commitment": the White House would rather see Tzipi Livni in power than Netanyahu, but such a hope is outside the lines of policy allowed by AIPAC. So, in order to have proof for any decline in the lobby's power, we need to witness a new readiness by the American administration to challenge and confront fundamental issues, which lie at the heart of the Israeli Zionist consensus.

The second point about this issue that is noteworthy is that one cannot single out AIPAC as the constitutive element defining American foreign policy. There are other factors such as the military-industrial complex, Christian Zionism, neoconservatism, and more. AIPAC's role is to fuse these many influences together and channel them effectively on Israel's behalf.

Chomsky: It is not the lobby that induces major U.S. high-tech corporations to increase their investments in Israel, or that leads the U.S. military and intelligence to strengthen their relations with Israel and to pre-position weapons in Israel for U.S. intervention in the region. The lobby indeed has influence, but typically when it pursues goals that are of little concern to U.S. elite opinion and concentrations of power, like crushing Palestinians. When U.S. power rejects its goals, the lobby disappears. In fact, an important example occurred just at the time when Obama and McCain were disgracing themselves by their odes to Israel. AIPAC was strongly supporting a congressional resolution (H.R. 362) calling for a virtual blockade of Iran, an act of war. They had mustered considerable congressional support, but the resolution vanished when the administration made it clear, quietly, that it opposed the resolution—antiwar lobbyists also had some effect.

A minor illustration of the same understandable phenomenon was Obama's speech to AIPAC, when he declared that Jerusalem must be the eternal and indivisible capital of Israel, to the great enthusiasm of the lobby. When his advisers recognized that such outlandish positions harm U.S. state interests, his campaign explained that his words didn't mean what they said.[10]

Barack Obama has announced his new team of secretaries and advisers on economic and foreign policy issues. How much do we know about these people and do their nominations fulfill Obama's promise of change?

Pappé: I think that between them, the vice president, the secretary of state, and the chief of the White House staff are a Zionist dream team. Will they be deprogrammed to such an extent that they will become proponents of the opposite view? Hard to see how this could happen, leaving aside unforeseen developments of such a magnitude that we all would be unable to maintain our conventional way of thinking and acting.

Chomsky: I have reviewed the choices, and will not repeat them.[11] His choices were old-time Washington insiders, mostly representing the financial institutions that provided the major financial support for his candidacy, including those who had primary responsibility for creating the financial crisis. On foreign policy, the advisers are mostly toward the hawkish end. On Israel-Palestine, they are drawn almost exclusively from long-term opponents of the international consensus on political settlement. More important, Obama's few pronouncements reject the consensus.[12]

CounterPunch had an interesting debate on the one-state versus two-state solution in March 2008. It started with a Michael Neumann article stating that "the one-state solution was an illusion" and was followed by articles by Assaf Kfoury entitled "'One-State or Two-State?' A Sterile Debate on False Alternatives" and Jonathan Cook entitled "One State or Two? Neither. The Issue Is Zionism." What's your opinion on this and do you think that in view of the "facts on the ground" (settlements, bypass roads) created by Israel a two-state solution is still possible?

Pappé: The facts on the ground have rendered a two-state solution impossible a long time ago. The facts indicated that there was never and will never be Israeli consent to a Palestinian state apart from a stateless state within two bantustans in the West Bank and Gaza, totally under Israeli control.

There is already one state and the struggle is to change its nature and regime. Whether the new regime and constitutional basis would be binational or democratic, or maybe even both, is less significant at this point. Any political outfit that would replace the present racist state of affairs is welcome. Any such outfit should also enable the refugees to return and even the most recent immigrants to remain.

But let me add two points: One is that the country as a whole is on the verge of a civil war that could engulf the Palestinians inside Israel. This would be a terrible development, but might hasten the final burial of the two-state solution and its distorted logic and justice. Two, the principle to which all should adhere is not imposing an ideal model at this point as a litmus test for loyalty to the cause or commitment to peace. Rather one should seek out an inclusive approach that would bring to the fore the significant common agenda that exists between various camps that are now part of the struggle for Palestine. It is better to hammer out these divergences of opinion now than to leave it for a future battle.

Chomsky: Today there are two options for Palestinians. One is U.S.-Israeli abandonment of their rejectionist stance, and a settlement roughly along the lines of what was being approached at Taba. The other option is continuation of current policies, which lead, inexorably, to incorporation into Israel of what it wants: at least, Greater Jerusalem, the areas within the separation wall (now an annexation wall), the Jordan Valley, and the salients through

Ma'aleh Adumim and Ariel and beyond that effectively trisect what remains, which will be broken up into unviable cantons by huge infrastructure projects, hundreds of checkpoints, and other devices to ensure that Palestinians live like dogs.

There are those who believe that Palestinians should simply let Israel take over the West Bank completely and then carry out a civil-rights/anti-apartheid-style struggle. That is an illusion, however. There is no reason why the U.S.-Israel would accept the premises of this proposal. They will simply proceed along the lines now being implemented, and will not accept any responsibility for Palestinians who are scattered outside the regions they intend to incorporate into Israel.

Could you both expand on this and tell us what, in your opinion, would be an acceptable and manageable step-by-step "road map"?

Pappé: It's probably too early to talk about steps, but I will use the term *step* to depict what is in practice a rough map forward.

The first step is to try and stop the escalation of Israeli next steps. The Hamas style of resistance only determines the pace of this Israeli policy, not its direction or its ferocity. The massive killings will expand, the occupation deepen, and the next stages of Palestine's ethnic cleansing continue. Therefore, there is no point in moving forward with any peace effort without an immediate end to the Israeli military presence in the West Bank and the end of the Gaza blockade. This could only be achieved by strong external pressure on Israel in the form of sanctions and other drastic measures.

In the second step, the civil society has to find ways to prepare for that moment by conducting a fruitful dialogue about the future political structure that will accommodate all the outstanding questions the "peace process" hitherto ignored: the right of the refugees to return, the construction of a political system of equality for all, and mutual respect for collective religious and cultural identities. If successful, it can be fed back into the political system and inspire a more valuable peace process in a long and contracted process.

Chomsky: The crucial step would be for the United States to join the overwhelming international consensus: to call for an agreement in those terms, and to put an end to all support to Israel that is used to undermine those possibilities. Israel will have no choice but to accede to such demands. There are those who claim that for Israel to forcibly remove settlers would lead to civil war. That is true but irrelevant. If Israel is compelled to abandon its rejectionism, it can simply announce that the IDF will leave the occupied territories on such-and-such a date. The great mass of settlers will pack up and return to Israel, and those who refuse can remain within a Palestinian state. The few thousand Israelis subsidized illegally to settle in Gaza could have been removed the same way, with no violence or conflict. But the staged "national trauma" was useful for propaganda purposes, to gain support for increased settlement in the West Bank. No "national trauma" would have to be staged if the United States and Israel agree to the kind of settlement that was rather close at Taba (Egypt), and that is supported by virtually the entire world.

During my recent trip to Israel/Palestine it became obvious (talking to people, reading newspapers, watching the news) that something scared Israel a lot: a boycott. Are you in favor of this type of action and do you think that it could bear fruit?

Pappé: Yes I am and I do think it has a chance of triggering processes of change on the ground. For me supporting a boycott was not easy and as a decision only matured after a long process of deliberation. But it seems now to be the best way forward and there are already signs that there are already considerable achievements on the ground, indicating this is an effective way to impact pubic opinion in the future.

There are three good reasons for us to think about a boycott campaign positively: 1) There are no dynamics of change from within Israel. The few that are there cannot effect change unless empowered and enhanced from the outside by a powerful voice that legitimizes these internal forces' readiness to challenge the most basic truisms of their society. 2) This is the only nonviolent strategy open for the Palestinians at this stage that does not question or delegitimize the struggles of the past, but rather complements them. It gives some hope for a modus operandi that is not desperate and self-destructive. 3) It has a track record in the past of some success in the struggle against apartheid in South Africa.

Chomsky: Boycotts sometimes make sense. For example, such actions against South Africa were effective, even though the Reagan administration evaded congressional sanctions while declaring Mandela's ANC to be one of the "more notorious terrorist groups" in the world (in 1988). The actions were effective because the groundwork had been laid in many years of education and activism. By the time they were implemented, they received substantial support in the United States within the political system, the media, and even the corporate sector, and there was no support for apartheid. Nothing remotely like that has been achieved in this case. As a result, calls for boycott almost invariably backfire, reinforcing the harshest and most brutal policies toward Palestinians.

Selective boycotts, carefully formulated, might have some effect. For example, boycotts of military producers who provide arms to Israel, or of the Caterpillar Corporation, which provides the equipment for destroying Palestine. All of their actions are strictly illegal, and boycotts could be made understandable to the general public, so that they could be effective. If enough support could be mobilized for a South African–style boycott and divestment effort, it would be unnecessary, because that very same support could impel Washington to abandon the rejectionist policies that bar a peaceful settlement.

Selective boycotts could also be effective against states with a far worse record of violence and terror than Israel, such as the United States. And, of course, without its decisive support and participation, Israel could not carry out illegal expansion and other crimes. There are no calls for boycotting the United States, not for reasons of principle, but because it is simply too powerful—facts that raise some obvious questions about the moral legitimacy of actions targeting its clients.

Coming back from Israel/Palestine a few weeks ago, the director of ICAHD [the Israeli Committee Against House Demolitions] UK told me that, in spite of Annapolis, "not one thing on the ground has improved…witnessing Israel judaisation of the country left me feeling cold and angry." Seeing this, could Palestinian resistance (which has mainly been nonviolent so far) revert to armed struggle and start a third intifada?

Pappé: It is difficult to understand the "could"—theoretically they can and they may, the question is whether it is going to produce different results from the previous two uprisings. The feeling is that it is not likely.

Chomsky: My opinion all along has been that the Palestinian leadership is offering Israel and its U.S. backers a great gift by resorting to violence and posturing about revolution—quite apart from the fact that, tactical considerations aside, resort to violence carries a very heavy burden of justification. Today, for example, nothing is more welcome to Israeli and U.S. hawks than Qassam rockets, which enable them to shriek joyously about how the ratio of deaths should be increased to infinity (all victims being defined as "terrorists"). I have also agreed all along with personal friends who had contacts with the Palestinian leadership (in particular, Edward Said and Eqbal Ahmad) that a nonviolent struggle would have had considerable prospects for success. And I think it still does, in fact, the only prospects for success.

Where is the Palestinian voice and what is its vision for the future?

Pappé: A heavy responsibility lies on the shoulders of the Palestinian leadership and activists in two respects. First, there is the need to unite and form a consensual point of gravity that can serve as a compass and conscience for the struggle as a whole. Second, there is a need for a more elaborate and expanded post-conflict vision on the Palestinian side, especially with regard to Israeli society as individuals and as a collective group. This is a process of decolonization in many ways that in so many places went sour for lack of planning and proper preparation for the day after.

Chomsky: It is remarkable that Palestinian society has managed to remain steadfast—even to survive—in the face of crushing blows and unremitting cruelty, and hostility and abandonment from all sides. One consequence is that it is hard to identify "the Palestinian voice and its vision." At least hard for me to do so. And apart from lack of competence, it is also not my right. The choices will have to come from within Palestinian society. From outside, all we can try honestly to do is to remove the constraints, alleviate the suffering, and help free the victims to find their own way in peace and with the opportunities they so richly deserve.

What should NGOs and charities working for justice in Palestine be focusing on?

Pappé: They know best and I hesitate to advise them. I think they gave us guidance with their call for a boycott and if they continue with initiatives like this, it can be very helpful. But most importantly it would be great if they could continue to work for reconciliation and unity in the Palestinian camp.

Chomsky: The daily and urgent task is to focus on the terrible ongoing violations of the most elementary human rights and the illegal U.S.-backed settlement and development projects that are designed to undermine a diplomatic settlement. A more general task is to try to lay the basis for a successful struggle for a settlement that takes into account the just demands of contesting parties—the kind of hard, dedicated, persistent educational and organizational work that has provided the underpinnings for other advances toward peace and justice. I have already indicated what I think that entails—not least, effective democracy promotion in the reigning superpower.

On May 31, 2010, in the early hours, Israeli commandos boarded six "Freedom Flotilla" ships carrying humanitarian help, in international waters, to stop them entering Gaza. Fighting ensued and at least nine people were killed. What do you make of this event?

Pappé: More than anything else this is a criminal act of piracy. It is twice illegal: it was meant to protect an illegal blockade of the Gaza Strip and it was violation of the international laws of navigation by storming a Turkish ship in international waters.

What is, however, most significant about this event is the gap between the Israeli Jewish perception of the event and the vast majority of people in the world. When one reads the Israeli responses, of politicians and citizens alike, one is reminded of the various interviews given by South African leaders in the 1970s. The gist of those interviews was we know that the world condemns us but we do not care, apartheid is the best system for all of us.

While the civil society in the West, and one should say for the first time quite prominent politicians as well, viewed the attack on the flotilla as unprecedented violation of international law and standards, the reaction in Israel was diametrically opposed. And while in the West, the illegality of the blockade was stressed as being at the heart of the problem, the reactions of Israel were to strengthen the support for the blockade and similar policies of strangulation.

This difference is manifested in the adjectives used by the Israeli media and political elite. This was not a peaceful flotilla, this was a unit of fanatic, pro-al-Qaeda terrorists wishing to destroy the State of Israel. What followed was that if Palestinians in Israel for instance chose to support this flotilla, as did Sheikh Raid Salah or the MK [Member of Knesset] Hanin Zu'ubi, then they are collaborating with the terrorists. The event trigged an already murky and dangerous wave of legislations and acts of persecution meant to delegitimize the Palestinian citizens in Israel and exclude them from citizenship in Israel. It is also not surprising that this was followed by legislations against Israeli Jews supporting the flotilla and the BDS movement.

So while the world's attention is focused on the act itself, it should in fact revisit its basic attitude to Israel as an obstacle for peace. Below is an attempt to understand that basic position through the process of decision making in Israel on the Gaza peace flotilla.

At the top of Israel's political and military systems stand two men, Ehud Barak and Binyamin Netanyahu, who are behind the brutal attack on the Gaza flotilla that shocked the world but seemed to be hailed as a pure act of self-defense by the Israeli public.

Although they come from the left (Defense Minister Barak from the Labor Party) and the right (Prime Minister Netanyahu from the Likkud) of Israeli politics, their thinking on Gaza in general and on the flotilla in particular is informed by the same history and identical world view.

At one time, Ehud Barak was Binyamin Netanyahu's command-
ing officer in the Israeli equivalent of the British SAS (or American
Navy Seals). More precisely, they served in a unit similar to the one
sent to assault the Turkish ship. Their perception of the reality in
the Gaza Strip is shared by other leading members of the Israeli
political and military elite, and is widely supported by the Jewish
electorate at home.

And it is a simple take on reality. Hamas, although the only government in the Arab world that was elected democratically by the
people, has to be eliminated as a political as well as a military force.
This is not only because it continues the struggle against the forty-
year Israeli occupation of the West Bank and the Gaza Strip by
launching primitive missiles into Israel—more often than not in
retaliation to an Israeli killing of its activists in the West Bank. But
it is mainly due to its political opposition to the kind of "peace" Israel wants to impose on the Palestinians.

The forced peace is not negotiable as far as the Israeli political
elite is concerned, and it offers the Palestinians a limited control and
sovereignty in the Gaza Strip and in parts of the West Bank. The
Palestinians are asked to give up their struggle for self-determination
and liberation in return for the establishment of three small bantustans under tight Israeli control and supervision.

The official thinking in Israel, therefore, is that Hamas is a formidable obstacle to the imposition of such a peace. And thus the
declared strategy is straightforward: starving and strangulating
the million and a half Palestinians living in the densest space in
the world.

The blockade that was imposed in 2006 is supposed to lead the
Gazans to replace the current Palestinian government with one that
would accept Israel's dictate—or at least would be part of the more
dormant Palestinian Authority in the West Bank. In the meantime

Hamas captured an Israeli soldier, Gilad Shalit, and so the blockade became tighter. It included a ban of the most elementary commodities without which human beings find it difficult to survive. From want of food to medicine to want of cement and petrol, the people of Gaza live in conditions that international bodies and agencies have described as catastrophic and criminal.

As in the case of the flotilla, there are alternative ways for releasing the captive soldier, such as swapping with Shalit the thousands of political prisoners Israel is holding. Many of them are children, and quite a few are being held without a trial.

The Israelis have dragged their feet in negotiations over such a swap, which are not likely to bear fruit in the foreseeable future.

But Barak and Netanyhau, and those around them, know too well that the blockade of Gaza is not going to produce any change in the position of Hamas and one should give credit to the British prime minister, David Cameron, who remarked in Prime Minister's Questions in parliament that the Israeli policy, in fact, strengthens, rather than weakens, Hamas's hold on Gaza. But this strategy, despite its declared aim, is not meant to succeed, or at least no one is worried in Jerusalem if it continues to be fruitless and futile.

One would have thought that Israel's drastic decline in international reputation would prompt new thinking by its leaders. But the responses to the attack on the flotilla have clearly indicated that there is no hope for any significant shift in the official position. A firm commitment to continue the blockade, and a heroes' welcome to the soldiers who pirated the ship in the Mediterranean show that the same politics will continue for a long time.

And this is not surprising. The Barak-Liberman-Netanyahu government does not know any other way of responding to the reality in Palestine and Israel. The use of brutal force to impose your will and a hectic domestic and foreign propaganda machine that describes it as self-defense, while demonizing as terrorists the half-starved people in Gaza and those who come to their aid, is the only possible course for these politicians. The terrible consequences in human death and suffering of this determination do not concern them, nor does international condemnation.

The real—unlike the declared—strategy is to continue this state of affairs. As long as the international community is complacent, the Arab world impotent, and Gaza contained, Israel can still have a thriving economy and an electorate that regards the dominance of the army in its life, the continued conflict, and the oppression of the Palestinians as the exclusive past, present, and future reality of life in Israel. The U.S. vice president Joe Biden was humiliated by the Israelis recently when they announced the building of 1,600 new homes in the disputed Ramat Shlomo district of Jerusalem, on the day he arrived to try to freeze the settlement policy. But his unconditional support now for the latest Israeli action makes the leaders and their electorate feel vindicated.

It would be wrong, however, to assume that American support and a feeble European response to Israeli criminal policies such as those pursued in Gaza are the main reasons for the protracted blockade and strangulation of Gaza. What is probably most difficult to explain to readers around the world is how deeply these perceptions and attitudes are grounded in the Israeli psyche and mentality. And it is indeed difficult to comprehend how diametrically opposed are the common reactions in the UK, for instance, to such events to the emotions they trigger inside the Israeli Jewish society.

The international response is based on the assumption that more forthcoming Palestinian concessions and a continued dialogue with the Israeli political elite will produce a new reality on the ground. The official discourse in the West is that a very reasonable and attainable solution is just around the corner if all sides would make one final effort: the two-state solution.

Nothing is further from the truth than this optimistic scenario. The only version of this solution that is acceptable to Israel is the one that both the tamed Palestine Authority in Ramallah and the more assertive Hamas in Gaza could never ever accept. It is an offer to imprison the Palestinians in stateless enclaves in return for ending their struggle.

Thus even before one discusses either an alternative solution—a single democratic state for all, which I support—or explores a more plausible, two-state settlement, one has to transform fundamentally the Israeli official and public mindset. This mentality is the principal barrier for a peaceful reconciliation in the torn land of Israel and Palestine.

Chomsky: Hijacking boats in international waters and killing passengers is, of course, a serious crime. The editors of the London *Guardian* are quite right to say that "if an armed group of Somali pirates had yesterday boarded six vessels on the high seas, killing at least 10 passengers and injuring many more, a NATO taskforce would today be heading for the Somali coast."[13] It is worth bearing in mind that the crime is nothing new.

For decades, Israel has been hijacking boats in international waters between Cyprus and Lebanon, killing or kidnapping passengers, sometimes bringing them to prisons in Israel including secret prison-torture chambers, sometimes holding them as hostages for many years.

Israel assumes that it can carry out such crimes with impunity because the United States tolerates them and Europe generally follows the U.S. lead. Much the same is true of Israel's pretext for its latest crime: that the Freedom Flotilla was bringing materials that could be used for bunkers for rockets. Putting aside the absurdity, if Israel were interested in stopping Hamas rockets it knows exactly how to proceed: accept Hamas offers for a cease-fire. In June 2008, Israel and Hamas reached a cease-fire agreement. The Israeli government formally acknowledges that until Israel broke the agreeement on November 4, invading Gaza and killing half a dozen Hamas activists, Hamas did not fire a single rocket. Hamas offered to renew the cease-fire. The Israeli cabinet considered the offer and rejected it, preferring to launch its murderous and destructive Operation Cast Lead on December 27. Evidently, there is no justification for the use of force "in self-defense" unless peaceful means have been exhausted. In this case they were not even tried, although—or perhaps because—there was every reason to suppose that they would succeed. Operation Cast Lead is therefore sheer criminal aggression, with no credible pretext, and the same is true of Israel's current resort to force.

The siege of Gaza itself does not have the slightest credible pretext. It was imposed by the United States and Israel in January 2006 to punish Palestinians because they voted "the wrong way" in a free election, and it was sharply intensified in July 2007 when Hamas blocked a U.S.-Israeli attempt to overthrow the elected government in a military coup, installing Fatah strongman Muhammad Dahlan. The siege is savage and cruel, designed to keep the caged animals barely alive so as to fend off international protest, but hardly more than that. It is the latest stage of long-standing Israeli plans, backed by the United States, to separate Gaza from the West Bank.

These are only the bare outlines of very ugly policies, in which Egypt is complicit as well.

SEVEN

THE KILLING FIELDS OF GAZA 2004–2009

Preface

The Gaza Strip is a little bit more than 2 percent of Palestine. This small detail is never mentioned whenever the Strip is in the news nor has it been mentioned during the Israeli onslaught on Gaza in January 2009. Indeed it is such a small part of the country that it never existed as a separate region in the past. Gaza's history before the Zionization of Palestine was not unique and it was always connected administratively and politically to the rest of Palestine. It was until 1948 an integral and natural part of the country. As one of Palestine's principal land and sea gates to the rest of the world it tended to develop a more flexible and cosmopolitan way of life, not dissimilar to other gateways societies in the eastern Mediterranean in the modern era. This location near the sea and on the Via Maris to Egypt and Lebanon brought with it prosperity and stability until this life was disrupted and nearly destroyed by the Israeli ethnic cleansing of Palestine in 1948.

Between 1948 and 1967, Gaza became a huge refugee camp restricted severely by the respective Israeli and Egyptian policies:

both states disallowed any movement out of the Strip. Living conditions were already harsh then as the victims of the 1948 Israeli
politics of dispossession doubled the number of the inhabitants
who had lived there for centuries. On the eve of the Israeli occupation in 1967, the catastrophic nature of this enforced demographic
transformation was evident all over the Strip. This once pastoral
coastal part of southern Palestine became within two decades one
of the world's densest areas of habitation, without any adequate
economic infrastructure to support it.

The first twenty years of Israeli occupation allowed at least
some movement outside an area that was closed off as a war zone
in the years 1948 to 1967. Tens of thousands of Palestinians were
permitted to join the Israeli labor market as unskilled and under-
paid workers. The price Israel demanded for this slave market was
a total surrender of any national struggle or agenda. When this was
not complied with, the "gift" of laborers' movement was denied
and abolished. All these years, leading to the Oslo Accord in 1993,
were marked by an Israeli attempt to construct the Strip as an enclave, which the Israeli peace camp hoped would be either autonomous or part of Egypt and the nationalist camp wished to
include in the Greater Eretz Israel they dreamed of establishing instead of Palestine.

The Oslo agreement enabled the Israelis to reaffirm the Strip's
status as a separate geopolitical entity—not just outside of Palestine as a whole, but also cut off from the West Bank. Ostensibly,
both the Gaza Strip and the West Bank were under the Palestinian
Authority but any human movement between them depended on
Israel's good will, a rare Israeli trait that almost disappeared when
Binyamin Netanyahu came to power in 1996. Moreover, Israel held,
as it still does today, the water and electricity infrastructure. Since
1993 it used, or rather abused, this possession in order to ensure, on

the one hand, the well-being of the Jewish settler community and, on the other, to blackmail the Palestinian population into submission and surrender. The people of the Gaza Strip thus vacillated in the last sixty years between being internees, hostages, or prisoners in an impossible human space.

It is within this historical context that we should view the massacre that took place in January 2009 and the violence raging in Gaza in the preceding five years. The violence was not only meted out by Israeli forces, there was a fair share of inter-Palestinian fighting for a short while, although one should say that given the nature of the Israeli occupation and policy this internal violence was far less than would be expected under such circumstances. But this internal phase is a minor aspect of a far more important issue: Israeli violence against the Gaza Strip.

When we look back from our current vantage point, we see more clearly than ever before the fallacy of the Israeli discourse and justification for its actions in Gaza. Its politicians and diplomats defined the policies against Gaza as a "war against terror," directed against a local branch of al-Qaeda and one that was meant to fend off a seditious Iranian penetration into this part of the world. Its academics preferred to depict Gaza as another arena in the dreaded Clash of Civilizations. However, the origins of the particular violent history of the Gaza Strip lie elsewhere. The recent history of the Strip—sixty years of dispossession, occupation, and imprisonment—inevitably produced internal violence such as we witnessed in the last few years as it produced other unbearable features of life lived under such impossible conditions.

In fact, if we take even a closer look at the five years preceding the Cast Lead operation we can provide a sure analysis of the motivation for the violence directed against the Palestinians in 2009. There are two historical contexts for what happened in Gaza in

January that year. One takes us back to the foundation of the State of Israel through the occupation of the Strip by Israel in 1967 and up to the failed Oslo Accord of 1993. The second is the one presented here, an escalation of an Israeli policy that culminated with the events of 2009. The ideology of ethnic cleansing adopted in 1948 as the main tool for implementing the dream of a safe and democratic Jewish state led to the occupation of the Gaza Strip in 1967, which lasted until 2005, when Israel allegedly withdrew. The Gaza Strip was already encircled with an electric fence in 1994 as part of the preparation for peace with the Palestinians and became a ghetto in 2000 when the peace process was declared dead. The decision of the people of Gaza to resist this closure, by violent and nonviolent means, confronted the Israeli military and political elite with a new dilemma. They assumed that locking Gazans in a huge prison would settle the problem for a long while, but this turned out to be wrong. So they were looking for a new strategy.

The bitter fruits of this strategy were revealed in January 2009 and the international community reacted furiously but ineffectively. The main by-product of this international fury was the Goldstone report. It summarizes well, although in a very cautious and limited way, the scope of the carnage left by Israel after hostilities subsided. The international community, however, did not inquire why such a ruthless policy was pursued and what were its immediate origins.

MOVING TO A NEW STRATEGY, 2000–2005

Ever since 2000, the Israeli military escalated its actions against the Palestinians and the anti-Israeli forces in Lebanon. It began with military operations in the West Bank in reaction to the second intifada—which also included the construction of the apartheid or segregation wall and culminated in the attack on

Lebanon in 2006 and the assault on Gaza in 2009. This was accompanied by an equally ruthless policy of dispossession and incremental transfer of Palestinians from the Greater Jerusalem area in the same years.

One pretext for action all over the country was the increasing political power by Islamic groups such as Hamas in the occupied territories, Hezbollah in Lebanon, and the Islamic movement inside Israel. The reasons for these draconian policies go back to the formative years of Zionism and the conception of an ideology that moved successive Israeli governments to seek unchallenged domination in Palestine and beyond, all over the eastern Mediterranean.

The number of regional states and local Palestinian movements willing to confront this domination seemed to have gradually decreased before 2006 and Israeli policy makers sensed that their overall strategy was winning the day. They were particularly satisfied with the situation in the occupied West Bank and Gaza Strip after the second intifada subsided around the year 2005. The matrix of walls, fences, checkpoints, colonial settlements, Israeli-only bypass roads, and military bases Israel has spread all over the West Bank turned it in their eyes into a "pacified" territory. However, the situation in Gaza was different. There the Israelis were facing determined resistance, as the Hamas movement, like Hezbollah in Lebanon before it, refused to succumb to Israel's will. For the then Israeli prime minister, Ariel Sharon, and the main political class of those days, which remains even more at the center of Israeli politics today— Ehud Barak, Shimon Peres, Tzipi Livni, and Binyamin Netanyahu— controlling the Gaza Strip from the outside while carving the West Bank into manageable bantustans seemed the best solution for the "Palestine problem." The new strategy was conceived on the training grounds of the Israeli Army in the dummy city built by the army in the Negev.

2004: THE DUMMY CITY

In 2004, the Israeli Army began building a dummy Arab city in the Negev desert. It was the size of a real city, with streets (all of them given names), mosques, public buildings, and cars. Built at a cost of $45 million, this phantom city became a dummy Gaza in the winter of 2006, after Hezbollah fought Israel to a draw in the north, so that the IDF could prepare to fight an "improved war" against Hamas in the south after the fiasco in the north.[1]

When the Israeli chief of general staff Dan Halutz visited the site after the Lebanon war, he told the press that soldiers "were preparing for the scenario that will unfold in the dense neighbourhood of Gaza City."[2] A week into the bombardment of Gaza, Ehud Barak attended a rehearsal for the ground war. Foreign television crews filmed him as he watched ground troops conquer the dummy city, storming the empty houses and no doubt killing the "terrorists" hiding in them.[3]

More often than not such maneuvers ended in the destruction of the enemy base. The Israeli NGO Breaking the Silence (Shoverim Shetika) published in 2009 a report about its members'—mostly reserve soldiers—experiences in Operation Cast Lead. The gist of the evidence was that the soldiers had orders to attack Gaza as if they were assaulting a massive and fortified enemy line: this transpired from the firepower and troops formation employed, the absence of any orders or procedures about acting within a civilian space, and the synchronized effort from the land, sea, and air conventional armies employed against huge armadas of tanks, armored cars, and hundred of thousands of ground troops. Among the worst were the senseless demolition of houses, the spraying of civilians with phosphorus shells, the killing of innocent civilians by light weaponry, and orders by the commanders to act without moral inhibitions.

"You feel like an infantile child with a magnifying glass that torments ants, you burn them," testified one soldier.[4] In short as they were trained in practice to deal with the dummy city, they enacted the total destruction of the real city.

2005: "FIRST RAINS"

The militarization of Israeli policy toward the Gaza Strip began in 2005. Gaza became in that year a military target in the official Israeli view, as if it were a huge enemy base and not a civilian and human space. Gaza is a city as any other city in the world, and yet for the Israelis it became a dummy city on which soldiers experimented with the most recent and updated weapons.

This policy was enabled by the Israeli government's decision to evict the Jewish settlers who colonized the Gaza Strip since 1967. The settlers were moved allegedly as part of what the government described as a unilateral policy of disengagement: the argument was that since there was no progress in the peace talks with the Palestinians, it was up to Israel to determine what its final borders with the Palestinian areas would look like.

But things did not turn out the way they were expected to. The eviction was followed by a Hamas takeover, first in democratic elections, then in a preemptive coup staged to avert an American and Israeli-backed seizure by Fatah. The immediate Israeli response was to impose an economic blockade on the Strip to which Hamas retaliated by firing missiles at the nearest town to the Strip, Sderot. This gave Israel a pretext to use its air force, artillery, and gunships. Israel claimed to be shooting at the launching areas of the missiles, but in practice this meant anywhere and everywhere in Gaza.

Creating the prison and throwing the key into the sea, as UN Special Rapporteur John Dugard has put it,[5] was an option the

Palestinians in Gaza reacted against with force already in September 2005. They were determined to show at the very least that they were still part of the West Bank and Palestine. In that month, they launched the first significant, in number not quality, barrage of missiles into the western Negev—as often, these resulted in damage to some property but very rarely in human casualties. The events of that month deserve a detailed mention, because the early Hamas response before September was a trickle of sporadic missiles. The launch in September 2005 was in response to an Israeli campaign of mass arrests of Hamas and Islamic Jihad activists in the Tul Karem area; one could not escape the impression at the time that the army was looking to trigger a Hamas reaction that would allow Israel to escalate its attacks. And indeed Israeli retaliation came in the form of a harsh policy of massive killing, the first of its kind, code-named First Rains. It is worth dwelling for a moment on the nature of that operation. The discourse that accompanied it was that of punishment and it resembled punitive measures inflicted in the more distant past by colonialist powers, and more recently by dictatorships, against rebellious imprisoned or banished communities. A frightening show of the oppressors might end with a large number of dead and wounded among the victims. In First Rains, supersonic planes were flown over Gaza to terrorize the entire population, succeeded by the heavy bombardment of vast areas from the sea, sky, and land. The logic, the Israeli Army explained, was to create pressure so as to weaken the Gaza community's support for the rocket launchers.[6] As was expected, by the Israelis as well, the operation only increased the support for the rocket launchers and gave impetus to their next attempts. In hindsight, and especially given the Israeli military commanders' explanation that the army had long been preparing the Cast Lead operation,[7] it is possible that the real purpose of that particular operation was experimental. And if the Israeli generals wished to know how such operations would be received at home, in the region, and in the world, it seems that instantly the answer was "very well"; namely, no one took an interest in the scores of dead and hundreds of wounded Palestinians left behind after First Rains subsided.[8]

And hence since First Rains and until June 2006, all the following operations were similarly modeled. The difference was in their escalation: more firepower, more casualties, and more collateral damage and, as to be expected, more Qassam missiles in response. Accompanying measures in 2006 were more sinister means of ensuring the full imprisonment of the people of Gaza through boycott and blockade, while the world at large kept silent.

2006: "SUMMER RAINS" AND "AUTUMN CLOUDS"

The eviction of the settlers from the Strip in 2005 and the victory of Hamas there in early 2006 seemed to transform this region into a battlefield. No longer under the authority of the PA and without the presence of vulnerable settlers, it became a purely "military" problem.

However, 2006 was not such a good year for the Israeli Army. It failed to deter and defeat Hezbollah in southern Lebanon in a war Israel initiated. This coincided with the capture of an Israeli soldier in a daring military operation by Hamas.

Israeli actions were motivated by the dual sense of humiliation on the one hand and a sense of immunity, at least from the society at home, to react vehemently to any show of Palestinian resistance in Gaza. With the help of an inciting media and jingoistic public mood the events in the summer of 2006 allowed the policy makers to use brutal military power as a short-term reaction to a problem they had no idea how to solve politically. The frustration that propelled the strongest army in the Middle East against civilians in Gaza could only end in a disastrous way, as indeed it did.

Let us analyze closely these three elements that led to further escalation in the operations against Gaza and to the barbarization of this front in an unprecedented way. These elements were frustration, the search for a pretext, and the absence of a political strategy.

Israeli experts and pundits were the first to make the point that the escalation of firepower and military action in 2006 was a direct response to the frustration of the army due to its relative defeat in the north.[9] The army needed to demonstrate its superiority and deterrence capability—still broadcast by its chiefs as the main safeguards for the Jewish state's survival in a "hostile" world. The Islamist character of both Hamas and Hezbollah and an alleged, and totally fabricated, association of both with al-Qaeda, enabled the army to imagine Israel spearheading a global war against jihadism in Gaza. While George W. Bush was in power, the killing of women and babies in Gaza could be justified by the American administration as being part of a holy war against Islam (a practice not alien to the American forces in Iraq and Afghanistan) under the banner of fighting terrorism.

The humiliation did not end with the debacle in Lebanon but continued with the capture by the Hamas of an Israeli soldier, Gilad Shalit, in the summer of 2006. "One Humiliation Too Many!" cried *Haaretz* after the abduction. The paper reported furious generals demanding brutal reaction to both Hezbollah and Hamas.[10]

The ruthless Israeli reaction was also due to the absence of a clear policy. The Israeli leadership in September 2006 seemed to be at a loss for what to do with the Gaza Strip. Reading its statements at the time, one gathers the government of that year was quite confident about its policy toward the West Bank, but not toward the Strip.

The Israeli official line is that the final delineation of Israel's eastern border has nearly been completed. This is probably why the "West Bank" or the "occupation" as issues have been removed from the domestic agenda and ceased to be a divisive factor in Israel's political life as it had been for a while after 1967. The unilateral policy of annexing about half of the West Bank continued with extra zeal in 2007 and was fully supported by the Jewish electorate. It was somewhat delayed by the promises Israel made, under the Road Map, to stop building new settlements. Israel found two ways of circumventing this impediment. First, it defined a third of the West Bank as Greater Jerusalem, which allowed it to build towns and community centers within this new annexed area. Second, it expanded old settlements to such proportions that there was no need to build new ones. This trend was given an additional push in 2006 (hundreds of caravans in "outposts" [*mitzpim* in Hebrew] were installed to delineate the boundaries of the Jewish "sphere" within the Palestinian territories). The master plans for the new towns and neighborhoods were finalized and the apartheid bypass roads and highway system were completed. In all, the settlements, army bases, roads, and wall prepared the ground for the final stages in this strategy. Within the territories informally annexed to Israel, and those that might still be incorporated in the Jewish state, there is still a considerable number of Palestinians against whom, at the end of 2006, the Israeli authorities began pursuing a policy of a creeping transfer. Very little international attention has been paid to this de-Arabization of Jerusalem—too boring a subject for the Western media to bother with and too elusive for human rights organizations to make a general point about. There was no rush as far as the Israelis were concerned: they felt in the beginning of 2007 that they had the upper hand there. The daily abusive and

dehumanizing heavy military and bureaucratic hands of the
regime were as effective as ever in furthering the process of dis-
possessing Palestine.

This strategy was first conceived by Ariel Sharon in 2001 and
became the cornerstone of all the successive governments' policies.
It won the day, and international immunity, in particular, since the
only other meaningful political alternative the Israeli political
scene offered was a crude "transferist" policy, advocated by the
popular Israeli Beitenu party and its leader, Avigdor Liberman,
and by a coalition of right-wing parties.

In 2005, Prime Minister Ehud Olmert named this strategy "ingathering." This was a self-justification for pursuing unilateral action in the West Bank, since there was no progress in the peace
process.[11] In practice it meant that the 2006 Israeli government
wished to annex the parts it coveted—more or less half of the West
Bank—and try and push out, or at least enclave within it, the native population, while allowing the other half of the West Bank to
develop in a way that would not endanger Israeli interests (either
by being ruled by a submissive Palestinian Authority or by associating directly with Jordan). This was a fallacy, but nonetheless it
won the enthusiastic vote of most of the Jews in the country when
Olmert turned it into an essential part of his election campaign.

The clear policy toward the West Bank highlighted the confu-
sion about the Gaza Strip. The Gaza Strip, in the eyes of the Israelis, was a very different geopolitical entity from that of the West
Bank. Hamas had already controlled the Gaza Strip for almost a
year, while the leader of the Fatah faction, Abu Mazin, was running
the fragmented West Bank with Israeli and American blessing. Unlike in the West Bank there was no chunk of land in Gaza that Israel
coveted and there was no hinterland, like Jordan, to which the
Palestinians of Gaza could be expelled.

Egypt, unlike Jordan, succeeded in persuading the Israelis, already in 1967, that for them the Gaza Strip was a liability and would never form part of Egypt. So a million and half Palestinians remained an "Israeli" problem and responsibility—although geographically the Strip is located on the margins of the state of Israel, psychologically it was still in 2006 very much in its midst.

The Israeli tactics, as different from strategy, were clearer. Should the people in Gaza reconcile with the imprisonment until either the PA retook the Strip or Israel found a better solution, then the area could be managed the way Palestinians are treated in the West Bank. Should they resist, as indeed they did, ghettoization and strangulation, then the policy of "punitive" actions would continue.

The inhuman living conditions in the Strip disabled the people who lived there from reconciling with the imprisonment Israel had imposed on them ever since 1967. There were relative better periods when movement to the West Bank and into Israel for work was allowed, but these better times were gone by 2006. Harsher realities were in place since 1987. Some access to the outside world was allowed as long as there were Jewish settlers in the Strip, but once they were removed the Strip was hermetically closed. Ironically, most Israelis, according to 2006 polls, looked at Gaza as an independent Palestinian state that Israel has graciously allowed to emerge.[12] The leadership, and particularly the army, saw it as a prison with the most dangerous community of inmates, which had to be managed ruthlessly one way or another.

Thus, the ghettoization of the Palestinians in Gaza did not reap any dividends. The ghettoized community continued to express its will for life by firing primitive missiles into Israel. Ghettoizing or quarantining unwanted communities, even if they were regarded as dangerous, has never worked in history as a solution. The Jews know it best from their own history.

The final strategy was not articulated and in its stead it seemed that the daily military activity began to emerge as the new strategy itself and thus the "punitive" tactics turned into genocidal strategy in 2006. What was missing for a significant escalation was a pretext. The history of the most brutal Israeli actions against the Palestinians is loaded with such pretexts. Ever since 1948, the Israeli Army and government searched for adequate pretext for any massive operations against the Palestinians. This was the case in 1947 and 1948. The actual ethnic cleansing began only after the Palestinians reacted angrily against the UN partition resolution of November 1947 and attacked isolated Jewish settlements and assaulted Jewish transport on Palestine's roads. This spontaneous reaction subsided after a short while but was enough to provide the pretext for a massive operation of ethnic cleansing (conceived as an option already in the 1930s).[13]

Similarly, the invasion of Lebanon in 1982 was presented as retaliation for the PLO struggle against Israel—a very late in the day and limited Palestinian resistance in the occupied territories after twenty years of oppression.

These pretexts were never convincing to the international community yet they never led to any actions against Israel. This is the lesson the Israelis learned in 1982. The international community did not then accept the Israeli justification for the third invasion of its northern neighbor (the previous two invasions were in 1948 and 1978). An international commission of six jurists headed by Sean MacBride described that attack, as would Judge Goldstone a quarter of century later when reporting on Gaza, as a series of war crimes. However the MacBride committee was much more explicit: it accused Israel of genocide of the Palestinian communities in Lebanon (although two members of the commission asked to differ on this conclusion but not on the facts). It accused Israel of using forbidden weapons against civilians and the indiscriminate and reckless bombing of civilian targets: schools and hospitals as well as cities, villages, and refugee camps, and it culminated in the Sabra and Shatila massacre, which for a while focused world public opinion on the nature of Israeli policy.[14]

It took a while for the Palestinian national movement to recover, but the next attempt to shake off (*intifada* in Arabic) the Israeli occupation also failed and triggered escalated Israeli reactions. One uprising in 1987 was easily crushed while the other of 2000 took more time to control but also provided the pretext for the renewal of ruthless policies.

The pretext for the operations in 2006 was the capture of Gilad Shalit. One should not venture too much in any kind of counterfactual history, but it is quite probable that had Shalit not been captured by Hamas, any of that organization's military operations against Israeli policies of strangulation would have served as a pretext for expanded Israeli assaults on the Gaza Strip.

The reaction, or rather the initiation, of the next stage, was codenamed operation Summer Rains, which commenced on June 28, 2006, and ended in November that year. The employment of such names by the Israeli Army reveals the sinister nature of its intentions and attitudes. The previous operation, as mentioned, was code-named First Rains, which turned into Summer Rains. Autumn Clouds would later follow. In a country where there is no rain in the summer, the only precipitation that one can expect are showers of F-16 bombs and artillery shells hitting the people of Gaza.

It was the most brutal attack on Gaza since 1967. In the past, the "punitive" Israeli actions against the 1.5 million Palestinians entrapped in the Strip were "limited" to massive bombardment from outside the Strip (from the land, the sea, and the air); this time the army invaded the Strip on the ground and added the firepower of its tanks to the overall bombardment of the most densely populated civilian center on the globe.

It was the first Israeli land incursion after the eviction of the settlers a year before. The worst part of it was the Israeli actions in September 2006, when the nature of the Israeli escalation revealed itself more clearly. On an almost daily basis civilians were killed by the Israeli Army. September 2 was a typical day in this horror show. Three citizens were killed and a whole family was wounded in Beit Hanoun. This was the morning harvest; before the end of day many more were killed. In September an average of eight Palestinians died daily in the Israeli attacks on the Strip. Many of them were children. Hundreds were maimed, wounded, and paralyzed.[15] The systematic slaughter more than anything else had the appearance of an inertia killing, when the continued employment of massive power is done as daily routine and not as the implementation of a policy.

On December 28, 2006, the Israeli human rights organization B'Tselem published its annual report about the Israeli atrocities in the occupied territories. In that year Israeli forces killed six hundred and sixty citizens.[16] The number of Palestinians killed by Israel in 2006 tripled in comparison to the previous year (around two hundred). According to B'Tselem, the Israelis killed 141 children in 2006. Most of the dead were from the Gaza Strip, where the Israeli forces demolished almost three hundred houses and slew entire families. This means that since 2000, Israeli forces killed almost four thousand Palestinians, a large number of them children; more than twenty thousand were wounded.

The land invasion enabled the army to kill citizens even more effectively and to present it as a result of heavy fighting within densely populated areas, an inevitable result, the army spokespersons claimed, of the circumstances but not of Israeli policies. A month and half later the operation Autumn Clouds was launched and proved to be even more lethal. On November 1, 2006, in less than forty-eight hours, the Israelis killed seventy civilians; by the end of that month, with additional mini operations accompanying it, almost two hundred were killed, half of them children and women.[17]

From First Rains to Autumn Clouds one could see escalation in every aspect. The first was the disappearance of the distinction between civilian and non-civilian targets: the senseless killing turned the population at large into a legitimate military target. The second was the escalation in military means: employment of every possible killing machine the Israeli Army possessed. Third, the escalation was conspicuous in the number of casualties: with each operation, and each future operation, a much larger number of people were killed and wounded. Finally, and most importantly, the operations became a strategy—this was now clearly the way Israel intended to solve the problem of the Gaza Strip.[18]

2007–2008: THE POLICY BECOMES A STRATEGY

A creeping transfer in the West Bank and a measured policy of systematic killings in the Gaza Strip were the two strategies Israel continued to employ in 2007 as well. From an electoral point of view, the one in Gaza was more problematic as it did not reap any tangible results, while the West Bank under Abu Mazin was yielding to Israeli pressure and there seemed to be no significant force that could arrest the Israeli strategy of annexation and dispossession. But Gaza continued to fire back. On the one hand, this enabled the Israeli Army to initiate more massive operations, but there was also the great danger, on the other, that as happened in 1948, the army would demand a more drastic and systematic "punitive" and collateral action against the besieged people of the Gaza Strip.

The casualties were rising in 2007. Three hundred people were killed in Gaza, dozens of them children. But even under Bush, and definitely in the post-Bush era, the myth of fighting the World Jihad in Gaza was losing its credibility. So a new mythology was proposed in 2007: Gaza was a terrorist base determined to destroy Israel. The only way the Palestinians could be "de-terrorized," so to speak, was to consent to live in a Strip encircled by barbed wire and walls. Flour, cement, medicine, dairy products, and rice were barred, and movement in and out of the Strip restricted, as a result of the political choices made by Gazans. Should they persist in supporting Hamas, they would be strangled and starved until they changed their ideological inclination. Should they succumb to the kind of politics Israel wished them to adopt, they would have the same fate as that of the West Bank: life without basic civil and human rights. They could either be inmates in the open prison of the West Bank or incarcerated in the maximum-security one of the Gaza Strip. If they resisted, they were likely to be imprisoned without trial, or killed. This was Israel's message in 2007 and the people of Gaza were given a year to make up their minds.

In the summer of 2008 an official bilateral cease-fire was declared brokered by Egypt. The Israeli government did not achieve its goals. It needed to prepare more seriously for the next step and that year was used for such preparations. Its strategy depended not only on silencing Hamas in the Gaza Strip but consisted of a desperate attempt to prove to the Quartet (the UN, the EU, the United States, and Russia) and the Palestinian Authority that the situation in the Strip was under its control to the extent that its "solution" could be incorporated in an Israeli vision of the future peace.

The summer of 2008 was two years after the humiliation of Lebanon. There was no wish in a government, which was subjected to an aggressive inquiry and damning report by an official commission into its failure in the north, to allow the Israeli public to dwell on this open wound for too long. There were also winds of change blowing from Washington where it was feared a new administration would not be as sympathetic to the Israeli strategy, and all in all world public opinion, at least from the bottom up, as it had been since 2000, seemed restive and antagonistic.

The old method of waiting for the right pretext to move ahead and escalate the struggle against the only resistance still intact was at work again. Once the pretext was found the army strategists, we now know, intended to upgrade the reaction. The talk in the IDF was now of a new doctrine vis-à-vis Gaza: the "Dahiyya Doctrine." In October 2008, *Haaretz* referred for the first time to the doctrine. The gist of it was the comprehensive destruction of areas in their entirety and the employment of disproportional force in response to the launch of missiles. When *Haaretz* reported the doctrine, the paper referred to it as a future strategy toward Lebanon—hence the Dahiyya reference, the Shiite quarter that was bombarded to dust in the 2006 Israeli air attack on Beirut. Gadi Eizenkot, the then chief of the Northern Command, said, "for us villages are military bases." He talked about total destruction of villages as a punitive action. But his colleague, Colonel Gabi Siboni, told an academic conference at the Institute for National Security in Tel-Aviv University that this would apply to the Gaza Strip as well. He added that "this is meant to inflict damage that would take ages to recover from."[19]

The evidence the NGO Breaking the Silence found corroborates this description of the doctrine. In a press conference these soldiers convened after the events of January 2009, they explained that the Gaza Strip was tackled as an armed outpost that had to be hammered and wiped out with all the might that the Israeli Army could muster.[20]

It seems that the doctrine was not just about employing military might, but also achieving the same desired result by other means. In 2008, the Israeli Army tightened the blockade on Gaza. This tactical move if analyzed in detail is far more than a punitive action. It is a policy that produced, given the demographic circumstances in the Gaza Strip, genocidal realities: lack of basic food, absence of elementary medicine, and no source of employment. To this one can add a massive claustrophobic traumatization of a million and half people who were not allowed to move about and lacked essential commodities and building material, which left them without shelter in summer or winter. And if this were not enough, the Israelis cut off the water and electricity supplies.[21]

Hamas did not budge and refused to disappear in return for the lifting of the blockade. So another pretext was sought: Israel violated the cease-fire on a daily basis in June 2008 with several attacks from the air and incursions on the ground. Groups that were not affiliated with Hamas retaliated with several rockets, and public opinion in Israel was now ready for a larger operation.

And yet this was not enough. In November 2008, the Israeli Army attacked a tunnel, one of many dug in order to survive the blockade, and claimed that it was a Marxist strike against a future Hamas operation. This time Hamas fired the rockets. It lost six people in the attack and launched a foray of more than thirty rockets. At the end of the month, Hamas declared that such Israeli actions, which became a daily occurrence, terminated the cease-fire.

On November 18, 2008, Hamas declared the end of the cease-fire and on the 24th intensified the barrage of missiles for a short while as a response to the previous Israeli action and ceased soon after. As before there were hardly any casualties on the Israeli side, although houses and flats were damaged and the afflicted citizens traumatized.

The November 24 missile attack was the one the Israeli Army had waited for. From November 25 until January 21, 2009, the Israeli Army bombarded the million and half people of Gaza from the air, land, and sea. Hamas responded with missiles that ended with three casualties and another ten Israeli soldiers were killed, some by friendly fire.

A GENOCIDAL POLICY?

The evidence collected by Israeli-based human rights organizations, international agencies, and media (although the Israelis barred the media from entering the Strip) was perceived by many to be far more serious than just war crimes. Some referred to it as genocide. It is not often that the president of the UN General Assembly would accuse a member state of genocide.[22] But when the Israeli Army bombarded the civilian population of Gaza, invoking the right of self-defense against terrorists launching missiles into civilian targets, Miguel D'Escoto Brockmann did not hesitate to describe such actions as genocide. As a former Roman Catholic priest and Nicaragua's foreign minister his views carry considerable weight. Needless to say, these remarks were promptly dismissed by the Israelis as anti-Semitic, the standard reaction to such accusations. Had his voice been a lonely one in the wilderness, it would have had little resonance, but it was joined by similar expressions of outrage by other senior politicians, especially outside the Western corridors of power, who chose the term *genocide* as the only way to describe the tragedy visited upon the people of Gaza.

D'Escoto Brockmann's reaction came before the full-scale destruction of homes, schools, and hospitals in many parts of Gaza. A week later, the Turkish columnist and author Oktay Akbal described the Israeli actions as the "Real Genocide."[23] The Israeli daily *Haaretz* reported on December 29, 2008, that government and opposition leaders across the globe, but mainly in Southeast Asia, Africa, and South America, referred to the atrocities (even before they fully transpired) as genocide.

There were strong criticisms from the West as well, but these sources were more cautious in using the term *genocide*. Nonetheless, the G-word frequently surfaced in the commentaries conveyed through alternative media, bloggers, and Web sites. Even before the Gaza operations in January 2009 occasional references were made to Israeli armed forces committing acts of genocide. "Some 1.4 million people, mostly children, are piled up in one of the most densely populated regions of the world, with no freedom of movement, no place to run and no space to hide," UN relief official Jan Egeland and Swedish foreign minister Jan Eliasson noted of the Israeli forays into Gaza, writing in *Le Figaro*. Journalist John Pilger wrote in the *New Statesman*, "A genocide is engulfing the people of Gaza while silence engulfs its bystanders."[24] In that same month repeated Israeli actions against the children in Gaza prompted similar expressions of concern from some unlikely sources: the internationally renowned jurist and Princeton professor of law, Richard Falk, wrote in that year that "it is especially painful for me, as an American Jew, to feel compelled to portray the ongoing and intensifying abuse of the Palestinian people by Israel through a reliance on such an inflammatory metaphor as 'holocaust.'"[25]

The January 2009 events were referred to in similar terms by the pro-Western Arab media organs. One such source was the Dubai-based satellite network Al-Arabia. On December 28, 2008, when the massive Israeli killing had just begun, although already resulting in unprecedented numbers of dead children and women, the network reported the popular protests around the world against the Israeli actions. The headline was "World Stands United against

'Genocide' in Gaza." It reported that "protestors from Denmark, Turkey, Pakistan, Cyprus, Bahrain, Kuwait, Iran, Sudan and even Israel all called for an end to what most demonstrators termed as 'genocide' in Gaza." [26]

This was not the mainstream media's opinion in the West, nor was it voiced in such a manner by any members of the political elite in North America or Europe. But within the balance of power between hegemonic and counterhegemonic voices, the latter included senior politicians in the rest of the world, the widest coalitions of the political left and of human rights organizations in the West, coupled with some influential voices from within the Western media. The journalist John Pilger referred to the events in Gaza as genocide in the *New Statesman* again on January 21, 2009.

In the aftermath of the event more voices joined in. Participants in the main demonstration in London on January 19, 2009, carried placards about the "Genocide in Gaza." Similar banners were raised in a massive demonstration in Copenhagen. Elsewhere, the Malaysian foreign minister in April 2009 described the attack on Gaza as genocide. [27]

One can understand why Judge Goldstone refrained from such language. His report as noted corroborates the evidence collected by those who described these policies as genocidal but sums them up as war crimes that require further investigation. Goldstone's report also uses the same language for the Hamas missile attack on Israel. This seems to be more lip service than a genuine point. The imbalance of the aggressors' power and destruction and the victims' pathetic military response deserves different language.

Moreover, when one reads the thorough and brave report of Judge Goldstone, one should remember that the 1,500 killed, thousands of wounded, and tens of thousands who lost their homes do not tell the whole story. It is the decision to employ such fierce military force in a civilian space that should be discussed. This kind of firepower can only produce the kind of horrific destruction we have seen in Gaza. It was used for this purpose. The nature of the military operations also displayed an Israeli military wish to experiment with new weapons, all intended to kill civilians as part of what the former chief of the army's general staff, Moshe Ya'alon, termed as the need to brand in the Palestinian consciousness the fearsome might of the Israeli Army.[28]

EIGHT

A MIDDLE EAST PEACE THAT COULD HAPPEN
(BUT WON'T)

The fact that the Israel-Palestine conflict grinds on without resolution might appear to be rather strange. For many of the world's conflicts, it is difficult even to conjure up a feasible settlement. In this case, it is not only possible, but there is near universal agreement on its basic contours: a two-state settlement along the internationally recognized (pre-June 1967) borders—with "minor and mutual modifications," to adopt official U.S. terminology before Washington departed from the international community in the mid-1970s.

The basic principles have been accepted by virtually the entire world, including the Arab states (who go on to call for full normalization of relations), the Organization of Islamic States (including Iran), and relevant non-state actors (including Hamas). A settlement along these lines was first proposed at the UN Security Council in January 1976 by the major Arab states. Israel refused to attend the session. The United States vetoed the resolution, and did so again in 1980. The record at the General Assembly since is similar.

There was one important and revealing break in U.S.-Israeli rejectionism. After the failed Camp David agreements in 2000, President

Clinton recognized that the terms he and Israel had proposed were unacceptable to any Palestinians. That December, he proposed his "parameters": imprecise, but more forthcoming. He then stated that both sides had accepted the parameters, while expressing reservations.

Israeli and Palestinian negotiators met in Taba, Egypt, in January 2001 to resolve the differences and were making considerable progress. In their final press conference, they reported that, with a little more time, they could probably have reached full agreement. Israel called off the negotiations prematurely, however, and official progress then terminated, though informal discussions at a high level continued, leading to the Geneva Accord, rejected by Israel and ignored by the United States.

A good deal has happened since, but a settlement along those lines is still not out of reach—if, of course, Washington is once again willing to accept it. Unfortunately, there is little sign of that.

Substantial mythology has been created about the entire record, but the basic facts are clear enough and quite well documented.

The United States and Israel have been acting in tandem to extend and deepen the occupation. In 2005, recognizing that it was pointless to subsidize a few thousand Israeli settlers in Gaza, who were appropriating substantial resources and protected by a large part of the Israeli Army, the government of Ariel Sharon decided to move them to the much more valuable West Bank and Golan Heights.

Instead of carrying out the operation straightforwardly, as would have been easy enough, the government decided to stage a "national trauma," which virtually duplicated the farce accompanying the withdrawal from the Sinai desert after the Camp David agreements of 1978–79. In each case, the withdrawal permitted the cry of "Never Again," which meant in practice: we cannot abandon an inch of the Palestinian territories that we want to take in violation of international law. This farce played very well in the West, though it was ridiculed by more astute Israeli commentators, among them that country's prominent sociologist the late Baruch Kimmerling.

After its formal withdrawal from the Gaza Strip, Israel never actually relinquished its total control over the territory, often described realistically as "the world's largest prison." In January 2006, a few months after the withdrawal, Palestine had an election that was recognized as free and fair by international observers. Palestinians, however, voted "the wrong way," electing Hamas. Instantly, the United States and Israel intensified their assault against Gazans as punishment for this misdeed. The facts and the reasoning were not concealed; rather, they were openly published alongside reverential commentary on Washington's sincere dedication to democracy. The U.S.-backed Israeli assault against the Gazans has only been intensified since, thanks to violence and economic strangulation, increasingly savage.

Meanwhile in the West Bank, always with firm U.S. backing, Israel has been carrying forward long-standing programs to take the valuable land and resources of the Palestinians and leave them in unviable cantons, mostly out of sight. Israeli commentators frankly refer to these goals as "neocolonial." Ariel Sharon, the main architect of the settlement programs, called these cantons "Bantustans," though the term is misleading: South Africa needed the majority black work force, while Israel would be happy if the Palestinians disappeared, and its policies are directed to that end.

One step toward cantonization and the undermining of hopes for Palestinian national survival is the separation of Gaza from the West Bank. These hopes have been almost entirely consigned to oblivion, an atrocity to which we should not contribute by tacit consent. Israeli journalist Amira Hass, one of the leading specialists on Gaza, writes that

> The restrictions on Palestinian movement that Israel introduced in January 1991 reversed a process that had been initiated in June 1967. Back then, and for the first time since 1948, a large portion of the Palestinian people again lived in the open territory of a single country—to be sure, one that was occupied, but was nevertheless whole.... The total separation of the Gaza Strip from the West Bank is one of the greatest achievements of Israeli politics, whose overarching objective is to prevent a solution based on international decisions and understandings and instead dictate an arrangement based on Israel's military superiority.... Since January 1991, Israel has bureaucratically and logistically merely perfected the split and the separation: not only between Palestinians in the occupied territories and their brothers in Israel, but also between the Palestinian residents of Jerusalem and those in the rest of the territories and between Gazans and West Bankers/Jerusalemites. Jews live in this same piece of land within a superior and separate system of privileges, laws, services, physical infrastructure and freedom of movement.[1]

The leading academic specialist on Gaza, Harvard scholar Sara Roy, adds:

> Gaza is an example of a society that has been deliberately reduced to a state of abject destitution, its once productive population transformed into one of aid-dependent paupers.... Gaza's subjection began long before Israel's recent war against it [December 2008]. The Israeli occupation—now largely forgotten or denied by the international community—has devastated Gaza's economy and people, especially since 2006.... After Israel's December [2008] assault, Gaza's already compromised conditions have become virtually unlivable. Livelihoods, homes, and public infrastructure have been damaged or destroyed on a scale that even the Israel Defense Forces admitted was

indefensible. In Gaza today, there is no private sector to speak of and no industry. 80 percent of Gaza's agricultural crops were destroyed and Israel continues to snipe at farmers attempting to plant and tend fields near the well-fenced and patrolled border. Most productive activity has been extinguished.... Today, 96 percent of Gaza's population of 1.4 million is dependent on humanitarian aid for basic needs. According to the World Food Programme, the Gaza Strip requires a minimum of 400 trucks of food every day just to meet the basic nutritional needs of the population. Yet, despite a March [22, 2009] decision by the Israeli cabinet to lift all restrictions on foodstuffs entering Gaza, only 653 trucks of food and other supplies were allowed entry during the week of May 10, at best meeting 23 percent of required need. Israel now allows only 30 to 40 commercial items to enter Gaza compared to 4,000 approved products prior to June 2006.[2]

It cannot be too often stressed that Israel had no credible pretext for its 2008–9 attack on Gaza, with full U.S. support and illegally using U.S. weapons. Near-universal opinion asserts the contrary, claiming that Israel was acting in self-defense. That is utterly unsustainable, in light of Israel's flat rejection of peaceful means that were readily available, as Israel and its U.S. partner in crime knew very well.[3] That aside, Israel's siege of Gaza is itself an act of war, as Israel of all countries certainly recognizes, having repeatedly justified launching major wars on grounds of partial restrictions on its access to the outside world, though nothing remotely like what it has long imposed on Gaza.

One crucial element of Israel's criminal siege, little reported, is the naval blockade. Peter Beaumont reports from Gaza that "on its coastal littoral, Gaza's limitations are marked by a different fence where the bars are Israeli gunboats with their huge wakes, scurrying beyond the Palestinian fishing boats and preventing them from going outside a zone imposed by the warships."[4] According to reports from the scene, the naval siege has been tightened steadily since 2000. Fishing boats have been driven steadily out of Gaza's territorial waters and toward the shore by Israeli gunboats, often violently without warning and with many casualties. As a result of these naval actions, Gaza's fishing industry has virtually collapsed; fishing is impossible near shore because of the contamination caused by Israel's regular attacks, including the destruction of power plants and sewage facilities.

These Israeli naval attacks began shortly after the discovery by the BG (British Gas) Group of what appear to be quite sizeable natural gas fields in Gaza's territorial waters. Industry journals report that Israel is already appropriating these Gazan resources for its own use, part of its commitment to shift its economy to natural gas. The standard industry source reports:

> Israel's finance ministry has given the Israel Electric Corp. (IEC) approval to purchase larger quantities of natural gas from BG than originally agreed upon, according to Israeli government sources [which] said the state-owned utility would be able to negotiate for as much as 1.5 billion cubic meters of natural gas from the Marine field located off the Mediterranean coast of the Palestinian controlled Gaza Strip.
>
> Last year the Israeli government approved the purchase of 800 million cubic meters of gas from the field by the IEC…. Recently the Israeli government changed its policy and decided the state-owned utility could buy the entire quantity of gas from the Gaza Marine field. Previously the government had said the IEC could buy half the total amount and the remainder would be bought by private power producers.[5]

The pillage of what could become a major source of income for Gaza is surely known to U.S. authorities. It is only reasonable to suppose that the intention to appropriate these limited resources, either by Israel alone or together with the collaborationist Palestinian Authority, is the motive for preventing Gazan fishing boats from entering Gaza's territorial waters.

There are some instructive precedents. In 1989, Australian foreign minister Gareth Evans signed a treaty with his Indonesian counterpart Ali Alatas granting Australia rights to the substantial oil reserves in "the Indonesian Province of East Timor." The Indonesia-Australia Timor Gap Treaty, which offered not a crumb to the people whose oil was being stolen, "is the only legal agreement anywhere in the world that effectively recognises Indonesia's right to rule East Timor," the Australian press reported.

Asked about his willingness to recognize the Indonesian conquest and to rob the sole resource of the conquered territory, which had been subjected to near-genocidal slaughter by the Indonesian invader with the strong support of Australia (along with the United States, the United Kingdom, and some others), Evans explained that "there is no binding legal obligation not to recognise the acquisition of territory that was acquired by force," adding that "the world is a pretty unfair place, littered with examples of acquisition by force."[6]

It should, then, be unproblematic for Israel to follow suit in Gaza.

A few years later, Evans became the leading figure in the campaign to introduce the concept "responsibility to protect"—known as R2P—into international law. R2P is intended to establish an international obligation to protect populations from grave crimes. Evans is the author of a major book on the subject and was co-chair of the International Commission on Intervention and State Sovereignty, which issued what is considered the basic document on R2P.

In an article devoted to this "idealistic effort to establish a new humanitarian principle," the London *Economist* featured Evans and his "bold but passionate claim on behalf of a three-word expression which (in quite large part thanks to his efforts) now belongs to the language of diplomacy: the 'responsibility to protect.'" The article is accompanied by a picture of Evans with the caption "Evans: a life-long passion to protect." His hand is pressed to his forehead in despair over the difficulties faced by his idealistic effort. The magazine chose not to run a different photo that circulates in Australia, depicting Evans and Alatas exuberantly clasping their hands together as they toast the Timor Gap Treaty that they had just signed.[7]

Though a "protected population" under international law, Gazans do not fall under the jurisdiction of the "responsibility to protect," joining other unfortunates, in accord with the maxim of Thucydides—that the strong do as they wish, and the weak suffer as they must—which holds with its customary precision.

The kinds of restrictions on movement used to destroy Gaza have long been in force in the West Bank as well, less cruelly but with grim effects on life and the economy. The World Bank reports that Israel has established "a complex closure regime that restricts Palestinian access to large areas of the West Bank...The Palestinian economy has remained stagnant, largely because of the sharp downturn in Gaza and Israel's continued restrictions on Palestinian trade and movement in the West Bank."

The World Bank "cited Israeli roadblocks and checkpoints hindering trade and travel, as well as restrictions on Palestinian building in the West Bank, where the Western-backed government of Palestinian president Mahmoud Abbas holds sway."[8] Israel does permit—indeed encourage—a privileged existence for elites in Ramallah and sometimes elsewhere, largely relying on European funding, a traditional feature of colonial and neocolonial practice.

All this constitutes what Israeli activist Jeff Halper calls a "matrix of control" to subdue the colonized population. These systematic programs over more than forty years aim to establish Defense Minister Moshe Dayan's recommendation to his colleagues shortly after Israel's 1967 conquests that we must tell the Palestinians in the territories: "We have no solution, you shall continue to live like dogs, and whoever wishes may leave, and we will see where this process leads."[9]

Turning to the second bone of contention, settlements, there is indeed a confrontation, but it is rather less dramatic than portrayed. Washington's position was presented most strongly in Secretary of State Hillary Clinton's much-quoted statement rejecting "natural growth exceptions" to the policy opposing new settlements. Prime Minister Binyamin Netanyahu, along with President Shimon Peres and, in fact, virtually the whole Israeli political spectrum, insists on permitting "natural growth" within the areas that Israel intends to annex, complaining that the United States is backing down on George W. Bush's authorization of such expansion within his "vision" of a Palestinian state.

Senior Netanyahu cabinet members have gone further. Transportation Minister Yisrael Katz announced that "the current Israeli government will not accept in any way the freezing of legal settlement activity in Judea and Samaria."[10] The term "legal" in U.S.-Israeli parlance means "illegal, but authorized by the government of Israel with a wink from Washington." In this usage, unauthorized outposts are termed "illegal," though apart from the dictates of the powerful, they are no more illegal than the settlements granted to Israel under Bush's "vision" and Obama's scrupulous omission.

The Obama-Clinton "hardball" formulation is not new. It repeats the wording of the Bush administration draft of the 2003 Road Map, which stipulates that in Phase I, "Israel freezes all settlement activity (including natural growth of settlements)." All sides formally accept the Road Map (modified to drop the phrase "natural growth")— consistently overlooking the fact that Israel, with U.S. support, at once added fourteen "reservations" that render it inoperable.[11]

If Obama were at all serious about opposing settlement expansion, he could easily proceed with concrete measures by, for example, reducing U.S. aid by the amount devoted to this purpose. That would hardly be a radical or courageous move. The Bush I administration did so (reducing loan guarantees), but after the Oslo Accord in 1993, President Clinton left calculations to the government of Israel. Unsurprisingly, there was "no change in the expenditures flowing to the settlements," the Israeli press reported. "[Prime Minister] Rabin will continue not to dry out the settlements," the report concludes. "And the Americans? They will understand."[12]

Obama administration officials informed the press that the Bush I measures are "not under discussion," and that pressures will be "largely symbolic."[13] In short, Obama understands, just as Clinton and Bush II did.

At best, settlement expansion is a side issue, rather like the issue of "illegal outposts"—namely those that the government of Israel has not authorized. Concentration on these issues diverts attention from the fact that there are no "legal outposts" and that it is the existing settlements that are the primary problem to be faced.

The U.S. press reports that

> a partial freeze has been in place for several years, but settlers have found ways around the strictures…[C]onstruction in the settlements has slowed but never stopped, continuing at an annual rate of about 1,500 to 2,000 units over the past three years. If building continues at the 2008 rate, the 46,500 units already approved will be completed in about 20 years.… If Israel built all the housing units already approved in the nation's overall master plan for settlements, it would almost double the number of settler homes in the West Bank.[14]

Peace Now, which monitors settlement activities, estimates further that the two largest settlements would double in size: Ariel and

Ma'aleh Adumim, built mainly during the Oslo years in the salients that subdivide the West Bank into cantons.

"Natural population growth" is largely a myth, Israel's leading diplomatic correspondent, Akiva Eldar, points out, citing demographic studies by Colonel (res.) Shaul Arieli, deputy military secretary to former prime minister and incumbent defense minister Ehud Barak. Settlement growth consists largely of Israeli immigrants in violation of the Geneva Conventions, assisted with generous subsidies. Much of it is in direct violation of formal government decisions, but carried out with the authorization of the government, specifically Barak, considered a dove in the Israeli spectrum.[15]

Correspondent Jackson Diehl derides the "long-dormant Palestinian fantasy," revived by President Abbas, "that the United States will simply force Israel to make critical concessions, whether or not its democratic government agrees."[16] He does not explain why refusal to participate in Israel's illegal expansion—which, if serious, would "force Israel to make critical concessions"—would be improper interference in Israel's democracy.

Returning to reality, all these discussions about settlement expansion evade the most crucial issue about settlements: what the United States and Israel have already established in the West Bank. The evasion tacitly concedes that the illegal settlement programs already in place are somehow acceptable (putting aside the Golan Heights, annexed in violation of Security Council orders)—though the Bush "vision," apparently accepted by Obama, moves from tacit to explicit support for these violations of law. What is in place already suffices to ensure that there can be no viable Palestinian self-determination. Hence, there is every indication that even on the unlikely assumption that "natural growth" will be ended, U.S.-Israeli rejectionism will persist, blocking the international consensus as before.

Subsequently, Prime Minister Netanyahu declared a ten-month suspension of new construction, with many exemptions, and entirely excluding Greater Jerusalem, where expropriation in Arab areas and construction for Jewish settlers continues at a rapid pace. Hillary Clinton praised these "unprecedented" concessions on (illegal) construction, eliciting anger and ridicule in much of the world.[17]

It might be different if a legitimate "land swap" were under consideration, a solution approached at Taba and spelled out more fully in the Geneva Accord reached in informal high-level Israel-Palestine negotiations. The accord was presented in Geneva in October 2003, welcomed by much of the world, rejected by Israel, and ignored by the United States.[18]

Barack Obama's June 4, 2009, Cairo address to the Muslim world kept pretty much to his well-honed "blank slate" style—with little of substance, but presented in a personable manner that allows listeners to write on the slate what they want to hear. CNN captured its spirit by headlining a report "Obama Looks to Reach the Soul of the Muslim World." Obama had announced the goals of his address in an interview with *New York Times* columnist Thomas Friedman. "'We have a joke around the White House,' the president said. 'We're just going to keep on telling the truth until it stops working and nowhere is truth-telling more important than the Middle East.'" The White House commitment is most welcome, but it is useful to see how it translates into practice.[19]

Obama admonished his audience that it is easy to "point fingers… but if we see this conflict only from one side or the other, then we will be blind to the truth: the only resolution is for the aspirations of both sides to be met through two states, where Israelis and Palestinians each live in peace and security."

Turning from Obama-Friedman Truth to truth, there is a third side, with a decisive role throughout: the United States. But that participant in the conflict Obama omitted. The omission is understood to be normal and appropriate, hence unmentioned: Friedman's column is headlined "Obama Speech Aimed at Both Arabs and Israelis." The front-page *Wall Street Journal* report on Obama's speech appears under the heading "Obama Chides Israel, Arabs in His Overture to Muslims." Other reports are the same.

The convention is understandable on the doctrinal principle that though the U.S. government sometimes makes mistakes, its intentions are by definition benign, even noble. In the world of attractive imagery, Washington has always sought desperately to be an honest broker, yearning to advance peace and justice. The doctrine trumps truth, of which there is little hint in the speech or the mainstream coverage of it.

Obama once again echoed Bush's "vision" of two states, without saying what he meant by the phrase "Palestinian state." His intentions were clarified not only by the crucial omissions discussed elsewhere, but also by his one explicit criticism of Israel: "The United States does not accept the legitimacy of continued Israeli settlements. This construction violates previous agreements and undermines efforts to achieve peace. It is time for these settlements to stop." That is, Israel should live up to Phase I of the 2003 Road Map, rejected at once by Israel with tacit U.S. support, as noted—though the truth is that Obama has ruled out even steps of the Bush I variety to withdraw from participation in these crimes.

The operative words are "legitimacy" and "continued." It is useful to recall that it was Netanyahu's 1996 government that was the first in Israel to use the phrase "Palestinian state." It agreed that Palestinians can call whatever fragments of Palestine are left to them "a state" if they like—or they can call them "fried chicken."[20] By omission, Obama indicates that he accepts Bush's vision: the vast existing settlement and infrastructure projects are "legitimate," thus ensuring that the phrase "Palestinian state" means "fried chicken."

Always evenhanded, Obama also had an admonition for the Arab states: they "must recognize that the Arab Peace Initiative was an important beginning, but not the end of their responsibilities." Plainly, however, it cannot be a meaningful "beginning" if Obama continues to reject its core principles: implementation of the international consensus. To do so, however, is evidently not Washington's "responsibility" in Obama's vision; no explanation given, no notice taken.

On democracy, Obama said that "we would not presume to pick the outcome of a peaceful election"—as in January 2006, when Washington picked the outcome with a vengeance, turning at once to severe punishment of the Palestinians because it did not like the outcome of a peaceful election, all with Obama's apparent approval judging by his words before, and actions since, taking office.

Obama politely refrained from comment about his host, President Mubarak, one of the most brutal dictators in the region, though he has had some illuminating words about him. As he was about to board a plane to Saudi Arabia and Egypt, the two "moderate" Arab states,

> Mr. Obama signaled that while he would mention American concerns about human rights in Egypt, he would not challenge Mr. Mubarak too sharply, because he is a "force for stability and good" in the Middle East…Mr. Obama said he did not regard Mr. Mubarak as an authoritarian leader. "No, I tend not to use labels for folks," Mr. Obama said. The president noted that there had been criticism "of the manner in which politics operates in Egypt," but he also said that Mr. Mubarak had been "a stalwart ally, in many respects, to the United States."[21]

When a politician uses the word "folks," we should brace ourselves for the deceit, or worse, that is coming. Outside of this context, there are "people," or often "villains," and using labels for them is highly meritorious. Obama is right, however, not to have used the word "authoritarian," which is far too mild a label for his friend.

Just as in the past, support for democracy, and for human rights as well, keeps to the pattern that scholarship has repeatedly discovered, correlating closely with strategic and economic objectives. There should be little difficulty in understanding why those whose eyes are not closed tight shut by rigid doctrine dismiss Obama's yearning for human rights and democracy as a joke in bad taste.

ACKNOWLEDGMENTS

This book would not have been possible without the help and support of the following people:

Noam Chomsky, who answered my first email many years ago and has continued to do so throughout the years (in spite of their number). I still do not know how you do it. Thank you. Ilan Pappé, thank you for being approachable, an amazing speaker, and...also for answering my numerous emails. You are both true inspirations for being incredibly professional, sticking to your ethics, and "talking the talk, walking the walk."

Thanks to Anthony Arnove for helping me making the book what it is today. Thank you to Mikki Smith and Jessie Kindig, who spent many hours helping with research on endnotes. Many thanks to Dao Tran at Haymarket for turning a manuscript into a book and making the editing smooth and easy. Thanks to Caroline Luft for her detailed copyediting.

My brother Florent, for being my loyal companion throughout the years and without whom this book might never have existed. My friend Herve Landecker, for making me laugh, always, and being a great "manager." I wish I had met you earlier, but as the saying goes, "*mieux vaut tard que jamais*." Maria, thanks for your help with the interviews and for always having remained so enthusiastic about this project. Thanks to members of Lambeth and Wandsworth Palestine Solidarity Campaign for their contribution in the 2007 Chomsky interview. Huge thanks to Uhti Ewa Jasiewicz for her very constructive and helpful comments on the introduction and for everything she taught me in the last few months.

Mae, Mum, Dad, and Fay, thanks for being there, always. I love you. Jeanne, if God existed, I would kneel down and ask him not to intervene when it came to you, not to touch a hair on your head, to leave you as you are.

Finally, thanks to the people of Palestine for their steadfastness and thanks to all the international human rights activists supporting their universal struggle. You are the real heroes of this world.

A NOTE ON THE TEXT

"Clusters of History: U.S. Involvement in the Palestine Question" was previously published in *Race & Class* 48, no. 3 (2007): 1–28, Institute of Race Relations.

"'Exterminate All the Brutes': Gaza 2009" is based on a talk given at the Center for International Studies at MIT, January 19, 2009. Earlier versions appeared on ZNet and in *The Spokesman* (England) 103 (2009).

"A Middle East Peace That Could Happen (But Won't)" was previously published by TomDispatch, April 27, 2010, and is a revised excerpt of *Hopes and Prospects* (Chicago: Haymarket Books, 2010).

NOTES

CHAPTER ONE: 2007 INTERVIEW WITH CHOMSKY

1. Thomas Carothers, *Critical Mission: Essays on Democracy Promotion* (Washington, D.C.: Carnegie Endowment for International Peace, 2004), introduction and p. 7.

2. See Gilbert Achcar, Noam Chomsky, and Stephen Shalom, *Perilous Power* (Boulder, CO: Paradigm Publishers, 2007), epilogue, note 29 for review.

3. See Alistair Crooke, "Our Second Biggest Mistake in the Middle East," *London Review of Books* 29, no. 13 (July 5, 2007): 3–6; and Jonathan Steele, "Hamas Acted on a Very Real Fear of a US-Sponsored Coup," *Guardian*, June 22, 2007, 37. See also David Rose, "The Gaza Bombshell," *Vanity Fair*, April 2008; Norman Olsen, "An Inside Story of How the US Magnified Palestinian Suffering, *Christian Science Monitor*, January 12, 2009.

4. Richard Falk, "Slouching Toward a Palestinian Holocaust," ZNet, July 5, 2007, www.zcommunications.org/slouching-toward-a-palestinian-holocaust-by-richard-falk.

5. "Israel's Road Map Reservations," *Haaretz*, May 27, 2003, www.haaretz.com/hasen/pages/ShArt.jhtml?itemNo=297230.

6. Quoted in Helene Cooper, "Blair to Tackle Economics but Not Peace Efforts, a Task Reserved for Rice," *New York Times*, June 28, 2007.

7. Michael MccGwire, "The Rise and Fall of the NPT: an Opportunity for Britain," *International Affairs* 81, no. 1 (2005): 115–40.

8. Edward Said, "Palestinians under Siege," *London Review of Books* 22, no. 24 (December 14, 2000).

9. Marvin Kalb and Carol Saivetz, "The Israeli-Hezbollah War of 2006: The

Media as a Weapon in Asymmetrical Conflict," *Harvard International Journal of Press/Politics* 12, no. 3 (2007): 43–66, quote on p. 44.

10. See, for example, Aviv Lavie, "Inside Israel's Secret Prison," *Haaretz*, August 23, 2003.

11. Gilbert Achcar, *Eastern Cauldron: Islam, Afghanistan and Palestine in the Mirror of Marxism* (London: Pluto, 2004), 264.

CHAPTER TWO: CLUSTERS OF HISTORY
U.S. INVOLVEMENT IN THE QUESTION OF PALESTINE

1. John Mearsheimer and Stephen Walt, "The Israel Lobby," *London Review of Books* 28, no. 6 (March 23, 2006).

2. Quoted in Lawrence Davidson, *America's Palestine: Popular and Official Perceptions from Balfour to Israel's Statehood* (Gainesville: University Press of Florida, 2001), 2.

3. George Antonious, *The Arab Awakening* (Beirut: Khayats, 1945).

4. See Ilan Pappé, "Arab Nationalism," in Gerard Delanty and Krishan Kumar, eds., *The Sage Handbook of Nations and Nationalism* (London: Sage, 2006), 500–3.

5. Davidson, *America's Palestine*, 8, n. 25.

6. See Ruth Kark, "American Consular Reports as a Source for the Study of Nineteenth Century Palestine," *Cathedra* 50 (1989): 133–9.

7. Davidson, *America's Palestine*, 4, n. 13.

8. Joseph M. Canfield, *The Incredible Scofield and His Book* (Vallecito, CA: Ross House Books, 1988).

9. Stephen Sizer, *Christian Zionism: Road-Map to Armageddon* (New York: InterVarsity Press, 2005).

10. This whole episode can be read in a new light in Max Blumenthal, "Birth Pangs of a New Christian Zionism," *Nation*, August 8, 2006, www.thenation .com/article/birth-pangs-new-christian-zionism.

11. Quotation in Jerry Falwell, "Future-Word: An Agenda for the Eighties," in *The Fundamentalist Phenomenon: The Resurgence of Conservative Christianity*, ed. Jerry Falwell, with Ed Dobson and Ed Hindson (Garden City, NY: Doubleday, 1981): 186–223, quote p. 215.

For the political and theological program of Christian Zionism, see the "Proclamation of the Third International Christian Zionist Conference," held in Jerusalem from February 25–29, 2006, which called for Israeli defense of itself, an unpartitioned Jerusalem, and seizure of the Golan Heights: http://christianactionforisrael.org/congress.html.

For more on Christian Zionism, Falwell's central role in its promotion in America, and the combination of faith with Israeli security and expansion, see Merril Simon, *Jerry Falwell and the Jews* (Middle Village, NY: Jonathan David

Publishers, 1984); and Stephen Spector, *Evangelicals and Israel: The Story of American Christian Zionism* (New York: Oxford University Press, 2009).

12. Sizer, *Christian Zionism*.

13. Donald M. Love, *Henry Churchill King of Oberlin* (New Haven, CT: Yale University Press, 1956).

14. Davidson, *America's Palestine*, 6.

15. David Hapgood, *Charles R. Crane: The Man Who Bet on People* (New York: Xlibris Publications, 2000), 56–63.

16. Harry N. Howard, *The King Crane Commission: An American Inquiry into the Middle East* (Beirut: Khayats, 1963).

17. Davidson, *America's Palestine*, 146, n. 27.

18. Ilan Pappé, *The Making of the Arab-Israeli Conflict, 1947–1951* (London and New York: I. B. Tauris, 1994), 36.

19. Marc Lee Raphael, *Abba Hillel Silver: A Profile of American Judaism* (New York: Holmes and Meier, 1989).

20. H. Paul Jeffers, *The Napoleon of New York: Mayor Fiorello LaGuardia* (Toronto: John Wiley and Sons, 2002).

21. W. Brooke Graves, *Administration of the Lobby Registration Provision of the Legislation Reorganization Act of 1946: An Analysis of Experience During the 80th Congress* (Washington, D.C.: U.S. Government Printing Office, 1949).

22. Abraham Ben-Zvi, *Eisenhower, Kennedy, and the Origins of the American-Israeli Alliance* (New York: Columbia University Press, 1998).

23. Cheryl Rubenberg, *Israel and the American National Interest: A Critical Examination* (Chicago: University of Illinois Press, 1989), 329–77.

24. Alfred Lilienthal, "J. William Fulbright: A Giant Passes," *Washington Report on Middle Eastern Affairs* (April–May 1995): 92–3.

25. Douglas Little, "The Making of a Special Relationship: The United States and Israel, 1957–1968," *International Journal of Middle East Studies* 25, no. 4 (November 1993): 563–85.

26. Joel Beinin, "Pro-Israeli Hawks and the Second Gulf War," Middle East Report Online, April 6, 2003, www.merip.org/mero/mero040603.html.

27. Andrew I. Killgore, "According to Indictment, AIPAC Has Been under Investigation since 1999," Washington Report on Middle East Affairs, November 2005, www.washington-report.org/archives/November_2005/0511019.html.

28. Juan Cole, "AIPAC's Overt and Covert Ops," Antiwar.com, August 30, 2004, www.antiwar.com/cole/?articleid=3467.

29. Hannah Arendt, *The Jew as Pariah: Jewish Identity and Politics in the Modern Age* (New York: Grove, 1978).

30. Seymor Martin Lipset and Earl Raab, *Jews and the New American Scene* (Cambridge, MA: Harvard University Press, 1995), 26–7.

31. Full report in William River Pitt and Scott Ritter, *War on Iraq* (New York: Context Books, 2003).

32. Naseer Aruri, *Dishonest Broker: The US Role in Israel and Palestine* (Cambridge, MA: South End Press, 2003), 127–48.

33. Ibid.

34. Senate Committee on Foreign Relations, *High Costs of Crude: The New Currency of Foreign Policy*, 109th Cong., 1st sess., November 16, 2005 (Washington, D.C.: U.S. Government Printing Office, 2006).

35. David Ben-Gurion, diary, October 27, 1948.

36. Dana Milbank, "AIPAC's Big, Bigger, Biggest Moment," *Washington Post*, May 24, 2005, 14.

37. Aruri, *Dishonest Broker*, 37.

38. Gary Leupp, "'An American Strike on Iran Is Essential for Our Existence': AIPAC Demands 'Action' on Iran," CounterPunch, February 24–25, 2007, www.counterpunch.org/leupp02242007.html.

CHAPTER THREE: STATE OF DENIAL

1. Edward Said, *Culture and Imperialism* (New York: Alfred K. Knopf, Inc., 1993).

2. The scope of the tragedy is well described in a collection of articles in Ghada Karmi and Eugene Cortran, eds., *The Palestinian Exodus, 1948–1988* (London: Ithaca Press, 1999).

3. Pappé, *Making of the Arab-Israeli Conflict*, 124–43.

4. See, in particular, Nur Masalha's *Expulsion of the Palestinians: The Concept of "Transfer" in Zionist Political Thought, 1882–1948*, and his *A Land without a People: Israel, Transfer and the Palestinians 1949–96* (London: Faber and Faber, 1997). Masalha's later book, *Imperial Israel and the Palestinians: The Politics of Expansion, 1967–2000* (London: Pluto Press, 2000) is a comprehensive treatment of the imperial imperative within Herzlian Zionism. His recent book, *The Politics of Denial: Israel and the Palestinian Refugee Problem* (London: Pluto Press, 2003) exposes Israel's pretense to innocence on the question of the expelled Palestinians.

5. This is Michael Prior's translation, in *Zionism and the State of Israel: A Moral Inquiry* (London and New York: Routledge, 1999), 9, of "*Die arme Bevölkerung trachten wir unbemerkt über die Grenze zu schaffen, indem wir in den Durchzugsländern Arbeit verschaffen aber in unserem eigenen Lande jederlei Arbeit verweigern*" (Theodor Herzl, *Briefe und Autobiographische Notizen, 1886–1895*, vol. II, eds. Johannes Wachten et al. (Berlin: Propylaen Verlag, 1983), 117–18.

6. Masalha, *Expulsion of the Palestinians*, 93–141.

7. Shabtai Teveth, *Ben-Gurion and the Palestinian Arabs* (Oxford: Oxford University Press, 1985), 189.

8. See, for example, Masalha, *Expulsion of the Palestinians*.

9. Simha Flapan, *Zionism and the Palestinians 1917–1947* (London: Croom

Helm, 1979); Simha Flapan, *The Birth of Israel: Myths and Realities* (London: Croom Helm, 1987); Baruch Kimmerling, *Zionism and Territory: The Socio-Territorial Dimensions of Zionist Politics* (Los Angeles and Berkeley: University of California, Institute of International Studies [Research Series, No. 51], 1983); Benny Morris, *The Birth of the Palestinian Refugee Problem, 1947–1949* (Cambridge: Cambridge University Press, 1987); Benny Morris, *1948 and After: Israel and the Palestinians* (Oxford: Oxford University Press, 1990); Benny Morris, *Israel's Border Wars* (Oxford: Oxford University Press, 1993); Ilan Pappé, *Britain and the Arab-Israeli Conflict 1948–1951* (London: Macmillan, 1988); Pappé, *Making of the Arab-Israeli Conflict*; Tom Segev, *The First Israelis,* English language ed. Arlen N. Weinstein (New York: The Free Press/London: Collier Macmillan, 1986); Tom Segev, *The Seventh Million: The Israelis and the Holocaust,* trans. Haim Watzan (New York: Hill and Wang, 1993); Israel Shahak, *Report: Arab Villages Destroyed in Israel,* 2nd ed. (Jerusalem: Shahak, 1975); Anita Shapira, *Land and Power: The Zionist Resort to Force* (Oxford: Oxford University Press, 1992); Avi Shlaim, *Collusion across the Jordan: King Abdullah, the Zionist Movement, and the Partition of Palestine* (New York: Columbia University Press, 1988).

10. The conference papers, with a number of additional invited papers, were published in Naseer Aruri, ed., *Palestinian Refugees and Their Right of Return* (London and Sterling, VA: Pluto Press, 2001).

11. Matthew Engel, "Senior Republican Calls on Israel to Expel West Bank Arabs," *Guardian,* May 4, 2002.

CHAPTER FOUR: "EXTERMINATE ALL THE BRUTES" GAZA 2009

1. Mouin Rabbani, "Birth Pangs of a New Palestine," Middle East Report Online, January 7, 2009, www.merip.org/mero/mero010709.html.

2. Uri Blau and Yotam Feldman, "How IDF Legal Experts Legitimized Strikes Involving Gaza Civilians," *Haaretz,* January 22, 2009; Yotam Feldman and Uri Blau, "Consent and Advise," *Haaretz,* January 29, 2009.

3. Sabrina Tavernise, "Rampage Shows Reach of Militants in Pakistan," *New York Times,* March 31, 2009; Feldman and Blau, "Consent and Advise."

4. Ethan Bronner, "Parsing Gains of Gaza War," *New York Times,* January 19, 2009. On the 1950s concept, "We will go crazy" (*nishtagea*) if crossed, see Chomsky, *Fateful Triangle: The United States, Israel, and the Palestinians* (Cambridge, MA: South End Press, 1999), 467f.

5. Craig Whitlock and Reyham Abdel Kareem, "Combat May Escalate in Gaza, Israel Warns; Operation in Densely Packed City, Camps Weighed," *Washington Post,* January 11, 2009.

6. For sources and details, see *Fateful Triangle,* and Cheryl Rubenberg, *Journal*

of Palestine Studies, special issue, "The War in Lebanon" vol. 11, no. 4–vol. 12, no. 1 (Summer–Autumn 1982): 62–68.

7.   Interview with General Mordechai Gur, *Al Hamishmar* (May 10, 1978), quoted in Noam Chomsky, *Towards a New Cold War* (New York: Pantheon, 1982), 320.

8.   Ze'ev Schiff, *Haaretz,* May 15, 1978.

9.   Eban quoted in *Jerusalem Post,* August 16, 1981. See also Meiron Benvinisti, *Sacred Landscape: The Buried History of the Holy Land since 1948* (Berkeley: University of California Press, 2000) and Ehud Sprinzak, *The Ascendance of Israel's Radical Right* (New York: Oxford University Press, 1991).

10.   Thomas Friedman, "Israel's Goals in Gaza?" *New York Times,* op-ed, January 14, 2009.

11.   Steven Erlanger, "Weighing Crimes and Ethics in the Fog of Urban Warfare," *New York Times,* January 17, 2009.

12.   Fawaz Gerges, "Gaza Notebook," *Nation,* January 16, 2009.

13.   Ethan Bronner, "Israel Lets Reporters See Devastated Gaza Site and Image of a Confident Military," *New York Times,* January 16, 2009; Chomsky, *Pirates and Emperors Old and New* (New York: Claremont Research and Publications, 1986; extended version, Boston: South End Press, 2002), 44f.

14.   Gerges, "Gaza Notebook."

15.   "Gaza Relief Boat Damaged in Encounter with Israeli Vessel," CNN.com, December 30, 2008, www.cnn.com/2008/WORLD/meast/12/30/gaza.aid .boat/index.html; "Mckinney on Boat in Gaza Crash," video, CNN.com, www.cnn.com/2008/WORLD/meast/12/30/gaza.aid.boat/index.html#cnnS TCVideo; "Israeli Patrol Boat Collides with Aid Ship off Gaza," Agence France-Presse December 30, 2008; Zeina Karam, "Gaza Protest Boat Sails into Lebanon," Associated Press (30 December 2008); "Israel Accused of Ramming Gaza Aid Ship," *Guardian Unlimited* (30 December 2008); and Stefanos Evripidou, "Gaza Mercy Mission Rammed by Israeli Navy," *Cyprus Mail,* December 31, 2008.

16.   See note 20, below. See also Gilbert Achcar, Noam Chomsky, and Stephen Shalom, *Perilous Power* (Boulder, CO: Paradigm, 2007), 239.

17.   "Arabs Fiddle and Squabble, Again, as Palestine Bleeds and Burns, Again," editorial, *Daily Star* (Lebanon), January 14, 2009.

18.   Amal Saad-Ghorayeb, "Will Hizbullah Intervene in the Gaza Conflict?" *Daily Star* (Lebanon), January 13, 2009 and Zeev Maoz, "The War of Double Standards," July 24, 2006, http://psfaculty.ucdavis.edu/zmaoz/The%20War %20of%20Double%20Standards.pdf.

19.   Ibid.

20.   Friedman, "Israel's Goals in Gaza?"; "Senator Kerry's Speech on the Middle East to the Brookings Institution," Senator Kerry's Online Office, release, http://kerry.senate.gov/cfm/record.cfm?id=309250, March 9, 2009; and *Pirates and Emperors,* 63, citing David Shipler, "Palestinians and Israelis

Welcome Their Prisoners Freed in Exchange," *New York Times*, November 25, 1983.

21. Idith Zertal and Akiva Eldar, *Lords of the Land* (New York: Nation Books, 2007), xii, 450.

22. Stefano Ambrogi, "U.S. Seeks Ship to Move Arms to Israel," Reuters, Alert-Net, January 9, 2009, www.alertnet.org/thenews/newsdesk/L9736369.htm.

23. Cited in Thalif Deen, "U.S. Weaponry Facilitates Killings in Gaza," Inter Press Service, January 8, 2009, http://ipsnews.net/news.asp?idnews=45337.

24. Cited in Nikos D.A. Arvanites, "U.S. Resupplying Israel from Port in Greece," Ekonom:east Media Group, January 13, 2009, www.emg.rs/en/news/region/75403.html.

25. Stephen Zunes, "Obama and Israel's Military: Still Arm-in-Arm," *Foreign Policy in Focus*, March 4, 2009, www.fpif.org/articles/obama_and_israels _military_still_arm-in-arm.

26. "US Cancels Israel Arms Shipment over Greek Objections," Agence France-Presse, January 13, 2009.

27. Quoted in Thalif Deen, "U.S. Weaponry Facilitates Killings in Gaza," Inter Press Service, January 8, 2009.

28. William Hartung and Frida Berrigan, "U.S. Weapons at War 2008: Beyond the Bush Legacy," NewAmerica.net, www.newamerica.net/publications/ policy/u_s_weapons_war_2008_0; Ali Gharib, "U.S. Arms Deployed in Wars Around the Globe," Inter Press Service, December 11, 2008; Jim Wolf, "U.S. Arms Sales Seen Booming in 2009," Reuters, December 15, 2008; and Geraldine Baum, "U.S. Opposes Arms Trade Treaty," *Los Angeles Times*, November 1, 2008.

29. Mads Gilbert, "Doctor Decries Israeli Attacks," video, YouTube.com, www. youtube.com/watch?v=Ev6ojm62qwA; and Bronner, "Parsing Gains of War in Gaza."

30. John Heilprin, "UN Contradicts Israel over Depth of Crisis in Gaza," Associated Press, January 6, 2009.

31. Ethan Bronner, "Israeli Attack Splits Gaza; Truce Calls Are Rebuffed," *New York Times*, January 4, 2009.

32. Quoted in Steven Lee Myers and Helene Cooper, "Gaza Crisis Is Another Challenge for Obama, Who Defers to Bush for Now," *New York Times*, December 29, 2008.

33. "22nd Day of Continuous IOF Attacks on the Gaza Strip," press release, Palestinian Centre for Human Rights, January 17, 2009. A later careful count revealed higher figures. "Israeli Troops Head Out of Devastated Gaza," Reuters, January 19, 2009; "IOF Unilaterally Ceases Fire; Redeploys inside Gaza—Dozens of Decomposed Bodies Found under Houses Rubble and Enormous Destruction in Neighborhoods," press release, Al Mezan Center for Human Rights, January 18, 2009.

34. Yoav Stern and Yossi Melman, "ABC: IAF Attacked 3 Times in Sudan," *Haaretz*, March 29; Charles Levinson and Jay Solomon, "U.S., Egypt Push Sudan about Arms," *Wall Street Journal*, March 29, 2009.

35. Akiva Eldar, "Israeli Rejection of Gaza Deal May Topple Abbas," Haaretz.com, January 9, 2009, www.haaretz.com/hasen/spages/1054143.html; quoted in Mark Landler, "U.S. Pact Seen as Step Toward Gaza Cease-Fire," *New York Times*, January 16, 2009.

36. Gerges, "Gaza Notebook."

37. Tobias Buck, "Gaza Offensive Boosted Hamas, Poll Concludes," *Financial Times*, February 6, 2009.

38. Andrew England, "Al-Jazeera Journalists Become the Faces of the Frontline," *Financial Times*, January 14, 2009; Noam Cohen, "Few in U.S. See Jazeera's Coverage of Gaza War,"*New York Times*, January 12, 2009.

39. If security of Israel were the concern, then the wall could be built at the Green Line, the internationally recognized border, and there would be no objections—except from Israelis whose free access to occupied territory would be impeded.

40. Quotes are from Chief of Staff Rafael Eitan and Prime Minister Yitzhak Shamir. See *Fateful Triangle* for these and other examples.

41. Charles Levinson, "Israelis Watch the Fighting in Gaza from a Hilly Vantage Point," *Wall Street Journal*, January 8, 2009. See also the photograph of orthodox Jews dancing on a hilltop, with the caption "From a hill just outside the Gaza Strip, Israelis watch the air assaults on Gaza and dance in celebration of the attacks, January 8, 2009. Newscom," at http://electronicintifada.net/v2/article10215.shtml.

42. Anshil Pfeffer, Haaretz.com, January 9, 2009, www.haaretz.co.il/hasite/spages/1056116.html (Hebrew). Matthew Wagner, "Rabbis Order Soldiers and Police to Refuse to Dismantle Outposts. But Major Insubordination Seen as Unlikely," *Jerusalem Post*, May 27, 2009. On the role of the religious nationalist Rabbis, see Zertal and Eldar, *Lords of the Land.* One of their most revered figures, Rabbi Tzvi Yehudah Kook, said, "we are in the middle of redemption," and the state is "entirely sacred and without blemish," extending over the entire Land of Israel; quoted in Gershom Gorenberg, *The Accidental Empire* (New York: Times Books, 2006), 275.

43. Alan Dershowitz, "Lebanon Is Not a Victim," *Huffington Post*, August 7, 2006, www.huffingtonpost.com/alan-dershowitz/lebanon-is-not-a-victim_b_26715.html?view=print; Alan Dershowitz (video), www.youtube.com/watch?v=HCShwgO6M1M.

44. Ehud Olmert, speech to Joint Session of (U.S.) Congress, May 24, 2006. For full transcript, see "Address by Prime Minister Ehud Olmert to Joint meeting of US Congress," Embassy of Israel Web site, www.israelnewsagency.com/israelolmertcongress48480524.html.

45. Likud Party platform, see the Knesset website, www.knesset.gov.il/elections/knesset15/elikud_m.htm.

46. In an interview in Israel as he was resigning under corruption charges, Olmert withdrew all his previous positions, accepting the international consensus for the first time. Ethan Bronner, "Olmert Says Israel Should Pull Out of West Bank," *New York Times*, September 30, 2008. It is hard to know what to make of this, since his subsequent actions continued to conform to his illegal expansionist programs.

47. *Report on Israeli Settlements*, Foundation for Middle East Peace, January–February 2009; Ghassan Bannoura, "Report: Peace Now Annual Settlement Report Shows an Increase of Constructions," International Middle East Media Center, January 28, 2009; Mark Landler, "Clinton Expresses Doubts about an Iran-U.S. Thaw," *New York Times*, March 3, 2009, A6; Sara Miller, "Peace Now: Israel Planning 73,300 New Homes in West Bank," *Haaretz*, March 2, 2009. Miller notes Knesset member Yaakov Katz of the right-wing National Union Party, who is expected to join Netanyahu's cabinet in April 2009, told Army Radio, "We will make every effort to realize the plans outlined by [Peace Now official Yariv] Oppenheimer...I expect that, with God's help, this will all happen in the next few years, and there will be one state here." What is critical, as always, is how much help he can expect from Washington. On the modes of settlement expansion, see Zertal and Eldar, *Lords of the Land*. On expanding "rings of land," see B'Tselem, *Access Denied: Israeli Measures to Deny Palestinians Access to Land around Settlements*, September 2008, www.btselem.org/english/Publications/Summaries/200809_Access_Denied.asp.

48. Quoted in Gorenberg, *Accidental Empire*, 82. Yossi Beilin, *Mehiro shel Ihud* (Tel-Aviv: Revivim, 1985), 42, an important review of cabinet records under the Labor governments that held power until 1977.

49. Quoted in Gorenberg, *Accidental Empire*, 99f, 110–1, 173. For careful analysis of the court decisions, see Norman Finkelstein, *Beyond Chutzpah* (Berkeley and Los Angeles: University of California Press, 2008, expanded paperback edition), postscript, 227–70.

50. Ran HaCohen, "Pacifying Gaza," Antiwar.com, December 31, 2008, http://antiwar.com/hacohen/?articleid=13970.

51. Shlomo Avineri, *Haaretz*, March 18, 2003. Perhaps this was intended as irony, though it seems not. It is often hard to tell. The term in Hebrew for Israeli propaganda is *hasbara* (explanation). Since whatever Israel does is necessarily right and just, it is only necessary to explain it to confused outsiders.

52. Ari Shavit, "Gaza Op May Be Squeezing Hamas, but It's Destroying Israel's Soul," *Haaretz*, January 16, 2009.

53. "UN Press Conference on Gaza Humanitarian Situation," United Nations, January 15, 2009, www.un.org/News/briefings/docs/2009/090115_Gaza.doc.htm.

Tobias Buck, Andrew England, and Heba Saleh, "Assault Kills Top Hamas Leader," *Financial Times*, January 15, 2009. Al Jazeera, "Gazans Count the Cost of War," January 16, 2009, http://english.aljazeera.net/news/middleeast/2009/01/2009116144139351463.html; Tamer Saliba and Patrick Quinn, "UN Says Gaza Faces Humanitarian Catastrophe," Associated Press, January 16, 2009.

54.   Amnesty International, "Israel/Occupied Palestinian Territories: Israel's Use of White Phosphorus Against Gaza Civilians 'Clear and Undeniable,'" January 19, 2009, www.amnesty.org/en/for-media/press-releases/israeloccupied -palestinian-territories-israel039s-use-white-phosphorus-a; and "Foreign- supplied Weapons Used Against Civilians by Israel and Hamas," February 20, 2009, www.amnesty.org/en/news-and-updates/foreign-supplied-weapons -used-against-civilians-israel-and-hamas-20090220. AI also called for an embargo on Hamas, but that is clearly meaningless.

55.   Sheera Frenkel, "Amnesty International: Gaza White Phosphorus Shells Were US Made," *Times* (London) online, February 24, 2009, www.timesonline .co.uk/tol/news/world/middle_east/article5792182.ece; "Amnesty Interna- tional Says Israel Misused US-Supplied Weapons in Gaza," VOA news, Feb- ruary 23, 2009, www.voanews.com/english/2009-02-23-voa17.cfm.

56.   Peter Beaumont, "Gaza Desperately Short of Food after Israel Destroys Farmland," *Observer*, February 1, 2009; Donald Macintyre, "An Assault on the Peace Process," *Independent*, January 26, 2009.

57.   IRIN—UN Office for Coordination of Humanitarian Affairs, "Tough Times for University Students in Gaza," March 26, 2009, www.irinnews.org/ PrintReport.aspx?ReportId=83655.

58.   Gideon Levy, "The Ebb, the Tide, the Sighs," *Haaretz*, November 16, 2008; "Al Mezan Center Condemns the Escalation of Israeli Violations against Palestinian Fishers and Calls on the International Community to Act, and Civil Society to Intensify its Solidarity Campaigns," Al Mezan Center for Human Rights, press release, March 25, 2009, www.mezan.org/en/details .php?id=8594&ddname=fishermen&id_dept=9&id2=9&p=center; Inter- national Solidarity Movement, "Gazan Coast Becoming a 'No-go' Zone," February 16, 2009; "Gaza Marine Project—and Who Owns It?" video, www.youtube.com/watch?v=cyPtd6qKLVE&feature=channel_page.

59.   *Platts Commodity News*, February 3, 2000. See also *Platts Commodity News*, December 3, 2008; "Israel Power Firm Sends Top Team to London for Talks with BG," *Platt's Commodity News*, February 16, 2009, reporting that IEC "is sending a high level delegation to London for talks with BG on purchase of natural gas from the Marine Gaza field"; *Economist Intelligence Unit*, January 20; Amotz Àsa-El, "Gas Discovery Tempers Israeli Recession Blues," *Market Watch* (Jerusalem), January 27, 2009; Steve Hawkes and Sonia Verma (Jerusalem), "BG Group at Centre of $4bn Deal to Supply Gaza Gas to Israel,"

Times (London), May 23, 2007; Michel Chossudovsky, "War and Natural Gas: The Israeli Invasion and Gaza's Offshore Gas Fields," Center for Research on Globalization, January 8, 2009, www.globalresearch.ca/index.php ?context=va&aid=11680. Also Martin Barillas, "Massive Natural Gas Deposits Found Off Israel," January 19, 2009, SperoNews, www.speroforum.com/a/ 17732/Massive-natural-gas-deposits-found-off-Isr.

60. See "Good News, Iraq and Beyond," chap. 5 in *Hopes and Prospects* (Chicago: Haymarket, 2010).

61. "Apocalypse Near," Noam Chomsky, interview by Merav Yudilovitch, *Ynet*, August 4, 2006, www.ynetnews.com/articles/0,7340,L-3286204,00.html.

62. Ali Abunimah, "We Have No Words Left," *Guardian*, December 29, 2008. Mustapha Barghouti, "Palestine's Guernica and the Myths of Israeli Victimhood," http://palestinethinktank.com/2008/12/29/mustafa-barghouti-palestines-guernica-and-the-myths-of-israeli-victimhood/, December 29, 2008.

63. Hillary Clinton's stern admonition when Israel demolished eighty more Arab homes in East Jerusalem in Sue Pleming and Mohammed Assadi, "Clinton Criticises Israel over E. Jerusalem Demolition," Reuters, March 4, 2009.

64. Among others, on Hamas see Ismail Haniyeh, "Aggression Under False Pretenses," *Washington Post*, July 11, 2006; Khalid Mish'al, "Our Unity Can Now Pave the Way for Peace and Justice," *Guardian*, February 13, 2007. Guy Dinmore and Najmeh Bozorgmehr, "Iran 'Accepts Two-state Answer' in Mideast," *Financial Times*, September 2, 2006; "Leader Attends Memorial Ceremony Marking the 17th Departure Anniversary of Imam Khomeini," The Center for Preserving and Publishing the Works of Grand Ayatollah Sayyid Ali Khamenei, June 4, 2006, http://english.khamenei.ir/index.php ?option=com_content&task=view&id=442&Itemid=2. See also Iran scholar Ervand Abrahamian, "Khamenei Has Said Iran Would Agree to Whatever the Palestinians Decide," in David Barsamian, ed., *Targeting Iran* (San Francisco: City Lights, 2007), 112. Hassan Nasrallah has repeatedly expressed the same position.

65. For brief review of the record, and sources, see *Failed States*. See further Norman Finkelstein, *Image and Reality of the Israel-Palestine Conflict* (London: Verso, 1996; new edition 2003). For a detailed critical analysis of Israel's security strategy from the outset, revealing clearly the preference for expansion over security and diplomatic settlement, see Zeev Maoz, *Defending the Holy Land* (Ann Arbor: University of Michigan Press, 2006).

66. Ethan Bronner, "Gaza War Role Is Political Lift for Ex-Premier," *New York Times*, January 8, 2009.

67. See *Failed States*, 193ff.

68. Gareth Porter, "Israel Rejected Hamas Ceasefire Offer in December," Inter Press Service, January 9, 2009, www.ipsnews.net/print.asp?idnews=45350. For detailed analysis of the record of violation of cease-fires in the past

decade, see Nancy Kanwisher, Johannes Haushofer, and Anat Biletzki, "Reigniting Violence: How Do Ceasefires End?" *Huffington Post*, January 6, 2009, www.huffingtonpost.com/nancy-kanwisher/reigniting-violence-how-d _b_155611.html. Their analysis "shows that it is overwhelmingly Israel that kills first after a pause in the conflict…Indeed, it is virtually always Israel that kills first after a lull lasting more than a week."

69. Dion Nissenbaum, "Israeli Ban on Sending Pasta to Gaza Illustrates Frictions," McClatchy Newspapers, February 25, 2009; Joshua Mitnick and Charles Levinson, "World News: Peace Holds in Gaza; U.N. Chief Blasts Israel," *Wall Street Journal*, January 21, 2009; and many others. On Hamas post-invasion truce offers, reiterating those rejected by Israel before the attack, see Khaled Abu Toameh, "Haniyeh: Hamas will consider cease-fire initiatives. Fatah official says leader in hiding has 'raised the white flag,'" *Jerusalem Post*, January 13, 2009; Stephen Gutkin, "Hamas Officials Signal Willingness to Negotiate," Associated Press, January 29, 2009. On Israel's rejection of truce offers shortly before the attack, see Porter, "Israel Rejected Hamas Ceasefire"; Peter Beaumont, "Israel PM's Family Link to Hamas Peace Bid: Olmert Rejected Palestinian Attempts to Set Up Talks through Go-Between Before Gaza Invasion," *Observer*, March 1, 2009, 33.

70. Amos Harel and Avi Issacharoff, "IDF Carries Out First Arrest in Gaza Strip Since Pullout," *Haaretz*, June 24, 2006, www.haaretz.com/news/idf-carries -out-first-arrest-in-gaza-strip-since-pullout-1.191233; Caleb Carr, "A War of Escalating Errors," *Los Angeles Times*, August 12, 2006. Noam Chomsky, *Interventions* (San Francisco: City Lights, 2007), 188.

71. Howard Friel and Richard Falk, *Israel-Palestine On Record* (New York: Verso, 2007), 136, citing Human Rights Watch, June 30, 2006.

72. Quoted in Jeremy Bowen, "Bowen Diary: The Days Before War," BBC News, January 10, 2009, http://news.bbc.co.uk/2/hi/middle_east/7822048.stm.

73. Regev interviewed by David Fuller, Channel 4, UK, (video), www.youtube .com/watch?v=N6e-elrgYL0. Editorial, "The Other Israel," *Holon Israel*, December 2008–January 2009.

74. Rory McCarthy, "Gaza Truce Broken as Israeli Raid Kills Six Hamas Gunmen," *Guardian*, November 5, 2008.

75. David Rose, "The Gaza Bombshell," *Vanity Fair*, April 2008. Norman Olsen, "An Inside Story of How the US Magnified Palestinian Suffering,"*Christian Science Monitor*, January 12, 2009.

76. Ethan Bronner, "U.S. Helps Palestinians Build Force for Security," *New York Times*, February 27, 2009. Kerry, "Speech on the Middle East."

77. On the origins of these methods in the Philippines after the U.S. invading army destroyed the popular forces that had effectively liberated the country from Spanish rule, slaughtering hundreds of thousands of Filipinos in the process, and the ways in which these new methods fed back to imposing

surveillance and population control at home, see Alfred McCoy, *Policing America's Empire: the United States, the Philippines, and the Rise of the Surveillance State* (Madison, WI: University of Wisconsin Press, 2009). Among other studies, see Martha Huggins, *Political Policing: the United States and Central America* (Chapel Hill, NC: Duke University Press, 1998); Patrice McSherry, *Predatory States: Operation Condor and Covert War in Latin America* (Lanham, MD: Rowman & Littlefield, 2005).

78. Sara Roy, "If Gaza Falls..." *London Review of Books*, January 1, 2009, 26; Sara Roy, "Israel's 'Victories' in Gaza Come at a Steep Price," *Christian Science Monitor*, January 2, 2009; Physicians for Human Rights–Israel, Emergency Gaza Update 28.12.2008, www.phr.org.il/default.asp?PageID=190&ItemID=430.

79. Porter, "Israel Rejected Hamas"; Beaumont, "Israel PM's family link to Hamas peace bid," *Observer* (UK), March 1, 2009.

80. Akiva Eldar, "White Flag, Black Flag," *Haaretz*, January 5, 2009, www.haaretz.com/hasen/spages/1052621.html.

81. David Remnick, "Homelands," *New Yorker*, January 12, 2009.

82. See *Fateful Triangle*, 201ff. *Pirates and Emperors*, 56f.

83. Stephen Lee Myers, "The New Meaning of an Old Battle," *New York Times*, January 4, 2009.

84. David Ben-Gurion, "the strongman of the Yishuv...accepted the UN partition plan, but he did not accept as final the borders it laid down for the Jewish state," expecting them to be established by "a clear-cut Jewish military victory." Avi Shlaim, *The Iron Wall* (New York: W.W. Norton, 2000), 28–9. In internal discussion Ben-Gurion made it clear that "there are no final arrangements in history, there are no eternal borders, and there are no ultimate political claims. Changes and transformations will still occur in the world." We accepted the loss of Trans-Jordan (Jordan), but "we have the right to the whole of western Palestine," and "we want the Land of Israel in its entirety." Uri Ben-Eliezer, *The Making of Israeli Militarism* (Bloomington: Indiana University Press, 1998), 150–1.

85. Maoz, *Defending the Holy Land*, 103.

86. Chomsky, *Towards a New Cold War*, 461–462n, citing *Toldot HaHaganah*, vol. 2, 251f. He was accused of "pathological" behavior for referring (correctly) to the opposition of native-born Jews to Zionism (and for homosexuality).

87. Amnesty International, "Gaza Ceasefire at Risk," November 5, 2008, www.amnesty.org/en/news-and-updates/news/gaza-ceasefire-at+risk-20081105.

88. *Fateful Triangle*, 64f. For substantial evidence supporting this conclusion, see Maoz, *Defending the Holy Land*.

89. Andrew Cordesman, "The War in Gaza: Tactical Gains, Strategic Defeat?" Center for Strategic and International Studies. January 9, 2009, http://csis.org/publication/war-gaza. For Turki al-Faisal's own words, see "Saudi Arabia's

Patience Is Running Out" *Financial Times*, January 23, 2009.

90.   Uri Avnery, "How Many Divisions?" Gush Shalom–Israeli Peace Bloc, January 10, 2009, http://zope.gush-shalom.org/home/en/channels/avnery/1231625457.

91.   Baruch Kimmerling, *Politicide: Ariel Sharon's War against the Palestinians* (London: Verso, 2003).

CHAPTER FIVE: BLUEPRINT FOR A ONE-STATE MOVEMENT A TROUBLED HISTORY

1.   See Ilan Pappé, *A History of Modern Palestine; One Country, Two Peoples*, 2nd ed. (Cambridge: Cambridge University Press, 2006), 115–16.

2.   I have written on the minority report in Ilan Pappé, *The Making of the Arab-Israeli Conflict, 1947-1951* (London and New York: I. B. Tauris, 2001), 16–46.

3.   United Nations Archives, UNSCOP Verbatim Report in United Nations General Assembly Files, Second Session, August–November 1947.

4.   See Ali Abuminah, *One Country: A Bold Proposal to End the Israeli-Palestinian Impasse* (New York: Holt McDougal 2007); Ghada Karmi, *Married to Another Man: Israel's Dilemma in Palestine* (London: Pluto Press, 2007); Joel Kovel, *Overcoming Zionism: Creating a Single Democratic State in Israel/Palestine* (London: Pluto Press, 2007); and Jamil Hilal, ed., *Where Now for Palestine? The Demise of the Two-State Solution* (London: Zed Books 2007).

5.   The Web site of that campaign is the Palestinian Campaign for the Academic & Cultural Boycott of Israel, www.pacbi.org.

6.   See Meron Benvisiti, "The Binationalism Vogue," *Haaretz*, April 30, 2009. This was written as a response to the March 2009 Boston conference declaration.

7.   The Italian journalist and writer Paolo Barnard is the senior political correspondent of RAI and he posted seven short clips titled "Palestine-Israel: the Missing Narratives," on YouTube in May 2009.

8.   Shimon Peres, *Now and Tomorrow* (Tel-Aviv: Mabat Books, 1978), 20.

9.   See David Landau, "Maximum Jews, Minimum Arabs," *Haaretz*, November 13, 2003.

CHAPTER SIX: THE GHETTOIZATION OF PALESTINE

1.   "UN Expert: Palestinian Terror 'Inevitable' Result of Occupation," Associated Press, November 15, 2009, www.haaretz.com/hasen/spages/958358 .html; "Situation in the Gaza Strip: Policy of Isolation Has Failed, Say MEPs," February 21, 2008, United Nations Information System on the Question of Palestine, http://unispal.un.org/UNISPAL.NSF/0/7B4D40F E41CDCB91852573FB0057F9F0; "Palestinians Suspend Contact with Israel," Sky News online, March 2, 2008, http://news.sky.com/skynews/Home/ Sky-News-Archive/Article/20080641307601.

2. Yossi Beilin, *Mehiro shel Ihud* (Revivim, 1985).

3. Michael Walzer, "On Arabs and Jews: The Chimera of a Binational State," *Dissent* XIX, no. 3 (Summer 1972): 492–99, quote page 497.

4. Alan Dershowitz (video), www.youtube.com/watch?v=HCShwgO6M1M.

5. Barak Ravid, "Israel to Boycott 'Durban II' Anti-racism Conference," November 21, 2008, Haaretz.com, www.haaretz.com/hasen/spages/1038984.html.

6. "Israeli Diplomat Postpones Meeting after Costa Rica Recognizes Palestinian State," Associated Press, February 27, 2008, www.haaretz.com/hasen/spages/958208.html.

7. "Views of China and Russia Decline in Global Poll," BBC World Service, February 6, 2009, www.worldpublicopinion.org/pipa/pdf/feb09/BBCEvals_Feb09_rpt.pdf.

8. "Israeli PM Olmert Addresses Congress," address transcript from CQ Transcriptions, Inc., printed in *Washington Post*, May 24, 2006, www.washingtonpost.com/wp-dyn/content/article/2006/05/24/AR2006052401420.html. The applause levels are recorded in the transcript.

9. Amir Oren, "Who's the Boss?" *Haaretz*, November 29, 2002, www.haaretz.com/print-edition/features/who-s-the-boss-1.26841.

10. See Glenn Kessler, The Trail blog, washingtonpost.com, June 5, 2008, http://blog.washingtonpost.com/44/2008/06/05/obama_backtracks_on_jerusalem.html.

11. See *Z Magazine*, February 2008. See also my *Hopes and Prospects* (Chicago, Haymarket Books: 2010).

12. See "Obama on Israel-Palestine," ZNet, January 25, 2009, www.zcommunications.org/obama-on-israel-palestine-by-noam-chomsky-1. See also my *Hopes and Prospects* (Chicago: Haymarket Books, 2010).

13. "Gaza: From Blockade to Bloodshed," editorial, *Guardian*, June 1, 2010, www.guardian.co.uk/commentisfree/2010/jun/01/gaza-blockade-bloodshed-editorial.

CHAPTER SEVEN: THE KILLING FIELDS OF GAZA 2004–2009

1. On the plans to establish the dummy city see the daily *Globes* (in Hebrew), May 20, 2002 (planning actually began in 2002); there is also an interesting report of a soldier who participated in the training on the blog on November 7, 2009, www.Dacho.co.il/showthered.php; see also the IDF's own announcement on its website an article by Ido Elazar, www.1.idf.il/elram.

2. See Ilan Pappé, "Responses to Gaza," *London Review of Books* 21, no. 2 (January 29, 2009): 5–6.

3. Ibid.

4. Breaking the Silence, *Report on Gaza*, July 15, 2009. The NGO has a Web site, www.shovrimshtika.org, where this report is available and has also published

a ninety-six-page booklet entitled *Soldiers' Testimonies from Operation Cast Lead: Gaza 2009*.

5.   John Dugard, *Report of the Special Rapporteur on the Situation of Human Rights in the Palestinian Territories Occupied by Israel since 1967*, UN Commission on Human Rights (Geneva: United Nations, March 3, 2005).

6.   See *Yediot Ahronoth* for an analysis by the Israeli journalist Roni Sofer on September 27, 2005.

7.   Avi Isaacharoff and Amos Harel, "Analysis: Gaza Gains Have Softened Israel Stance on Shalit Deal," *Haaretz*, January 25, 2009, www.haaretz.com/print -edition/news/analysis-gaza-gains-have-softened-israel-stance-on-shalit-deal -1.268774 .

8.   See the report by Amir Buhbut and Uri Glickman "The IDF Had Attacked in Gaza," *Maariv*, September 25, 2005.

9.   Several generals and ex-generals expressed this view in a collection of articles in a strategic journal published by the Israeli Institute for National Security Studies, *Adkan Estrategi* (Strategic Update) 11, no. 4 (February 2009).

10.   Amos Harel and Avi Issacharoff, "One Humiliation Too Many," *Haaretz*, July 13, 2006.

11.   Ilan Pappé, "Ingathering," *London Review of Books* 28, no. 8 (April 20, 2006): 15.

12.   Yehuda Ben Meir and Daphna Shaked, "Public Opinion and National Security," *Adkan Estrategi* 10, no. 1 (June 2007): 25–8.

13.   See Ilan Pappé, *The Ethnic Cleansing of Palestine* (Oxford: Oneworld Publications, 2006).

14.   Sean McBride et al., *Israel in Lebanon: The Report of the International Commission to Enquire into Reported Violations of International Law by Israel during Its Invasion of Lebanon* (London: Ithaca Press, 1983).

15.   See the United Nations Office for the Coordination of Humanitarian Affairs (OCHA) Special Report of August 2007.

16.   B'Tselem, "683 People Killed in the Conflict in 2006," press release, December 28, 2006, www.btselem.org/english/Press_Releases/20061228.asp.

17.   Ibid.

18.   See "Operation Autumn Clouds Has Ended," *Maariv*'s summary of the operation on November 7, 2006.

19.   Gabi Siboni, "The Third Threat," *Haaretz*, September 30, 2009.

20.   Breaking the Silence, "Report on Cast Lead Operation," July 15, 2009.

21.   B'Tselem, "Gaza: Power and Water Cuts and Bread Shortage," press release, November 27, 2008, www.btselem.org/English/Gaza_Strip/20081127_More _Sanctions_on_Gaza.asp; and B'Tselem, "B'Tselem to Attorney General Mazuz: Concern over Israel Targeting Civilian Objects in the Gaza Strip," press release, December 31, 2008, www.btselem.org/English/Gaza_Strip/ 20081231_Gaza_Letter_to_Mazuz.asp.

22.   "Israel Accused of Gaza Genocide," Al-Jazeera, January 14, 2009, http://

english.aljazeera.net/news/americas/2009/01/200911321467988347.html.

23. Quoted in Nurgul Bulbul, "Oktay Akbal: Israel Commits Genocide in Gaza," *Turkish Weekly*, January 5, 2009.

24. Egeland and Eliasson quoted in John Pilger, "Terror and Starvation in Gaza," *New Statesman*, January 22, 2007, www.newstatesman.com/media/2007/01/pilger-genocide-gaza-palestine.

25. Richard Falk, "Slouching Towards a Palestinian Holocaust," Transnational Foundation for Peace and Future Research, June 29, 2007, www.transnational .org/Area_MiddleEast/2007/Falk_PalestineGenocide.html.

26. "World Stands United Against 'Genocide' in Gaza," Al-Arabiya, December 28, 2008, www.alarabiya.net/articles/2008/12/28/62977.html.

27. Ibid.

28. Quoted in several places; see, for instance, Morton A Klein, "Ya'alon: We Need Chuchills, not Chamberlains," JewishPress, May 17, 2006, www.jewishpress .com/printArticle.cfm?contentid=17947.

CHAPTER EIGHT: A MIDDLE EAST PEACE THAT COULD HAPPEN (BUT WON'T)

1. Amira Hass, "An Israeli Achievement," BitterLemons.org, April 20, 2009, www.bitterlemons.org/previous/bl200409ed15.html#isr2.

2. Sara Roy, *Harvard Crimson*, June 2, 2009. For extensive review of the ugly details, see Roy's "Before Gaza, After Gaza: Examining the New Reality in Israel/Palestine," to appear in *Palestine & the Palestinians Today*, Center for Contemporary Arab Studies, Georgetown University. Abbreviated version of introduction to third edition of Roy, *Gaza Strip*.

3. See *Hopes and Prospects* (Chicago: Haymarket Books, 2010), pp. 150f and sources cited in note 16, chap. 6.

4. Peter Beaumont, "Gazans Look for a Place to Breathe by the Sea," *Guardian*, May 27, 2009.

5. "Israel Lets Power Firm Seek More Gaza Gas to Diversify Supplies," *Platt's Commodity News*, February 3, 2009; "Israeli Power Firm Sends Top Team to London for Gas Talks with BG," *Platt's Commodity News*, February 16, 2009.

6. For sources, and more on Evans's role in this regard, see *Year 501* (New York: South End Press, 1999), chap. 4; *Powers and Prospects* (New York: South End Press, 1999), chaps. 7 and 8. Also Australian Southeast Asian specialist and former intelligence officer Clinton Fernandes's review of Evans's record, 2009, MS.

7. International Commission on Intervention and State Sovereignty, Gareth Evans and Mohamed Sahnoun, Co-chairs, *The Responsibility to Protect: Report of the ICISS* (Ottawa, Canada: IDRC Books, December 2001). Gareth Evans, "An Idea Whose Time Has Come—and Gone," *Economist*, July 23,

2009. See "Human Rights in the New Millennium," talk at London School of Economics (October 29, 2009), www.chomsky.info/talks/20091029.htm; *Z Magazine*, January 2010; www.chomsky.info. Evans-Alatas photo there and at Edward Herman and David Peterson, "The Responsibility to Protest, the International Criminal Court, and *Foreign Policy in Focus*," MRZine, August 24, 2009, http://mrzine.monthlyreview.org/hp240809.html.

8. Avi Issacharoff, "World Bank: Aid Isn't Enough to Spark Palestinian Growth," *Haaretz*, May 6, 2009. Associated Press, May 6, 2009; Reuters, May 7, 2009; For analysis of the harsh and deterioriating conditions, see Nadim Kawach, International Solidarity Movement, January 17, 2010, http://palsolidarity .org/2010/01/10761.

9. Beilin, *Mehiro shel Ihud*, 42–3.

10. Quoted in Barak Ravid, "Israeli Ministers: No West Bank Settlement Freeze," *Haaretz*, May 31, 2009.

11. The first revelation to the general public of Israel's U.S.-backed rejection of the "road map"—it was known and discussed in activist circles—is in Jimmy Carter's book *Palestine: Peace Not Apartheid* (New York: Simon & Schuster, 2006). The "reservations" are given in an appendix. The book aroused a storm of protest. As far as I could determine, this important section—the one revelation new to the general informed public—was not mentioned. There were great efforts to find trivial errors, but the one serious error was also ignored: Carter's repetition of the conventional myth that Israel's 1982 invasion of Lebanon was in defense against PLO rockets, already discussed. See *Hopes and Prospects*, 153–54, and note 21, chap. 6.

12. Quoted in *Hadashot*, October 8, 1993; Yair Fidel, *Hadashot Supplement*, October 29, 1993.

13. Helene Cooper, "U.S. Weighs Tactics on Israeli Settlement," *New York Times*, June 1, 2009.

14. Isabel Kershner, "Israel and U.S. Can't Close Split on Settlements," *New York Times*, June 2, 2009.

15. Akiva Eldar, "Border Control/Nothing Natural about It," *Haaretz*, June 2, 2009.

16. Jackson Diehl, "Abbas's Waiting Game on Peace with Israel," *Washington Post*, May 29, 2009.

17. Karen DeYoung and Howard Schneider, "Israel Putting Forth 'Unprecedented' Concessions, Clinton Says," *Washington Post*, November 1, 2009.

18. Geneva Accord, October 31, 2003, Electronic Intifada, Historical Documents. See also Menachem Klein, *A Possible Peace Between Israel and Palestine: An Insider's Account of the Geneva Initiative* (New York: Columbia University Press, 2007).

19. Ed Hornick, "Obama Looks to Reach the Soul of the Muslim World," CNN, June 3, 2009, http://edition.cnn.com/2009/POLITICS/06/03/obama.muslim .outreach; Thomas Friedman, "Obama Speech Aimed at Both Arabs and Is-

raelis," *New York Times*, June 3, 2009.

20. David Bar-Illan, director of Communications and Policy Planning in the office of the prime minister, interview, *Palestine-Israel Journal*, Summer/ Autumn 1996.

21. Jeff Zeleny and Michael Slackman, "As Obama Begins Trip, Arabs Want Israeli Gesture," *New York Times*, June 4, 2009.

INDEX

"Passim" (literally "scattered") indicates intermittent discussion of a topic over a cluster of pages.

the Silence
Siboni, Gabi, 189
Silver, Aba Hillel, 34
Sinai, 17, 123
Sizer, Stephen, 28–29
Sneh, Ephraim, 76
Sofer, Arnon, 76
Somalia, 168
South Africa, 15, 143, 147–48, 160,
    161, 163, 197
Soviet Union, 43, 51, 52, 127, 128, 137
Standard Oil, 41
Straits of Tiran, 115
Sudan, 101
Suez Crisis, 37
Summer Rains. *See* Operation
    Summer Rains
Syria, 31, 32, 96, 122

T

Taba, Egypt, 14, 112, 157, 159, 196
Tal-Shahar, 48
Tantura, 65, 66
Tel Aviv, 98, 102
Tel Aviv University, 80
Tel-Megiddo, 25
Texas, 25
Thatcher, Ronald, 27
Theory of International Politics
    (Waltz), 48
Timor Gap Treaty, 202
Transjordan, 61, 68
Truman, Harry, 33–34, 152
Tul Karem, 178
Turkey, 30, 31
Twain, Mark, 24

U

UN. *See* United Nations
US. *See* United States

USSR. *See* Soviet Union
Ukraine, 93
Um Khaled, 65
United Kingdom. *See* Great Britain
United Nations, 33–39 passim, 60–66
    passim, 83, 87–94 passim, 112,
    184, 191; Durban human rights
    conference, 148–49; Gaza City
    compound, 105; Security
    Council, 82, 88, 94–98 passim,
    106, 111, 195, 205. *See also*
    World Food Programme
United Nations Human Rights
    Council, 146
United Nations Relief and Works
    Agency for Palestine Refugees in
    the Near East (UNRWA), 81,
    105, 106, 115
United Nations Special Committee on
    Palestine (UNSCOP), 127
United States, 18–56 passim, 70–76
    passim, 81–97 passim, 101–7
    passim, 111–23 passim, 129,
    146–63 passim, 168, 169, 189,
    195–209 passim; and Iraq, 109;
    Jews in, 36, 64; Pax Americana,
    137–38; State Department,
    32–34 passim, 39, 45, 48, 60, 112,
    117. *See also* CIA; Democratic
    Party; Republican Party
University and College Union, 14
University of Bogazici, 30

V

Versailles, 30, 31

W

Wall Street Journal, 207
Walt, Stephen, 19, 21, 46, 47
Waltz, Kenneth, 48

Walzer, Michael, 148
Washington Institute for Near East
        Policy, 38, 40, 44, 47
Weissman, Keith, 40
Weizmann, Chaim, 34, 41
White, Haden, 20
Wilson, Woodrow, 30, 31, 32
Wolfowitz, Paul, 47
World Bank, 202
World Court, 98, 103, 150
World Food Programme, 199
World Health Organization, 118
World Social Forum, 18
World Trade Center, 17

Y
Ya'alon, Moshe, 194

Z
Zaitun, 107
Zertal, Idith, 90, 99
Zimbabwe, 92
Zipori, 62
Zochrot, 77
Zu'ubi, Hanin, 164
Zunes, Stephen, 91

ABOUT THE CONTRIBUTORS

ILAN PAPPÉ is professor of history at the University of Exeter and is the author of *The Ethnic Cleansing of Palestine*, *A History of Modern Palestine*, and *The Israel/Palestine Question*.

NOAM CHOMSKY is Institute Professor (Emeritus) of Linguistics and Philosophy at the Massachusetts Institute of Technology. He is the author of numerous books, including the *New York Times* bestsellers *Hegemony or Survival* and *Failed States*, and *Hopes and Prospects*.

FRANK BARAT is a human rights activist. He lives in London, UK. He is the coordinator of the Russell Tribunal on Palestine. He has written for the Electronic Intifada, CounterPunch, *Zmagazine*, the *New Internationalist*, the *Palestine Chronicle*, *State of Nature*, and other Web sites and publications.

ALSO FROM HAYMARKET BOOKS

Between the Lines:
Readings on Israel, the Palestinians, and the U.S. "War on Terror"
Tikva Honig-Parnass and Toufic Haddad • This compilation of essays, edited by
a Palestinian writer and an Israeli journalist, constitutes a challenge to critically
rethink the Israeli-Palestinian conflict. • ISBN 9781931859448

Hopes and Prospects
Noam Chomsky • Exploring challenges such as the growing gap between North and
South, the fiascos of Iraq and Afghanistan, the U.S.-Israeli assault on Gaza, and the recent financial bailouts, he also sees hope for the future and a way to move forward—
in the democratic wave in Latin America and in the global solidarity movements that
suggest "real progress toward freedom and justice." • ISBN 9781931859967

The Struggle for Palestine
Edited by Lance Selfa • *The Struggle for Palestine* gets behind the myths about the occupation to expose the role of the U.S. government in sponsoring Israel's war against
the Palestinians. It documents the efforts of Palestinians to win their freedom, and it
presents a clear vision of a real solution: the creation of a secular, democratic state in
all of Palestine. • ISBN 9781931859004

The Palestine Communist Party 1919–1948:
Arab and Jew in the Struggle for Internationalism
Musa Budeiri • This history of the Palestinian Communist Party shows how the
complex history of the Palestinian Left before the Zionist destruction of historic
Palestine was defined by secularism and solidarity between Arab and Jewish work-
ers. With a new introduction and afterword by the author. • ISBN 9781608460724

The Pen and the Sword: Conversations with Edward Said
David Barsamian, introductions by Eqbal Ahmad and Nubar Hovsepian • Gathered
here are five wide-ranging interviews with the internationally renowned Palestinian
scholar and critic Edward Said, covering the Israeli-Palestinian conflict; Said's
groundbreaking work of literary scholarship, *Orientalism*; music; and much more. •
ISBN 9781931859950

Boycott, Divestment, Sanctions: The Civil Struggle for Palestinian Rights
Omar Barghouti • International boycott, divestment, and sanctions (BDS) efforts
helped topple South Africa's brutal apartheid regime. Omar Barghouti makes the
case for a rights-based BDS campaign to stop Israel's rapacious occupation and
colonization of the Palestinian people. • Spring 2011 • ISBN 9781608461141

ABOUT HAYMARKET BOOKS

Haymarket Books is a nonprofit, progressive book distributor and publisher, a project of the Center for Economic Research and Social Change. We believe that activists need to take ideas, history, and politics into the many struggles for social justice today. Learning the lessons of past victories, as well as defeats, can arm a new generation of fighters for a better world. As Karl Marx said, "The philosophers have merely interpreted the world; the point, however, is to change it."

We take inspiration and courage from our namesakes, the Haymarket Martyrs, who gave their lives fighting for a better world. Their 1886 struggle for the eight-hour day, which gave us May Day, the international workers' holiday, reminds workers around the world that ordinary people can organize and struggle for their own liberation. These struggles continue today across the globe—struggles against oppression, exploitation, hunger, and poverty.

It was August Spies, one of the Martyrs targeted for being an immigrant and an anarchist, who predicted the battles being fought to this day. "If you think that by hanging us you can stamp out the labor movement," Spies told the judge, "then hang us. Here you will tread upon a spark, but here, and there, and behind you, and in front of you, and everywhere, the flames will blaze up. It is a subterranean fire. You cannot put it out. The ground is on fire upon which you stand."

We could not succeed in our publishing efforts without the generous financial support of our readers. Many people contribute to our project through the Haymarket Sustainers program, in which donors receive free books in return for their monetary support. If you would like to be a part of this program, please contact us at info@haymarketbooks.org.

Shop online at www.haymarketbooks.org or call 773-583-7884.